Most people think of globalization as a religiously neutral economic phenomenon. This striking collection of essays is the best, most balanced treatment of the theological dimensions of globalization from a Christian point of view I have seen.

Max L. Stackhouse
De Vries Professor of Reformed Theology and Public Life Emeritus
Princeton Theological Seminary
Author/editor, *God and Globalization*

The twenty-first century is witnessing unprecedented levels of both economic interdependence and economic disparity, creating profound moral questions for policymakers, corporations, civil society, and individual citizens. What does loving our neighbor mean in a world characterized by massive financial flows, volatile exchange rates, asset price bubbles, offshoring, environmental degradation, multinational corporations, and large-scale immigration? *Economic Justice in a Flat World* is a serious attempt by a hall of fame list of Christian scholars to address some of the most pressing issues of our time. It is a must read by anybody wanting to live faithfully in our rapidly globalizing world.

Brian Fikkert, PhD
Executive Director of the Chalmers Cen
Development at Covenant College and (
Hurts: How to Alleviate Poverty without Hurting the Poor . . . and Yourself

D1019585

There is generally more heat than light in the debate about religion and globalization. This book increases the light considerably. Offering analysis, insight, challenge, and nuance on complex issues, I commend it without reservation.

Peter S Heslam MA BA DPhil FRSA
Director, Transforming Business
UNIVERSITY OF CAMBRIDGE

ECONOMIC JUSTICE
in a flat world

ECONOMIC JUSTICE in a flat world
Christian perspectives on globalization

steven rundle, editor

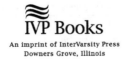

IVP Books

An imprint of InterVarsity Press
Downers Grove, Illinois

InterVarsity Press
P.O. Box 1400, Downers Grove, IL 60515-1426
World Wide Web: www.ivpress.com
E-mail: email@ivpress.com

InterVarsity Press® is the book-publishing division of InterVarsity Christian Fellowship/USA®, a movement of students and faculty active on campus at hundreds of universities, colleges and schools of nursing in the United States of America, and a member movement of the International Fellowship of Evangelical Students. For information about local and regional activities, write Public Relations Dept., InterVarsity Christian Fellowship/USA, 6400 Schroeder Rd., P.O. Box 7895, Madison, WI 53707-7895, or visit the IVCF website at <www.intervarsity.org>.

Originally published by Biblica.

Cover design: Nick Lee
Interior design: projectluz.com
Editorial team: Dana Bromley

ISBN 978-0-8308-5639-8

Printed in the United States of America ∞

Cataloging-in-Publication Data is available through the Library of Congress.

P	18	17	16	15	14	13	12	11	10	9	8	7	6	5	4	3	2	1
Y	27	26	25	24	23	22	21	20	19	18	17	16	15	14	13	12

CONTENTS

Part III
International Aid, Development, and the Church

Part IV
Global Economic Stability, Growth, and the Environment

This book was truly a group effort. In addition to the contributing authors, who were all exceedingly gracious and patient with me, I am deeply indebted to several friends who unreservedly spent many hours helping me craft the outline and purpose of this book. These include Neal Johnson of the Bakke Graduate School of Business, David Richardson of Syracuse University and the Peterson Institute of International Economics, Scott Rae of Biola University, and Stephen Smith of Gordon College.

I would also like to thank Volney James of Authentic Media/ Paternoster for recognizing the need for this book and for giving me the freedom to produce it as I saw fit.

I am also indebted to Larry Strand, dean of the Crowell School of Business at Biola University, for being a constant source of encouragement and to Lillian Minar and Merlinda Balmas who helped with so many of the administrative details and sustained me with the occasional brownie or chocolate chip cookie.

Finally, I can't say enough about my wife Wendy and daughter Olivia. As always, they were constant sources of encouragement and they made many personal sacrifices to give me the space necessary to complete this project.

—Steven Rundle

THE CHALLENGE OF GLOBALIZATION IN CHRISTIAN PERSPECTIVE

Steve Rundle

Many people have heard about the 2.5 billion people who live on less than two dollars per day (World Bank 2008). Less widely known is that much of this poverty is concentrated in countries experiencing the most rapid population growth. Specifically, the populations of the fifty poorest countries (average annual income below $765) are expected to more than *double* between 2005 and 2050, while remaining constant in the industrialized world (United Nations 2005). This presents an enormous challenge for policymakers. For if these trends continue, the world could become even more economically unbalanced, more polarized, and more unstable as an increasing number of people see mass migration or violence as the best response to their poverty. These trends also present a challenge for Christians, because, while there is widespread agreement about the intolerability of poverty, confusion often prevails when discussions turn to specific causes or policy responses. The recent global recession—which will almost certainly increase the number of people in poverty—has only increased the importance of understanding the benefits and costs of global economic integration, specifically as it relates to the problem of poverty.

Nearly everyone agrees that economic development is an essential part of the solution to global poverty. However, the discussions get complicated when we consider how to achieve that development. Is a globalized free-market economy part of the solution or part of the problem? Are the World Bank, International Monetary Fund, and World Trade Organization pursuing policies that will ultimately reduce poverty, or are they serving the interests of the wealthy? What do pro-poor policy reforms look like in the areas of trade, foreign investment, and outsourcing? What kinds of immigration restrictions or reforms are consistent with the teachings of the Christian faith? Should Christians support an overhaul of the international financial system? Should development aid be awarded only to countries that are well governed and democratic? These questions, and many more like them, are not as simple as they are often portrayed. And while many are technical questions that require the specialized expertise of economists, there are, undeniably, dimensions that require the assistance of ethicists and theologians, among others, who can help identify the essentials of a Christian perspective on globalization.

A survey of books written by Christians on the subject reveals an abundance of moral outrage but little discussion of the economics behind the trends or of the policy options. This book seeks to fill that gap by bringing together some of the leading Christian international economists to weigh in on some of the most pressing questions related to the globalization debate. The goal is to provide a better understanding of the economic causes and consequences of globalization, focusing on its impact on the poor and on policy challenges from a Christian perspective. The purpose of this chapter is to introduce the globalization debate, its main characters and trends, followed by a brief overview of the book itself.

The Globalization Debate

"Globalization" is a term now widely used, as it has become an important influence in almost every facet of life. Most commonly it refers to the process of economic and cultural integration, of becoming a barrier free, or "flat" world in which goods, services, finances, people, ideas, cultures, and social problems such as crime and disease cross borders with fewer restrictions. There are aspects to globalization that are probably inevitable. For example, technological advances, making it possible to communicate more easily with people from different cultures and from other parts of the world, are unlikely to go away. However, other dimensions are far from inevitable. Free trade, for example, requires continual, multilateral support, something that is critically dependent on how well policymakers respond to the challenges that accompany economic integration. Also, cultural and religious forces at work have the potential to derail the globalization process.

A strong case can be made that this is not our first experience with a global economy. By many measures—trade, capital flows, and immigration—the economy was remarkably integrated and barrier free before 1914. However, two World Wars and a Great Depression later, the world had retreated to more familiar patterns of economic isolationism with devastating results. Seeking to repair the damage, economists from the Allied nations met in 1944 in Bretton Woods, New Hampshire, and created the International Monetary Fund (IMF) and the World Bank. The primary purpose of the IMF was to promote exchange rate stability in order to facilitate the orderly flow of goods, services, and capital. The World Bank was created to finance the reconstruction of nations devastated by World War II, a mission that was later expanded to include the alleviation of poverty more generally. This was followed in 1947 by the creation of the General Agreement of Tariffs and Trade (GATT), which established rules for trade and a process by which further rounds of trade liberalization could be pursued. However, with no authority of its own to enforce those rules, the GATT was replaced in 1995 by the World Trade Organization (WTO), which administers and enforces existing trade agreements, handles trade disputes between member countries, and provides technical assistance to developing countries.

Evidence of a reemerging global economy can be seen in many recent statistics. For example, between 1990 and 2006 the real value of foreign direct investment (FDI) inflows increased by over 350 percent, and merchandise exports grew by 143 percent, both rates far exceeding the 65 percent increase in global production over that same period.[1] In the United States, the value of international securities transactions as a percent of GDP increased from an almost negligible 6 percent in 1977 to over 344 percent in 2003 (Stultz 2005). The United Nations Conference on Trade and Development (UNCTAD 2007) estimates that there are now over 76,000 multinational corporations, a figure that has more than doubled since 1994. Perhaps more significantly, over 20,000 of those firms are based in developing and transition (formerly communist) economies. And finally, the international migration of people more than doubled between 1975 and 2005, far outpacing the 50 percent increase in world population during that same period (Taylor 2006; United Nations 2005).

Supporters of this recent round of globalization believe the benefits of economic integration outweigh the costs. For example, they point to the many countries, particularly in East Asia, that have experienced dramatic reductions in poverty after opening their economies to the outside world. A compelling argument can also be made that economic integration enhances geo-political stability when, for example, it discourages countries from going to war, as in the case of Taiwan and China or Pakistan and India. In terms of the cultural impact, a case can be made that our cultures are being enriched rather than weakened, that any apparent homogenization of our cultures is merely on the surface, and that "hybridization" is a more accurate description of the process.

Opponents of globalization believe the contrary: the costs of globalization outweigh the benefits. For example, they point to the increasing gap between rich and poor as prima facie evidence that the only beneficiaries of globalization are the wealthy. In this camp are some Christians who, in the words of theologian Max Stackhouse (2007, 5), have "baptized" the class analysis of Marxist social thought and see globalization as a completely immoral phenomenon whereby the rich systematically increase their wealth at the expense of the world's poor.[2]

Some oppose economic integration on nationalistic grounds, believing that it undermines a nation's ability and right to govern itself. The WTO, for example, is seen by some critics as an undemocratic, competing government that seeks to usurp the power of democratically elected, national governments. Another concern has to do with the consumerist ethos that drives much of our modern global economy and the strain this creates for the earth's natural resources and environment. These critics are concerned that in the interest of promoting an ever-expanding global economy, we have unconsciously abandoned any sense of "enough" and are becoming unwitting evangelists for consumerism. If left unabated, we are not only guilty of "cultural imperialism," but we also run the risk of overtaxing the earth's ability to sustain human life.

Among the most vocal participants in the debate are nongovernmental organizations (NGOs) such as Oxfam, Human Rights Watch, Greenpeace, and the World Council of Churches. The problems they seek to address are as diverse as they are real. Some, like UK-based Oxfam, recognize that there are many benefits to globalization and seek to create a more equitable trading system. Others are staunch opponents of capitalism who see nothing good about the globalization of markets and seek instead to create a system of relatively autarkic, "localized" markets.

The volume at which these debates are conducted makes it appear that there is little agreement about anything. But in fact there are several areas of widespread agreement. For example, few people dispute that the benefits of globalization have been unevenly distributed or that the international trading system has been and continues to be biased against the least-developed countries. Indeed, one of the principle goals of the Doha Round of trade talks has been to remedy those structural biases. It is also widely recognized that the performance of the Bretton Woods institutions has been at times disappointing. In its handling of the East Asian financial crisis in the late 1990s, for example, the IMF often pursued rather inflexible, one-size-fits-all solutions that were especially burdensome for the poor. Similarly, the World Bank's efforts to facilitate economic development have been mixed at best, particularly in sub-Saharan Africa, where by some measures the quality of life is now lower than it was forty years ago.

Reaching a consensus about solutions, however, is a different matter. Some of the obstacles are scientific; that is, the empirical evidence is still mixed, and further study is necessary. More often, however, the primary obstacles are political or ideological. An unfortunate reality about the political process today is that it tends to favor well-organized interest groups with narrow, well-defined goals over groups that are less coordinated and not well represented. Politicians are not insensitive to the disenfranchised, of course, but given the often contradictory proposals, the more organized interest groups often prevail. The church is arguably the largest and most well-organized pro-poor interest group. For it to become an effective advocate for the poor, the church needs to begin speaking with one voice. At present it does not.

Several Christian scholars have identified the lack of agreement on economic issues as a significant problem for the church. For example, Catholic theologian Samuel Gregg (2001) warns that if there is no such thing as a uniquely Christian perspective on globalization, then the church risks becoming an uninteresting participant in this debate.

Similarly, Protestant ethicist David Krueger (1997, 20) says that the church must ask "whether it has anything substantive to say about . . . a global market economy." Stackhouse (1995, 11) once complained that the church's contribution often suffers from being either boring or ideological.

Drawing the world's attention to injustice is a vitally important role of the church. But moral outrage alone achieves only so much. For the church to become a truly effective participant in the debate, it needs to be able to contribute substantively, which requires a better understanding of the political-economic forces behind the problems and of potential solutions. This book will not necessarily resolve every difference of opinion, but the hope is that it will help the church become a more effective witness in these areas.

What Is "Economic Justice"?

Given the divisions within the church over economic matters, it is important to clarify what we mean by "economic justice." A full exposition would require its own book, and in fact many books have been written on the subject.[3] Instead, for the purposes of this volume, economic justice is understood to mean the elimination of poverty, broadly defined. This too requires some explanation.

The term "poverty" means different things to different people. Clearly it means not being able to meet certain basic needs. But what exactly do humans need? Food, clothing, and shelter seem obvious, but how much clothing? How much food? Is a thatched hut adequate shelter? What about education and the right to vote? As it turns out, our definitions of deprivation and poverty are highly subjective and conditioned on our own social context. Economist Bradley Schiller explains the problem this way:

People in industrialized communities tend to have more generous notions of "minimum" needs . . . In the 1930s no one felt particularly poor if he or she did not possess electric lights. Yet, today, a family without electricity will most likely be considered poor. So we include a provision for electricity in our minimum poverty-defining budget. But consensus is far more difficult to achieve on a television, much less on a VCR, a CD player, a car, or a six-pack of beer (2001, 16–17).

Any attempt to define poverty is therefore bound to be highly imperfect and controversial. The World Bank, which must track global poverty as part of its mission, bases its definition on the most primitive requirements for human life, a list that consists of the minimum caloric intake essential to human existence and some form of shelter and clothing. For the sake of uniformity, this figure is reported in U.S. dollars and is adjusted to account for variations in purchasing power (also known as the "purchasing power parity" threshold). This admittedly austere poverty line currently stands at $395 per year (in 1993 dollars), or $1.08 per day (commonly reported as $1 per day). Using this definition of poverty, there were 970 million people in 2004 classified as "poor," which is down from 1.2 billion in 1990 but still represents over 18 percent of the world's population (World Bank 2008). Using a more generous figure of $2 per day, roughly 2.5 billion people—40 percent of humanity—were defined as poor.

As useful as these figures may be, they only capture one dimension of poverty—income. Most experts now recognize there are other dimensions of poverty that are not measured in dollars and cents. Poor health, illiteracy, lack of access to credit, and political disenfranchisement are just a few other indications of poverty. Admittedly, there is a strong correlation between income poverty and these other forms of deprivation; but to focus only on income levels is to miss other potentially significant problems. Put another way, income poverty can be both a cause and a consequence of these other problems. An uneducated person, for example, has an increased likelihood of being poor and raising children who are themselves illiterate and poor.

Thus, an increasing number of experts now recognize that poverty has both material and social dimensions. In an attempt to quantify this broader definition of poverty, economists created the Human Development Index (HDI), which takes into account a country's average life expectancy and educational attainment in addition to its average income. Comparisons of a country's GDP ranking with its HDI ranking are sometimes revealing. For example, relatively poor countries that have a good educational or health care system can have a relatively high HDI ranking, suggesting a better quality of life than their GDP ranking would imply. Conversely, countries that have a relatively high GDP can have a lower HDI score based on deficiencies in these other areas.

One advantage of these other measures of poverty, notes Nobel Laureate Amartya Sen (1999), is that they are *intrinsically* valuable; that is, they are valuable in their own right. Income is only *instrumentally* valuable—valuable for what it can be used for. Many people believe that, as another wise man once said, "man does not live by bread alone," and they have no trouble adding some level of health care and education to the list of life's necessities.

A closely related concern is income *inequality*. However, unlike abject poverty, which is morally objectionable to any person of conscience, there has been less agreement as to the moral significance of inequality. An argument can be made, for example, that inequality is a natural and relatively benign consequence of economic progress. Before the Industrial Revolution, nearly everyone was poor, which is to say there was little inequality. Since then some economies have industrialized more quickly than others, and as they did, the gap between rich and poor increased both within and between countries. So long as all incomes are rising and the number of people below the poverty line is falling, some would argue that concerns about inequality are misplaced.

Recent economic research has shed new light on this debate. The World Bank, for example, has recently made a compelling argument that not only does an increasing gap between rich and poor violate many people's sense of fairness—that is, many see it as intrinsically important—but there is an instrumental dimension that should concern even the more callous observer (World Bank 2006). Specifically, chronic inequality is likely the result of market imperfections that ultimately waste resources and limit the growth potential of an economy. In many cases, these market imperfections are the result of an imbalance of political power that becomes self-reinforcing and detrimental to the long-term health of an economy.

> The central argument here is that unequal power leads to the formation of institutions that perpetuate inequalities in power, status, and wealth—and that typically are also bad for the investment, innovation, and risk-taking that underpin long-term growth (World Bank 2006, 8–9).[4]

This concern about unequal and self-reinforcing balances of power hints at another closely related indicator of a just society, though a far less discussed one—income *mobility*. That is, how easy is it for people to move from lower income levels to higher ones? Do people regularly and quickly move up from the lower income levels, or does poverty become their permanent station in life? Is there a middle class to which poor people can aspire, or is there a huge, impenetrable gulf between the small elite class and the poor masses? While it is seldom discussed outside of economic circles, income mobility is an essential characteristic of a stable and just society. As Novak (1996, 194) once noted:

> Poor families do not ask for paradise, but they do want to see tangible signs of improvement over time . . . The realistic hope of a better future is essential to the poor, and this hope is made realistic only through the provision of universal chances for upward mobility such that, in general, people see that hard

work, good will, ingenuity, and talent pay off. When people lose their faith in this probability, they become cynical and destructive.

History has shown that democratic, capitalistic societies tend to have greater income mobility, though not everyone would see that as a good thing. Income mobility can be good and bad; good because it means the poor have a tendency to pull themselves out of poverty relatively quickly on average, but bad because there is no guarantee one will remain well off. Mobility works in both directions, and therein lies the source of many ethical disagreements.

It is reassuring to know that as divided as the church may be on economic matters, there is some level of agreement on the holistic nature of poverty. Christians also generally view the ideals of freedom and democracy approvingly, although many remain wary of free markets. Yet, even if one agrees that democratic and capitalistic societies are more just than their alternatives, does it follow that the cause of justice is advanced by removing barriers between those societies? Does economic justice imply economic and social freedom on a global scale? It is that question that motivates this book.

Overview of the Book

This book is divided into four parts. Part I, "Theological Perspectives on Global Capitalism," presents the perspectives of two theologians— one Catholic and one Protestant. The first is by Michael Novak (chap. 1), who, like many Catholic scholars, draws heavily from the rich history of Catholic social teaching and generally treats those teachings as authoritative. In his chapter, Novak defends the ideal of global capitalism by showing its compatibility with Catholic social teaching, particularly the extensive writings on the subject by Pope John Paul II. Novak maintains that those writings not only offer a vision for a just globalization but also serve as "a vantage point of criticism for those times when globalization falls short of its potential for human well being."

By comparison, Protestants are more inclined toward individualized interpretations of the Bible, and their scholarship tends to emphasize specific passages of Scripture rather than historic teachings of church fathers. The essay by A. Sue Russell (chap. 2) is an excellent example of this. In it, she draws heavily from the familiar passage in Luke 10 about the good Samaritan, and she argues that globalization is expanding not only our markets but also the definition of "neighbor" as it applies to this passage. This points to another interesting difference between the two theological essays. In addition to their different points of theological reference, Novak defends an ideal—global capitalism—whereas Russell focuses on the practical implications of living out our faith in a globalizing world.

In Part II, "The International Flow of Goods, Services, Capital, and Labor," the attention shifts to some of the most divisive subjects of our day. Daniel Finn (chap. 3) begins the section by considering the rules of international trade. As he points out, creating rules that are universally accepted as "fair" is not a simple matter, because what one culture considers "fair play" can for another culture be unfair, immoral, or even illegal. He then identifies the essentials to a Christian perspective on a just trading system, and he concludes by discussing the specific challenges associated with fairness in the context of "dumping" and subsidies. Stephen L. S. Smith (chap. 4) follows with a look at foreign direct investment (FDI) and its ethical challenges. He argues that a blanket criticism of multinational corporations is simplistic and unfair. Rather, it is important to understand the different types of FDI and the unique challenges and development potential associated with each. He concludes by suggesting some areas of justice-promoting research for Christian social scientists. Next, Brad Christerson (chap. 5) takes on the controversial subject of immigration, which is another subject that is often treated simplistically and unfairly. Drawing from the economics research, Christerson argues that most economies benefit from immigration, although some controls are necessary and appropriate. He also makes a case for addressing the uneven distribution of costs and benefits in large, diverse countries like the United States. Wrapping up the section, and tying the three previous essays together, is one by J. David Richardson (chap. 6) that considers the interplay between trade, "offshoring," and immigration. After explaining how they are related and how wealthy and poor countries generally benefit from these forms of exchange, he argues in favor of expanding government-funded "trade adjustment assistance" programs to include dislocations from services trade and worker migration. He concludes the essay by identifying the opportunities these trends present for Christian ministries.

In Part III, "International Aid, Development, and the Church," the focus shifts to the challenges of economic development in the world's poorest countries. The section begins with an essay by Christopher B. Barrett (chap. 7) that addresses one of the most perplexing debates in development circles: Has foreign aid been an effective tool in reducing global poverty, and if not, why has it failed? Barrett identifies different types of aid and reasons for the mixed track record with respect to economic development. He concludes by identifying ways in which the allocation of aid can be improved, arguing that given our Christian understanding of human nature, we should advocate specifically targeted, bottom-up approaches that reinforce incentives for the poor to lift themselves and their communities out of poverty. Next, Roland Hoksbergen (chap. 8) looks at the role of small- and medium-sized enterprises (SMEs) in economic development and specifically the role of faith-based NGOs in promoting SME development. Christian development agencies often promote what they call "transformational" development: development that addresses the physical, social, and spiritual needs of a society. Hoksbergen evaluates that concept by drawing from his empirical study of SME development in Haiti, Kenya, and Nicaragua. The section concludes with an African perspective on economic development by Julius Oladipo (chap. 9) who makes a strong defense for the role of the church in Africa's fight against poverty. The essay contains an excellent discussion of the church's development track record, its core competencies, and the constraints it faces. He makes specific recommendations on how to leverage the church's unique advantages through international partnerships.

More than any of the others, Part IV, "Global Economic Stability, Growth, and the Environment," explores problems of a truly global nature, questions related to the governance and sustainability of the global economy. Stephen L. S. Smith (chap. 10) begins the section with an explanation of the benefits and limitations of the international financial system. He then discusses the roles of the IMF and World Bank, the challenges they face as they try to maintain order and stability in the international financial system, and the ethics and economics of the various proposals for reforming that system. John P. Tiemstra (chap. 11) presents a novel argument against financial globalization. Not only do globalized financial markets increase the risk of instability and unfairly restrict a nation's ability to control its own macroeconomic destiny (complaints that others have made), but they also impose Western-style solutions to asymmetric information and agency problems on countries that have historically handled those problems differently. He believes that globalization can better serve the interests of mankind, and be more consistent with the values of Christianity if the (relatively) free flow of goods was coupled with restrictions on the free movement of financial capital.

Closing out the book are three essays that consider the environmental impact associated with free trade and unrestrained economic growth. First, Judith M. Dean (chap. 12) considers the environmental impact of trade. Drawing on her extensive research on trade and investment in China, Dean rebuts the argument that free trade leads to environmental degradation. On the contrary, she argues that trade restrictions not only fail to benefit the environment but they also hurt the poor. In the interest of supporting the poor and the environment, Dean argues that Christians should promote trade while advocating for policies that address environmental problems directly. Donald Hay (chap. 13) follows with a detailed look at the economics of global climate change. Drawing from the most recent studies on global climate change, he explains why the church needs to show leadership in this area. Specifically, because the world's poorest countries will be the most negatively affected, he believes the church should advocate a response that is more aggressive, and more biased toward the poor, than what some wealthy nations are willing to support. He also identifies specific actions churches and individual Christians can take to reduce their carbon footprint. Finally, Bob Goudzwaard (chap. 14) concludes with a critical look at economic growth, expressing his concern that Christians have become "hypnotized" by an ideology that favors production over stewardship—increasing output rather than properly caring for inputs.

Conclusion

Few people dispute that over the last quarter century the percentage and number of people living below the poverty line has fallen considerably. Many observers credit the rapid development and growth that have occurred over that period, brought on by a sharp increase in the international flow of goods, capital, and people. However, a recurring question among many Christians is "At what price?" In the interest of bringing more of humanity into what Novak (chap. 1) calls "the circle of exchange," are some people being pushed out of that circle? In our relentless pursuit of economic growth are we becoming unwitting apologists for consumerism? How long can the earth's resources sustain such growth?

The essays contained in this volume reflect a range of perspectives, and that was intentional. To do otherwise would have been dishonest. Generally speaking, however, Christian economists agree that God cares about the poor and about environmentally sustainable development. They have a generally favorable view of markets and believe that trade, investment, and immigration are as a whole beneficial to society. They also tend to support in principle the selective use of government policy to correct problems associated with economic integration and market failure.

As Christians, these economists are keenly aware that we live in a fallen world and that neither markets nor governments can be expected to serve humankind perfectly. One will find little demagoguery in these essays. Instead, what the contributors have sought to explain is how market forces can work both *for* and *against* the poor and how those forces can be harnessed to achieve the greatest good. The hope is that this volume will help the church develop a more nuanced and balanced understanding of the issues to then become a more effective participant in the globalization debate.

Questions for Review

1. What is your opinion about globalization? Has it generally benefited mankind, been harmful, or a combination of both? Please explain.

2. Identify five specific ways your life is different today because of globalization, compared to what it would have been like thirty years ago.

3. Who are the key players in the globalization debate, and what are their roles?

4. How would you define economic justice? Do you believe economic freedom is an essential component of a just economy? Please explain.

Notes

[1] Merchandise exports and GDP calculations based on data from the *World Economic Outlook* (IMF May 1997, and April 2008). FDI calculations based on UNCTAD data available at http://www.unctad.org/Templates/Page.asp?intItemID=3152&lang=1. All figures were adjusted for inflation using the implicit GDP deflator provided by the St. Louis Federal Reserve Bank.

[2] Many of these same Christians advocate making globalization a confessional issue, that is, a litmus test that separates Christian from non-Christian. As Stackhouse explains, they hold that "if one believes that globalization bears within it any divinely blessed or grace-filled possibilities, one is a heretic and should be kept out or thrown out of the community of believers" (2007, p. 5).

[3] See Hartropp (2007) and van Til (2007) for two recent contributions.

[4] It is interesting to point out a classic philosophical step that has been taken here. Economics is woefully ill-equipped to evaluate questions about fairness. Therefore, any argument asserting the need for government intervention must first show that the existing order is inefficient (due to some market failure) and likely to undermine the long- term growth prospects of an economy. The World Bank skillfully dodges any discussion about fairness and focuses instead on the economic consequences of inequality.

References

Gregg, Samuel. 2001. "Globalization and the Insights of Catholic Social Teaching." *Journal of Markets and Morality* 4, no. 1 (Spring), 1–13.

Hartropp, Andrew. 2007. *What Is Economic Justice? Biblical and Secular Perspectives Contrasted.* Colorado Springs: Paternoster Theological Monographs.

Krueger, David A. 1997. The Business Corporation and Productive Justice in the Global Economy. In *The Business Corporation and Productive Justice*, by David A. Krueger, Donald W. Shriver, and Laura L. Nash. Nashville: Abingdon Press, 17–98.

Novak, Michael. 1996. Seven Corporate Responsibilities. In *Is the Good Corporation Dead? Social Responsibility in a Global Economy*, edited by John W. Houck and Oliver F. Williams. Lanham, MD: Rowman and Littlefield Publishers, 189–202.

Schiller, Bradley. 2001. *The Economics of Poverty and Discrimination.* Upper Saddle River, NJ: Prentice Hall.

Sen, Amartya. 1999. *Development as Freedom.* New York, NY: Alred A. Knopf, Inc.

Stackhouse, Max L. 1995. Christian Social Ethics in a Global Era: Reforming Protestant Views. In *Christian Social Ethics in a Global Era*, edited by Max Stackhouse, Peter L. Berger, Dennis P. McCann, and M. Douglas Meeks. Nashville: Abingdon Press, 11–73.

———. 2007. *God and Globalization, Volume IV: Globalization and Grace.* New York, NY: Continuum International Publishing Group.

Stultz, Rene M. 2005. "The Limits of Financial Globalization." National Bureau of Economic Research Working Paper 11070 (January). Cambridge, MA: National Bureau of Economic Research.

Taylor, J. Edward. 2006. "International Migration and Economic Development." Paper prepared for the Symposium on International Migration and Development, Turin, Italy (June 28–30). View at http://www.un.org/esa/population/migration/turin/Symposium_Turin_files/P09_SYMP_Taylor.pdf.

United Nations, Population Division of the Department of Economic and Social Affairs. 2005. *World Population Prospects: The 2004 Revision.* New York, NY: United Nations.

UNCTAD. 2007. *World Investment Report.* Geneva: United Nations Conference on Trade and Development.

van Til, Kent A. 2007. *Less Than Two Dollars a Day: A Christian View of World Poverty and the Free Market.* Grand Rapids, MI: Eerdmans.

World Bank. 2006. *World Development Report: Equity and Development.* Washington, D.C.: World Bank.

———. 2008. *Global Economic Prospects.* Washington, D.C.: World Bank.

WTO. 2007. *International Trade Statistics.* (Washington, DC: The World Trade Organization).

PART I

Theological Perspectives on Global Capitalism

CHAPTER 1

CATHOLIC SOCIAL TEACHING, MARKETS, AND THE POOR

Michael Novak

"Be not afraid!" is the favorite injunction of John Paul II to the peoples of the world. Under his leadership, the Catholic Church has made a remarkable new judgment about the institutions of democracy, such as the rule of law, the protection of rights, the separation of powers, and the principle of limited government. Following traditional Catholic social thought, it has also reaffirmed its guarded approval of the free economy—respect for the right of private property, the right of free association, and even the right of economic initiative. But John Paul II has gone farther. He has communicated with penetrating insight the roles of human capital, especially the roles of knowledge, know-how, and practical creativity in creating the wealth of nations. Neither democracy nor capitalism is to be identified as the highest earthly good in his thought. Both democracy and capitalism must conform to the rule of law and to sound moral criteria. If they do so, the Church approves of them and looks upon them with hope and expectation, not with fear.[1]

When we recall the murders, executions, and exiles the Church endured under the French Revolution of 1789, the Mexican Revolution of 1920, and many other "liberal" governments in

21

between, it is not hard to understand why the Church was for several decades hostile to tyrannies that called themselves "liberal." Much that went by that name was in fact illiberal.[2] Yet John Paul II, like his namesake John XXIII before him, has from the beginning of his pontificate chosen to regard the world of history—the world of our time—with hope and expectation. "Be not afraid!" He used those very words on his first visit to Poland in 1979, some six months after he became pope, when the Berlin Wall seemed high and solid. He used them with regard to "globalization" in September 1999. He uses them still.

John Paul II has been called by his biographer "a witness to hope" (Weigel 1999). If by "liberalism" we mean a philosophy that is materialist, persecutory, anti-Christian, closed to, or perhaps even opposed to belief in God, then such a philosophy runs counter to Christian thought. But if by "liberalism" we mean a commitment to the best institutions worthy of human dignity, such as limited government, protection of political and civil rights, respect for religious liberty and the free exercise of religion, and a free economy powered by knowledge, know-how, invention, and enterprise, then Catholic social thought sees much reason for hopeful cooperation with liberalism. Those are the commitments of "all men of good will," to whom the angels sang "Peace on earth!" in welcoming the Christ.

Catholic social thought has established critical grounds for a profound appreciation of the humanism that infuses the institutions of democracy and capitalism at their best, and for a vision in whose light their existing practice (and incomplete development) may be justly criticized and incited to further progress.

I want to unpack this thesis under five headings: *materialism,* or the primacy of the spirit; *solidarity;* the *subjectivity of society* (that is, the liberty, initiative, and creativity of the human subject); *subsidiarity;* and *breaking the chains of poverty.*

Foundations of the Catholic Understanding of Democratic Capitalism

Materialism. In 1997, the Synod of America, which brought together the bishops of North and South America, disparaged those it called "neoliberals." A tradition in Latin America and in Spain describes "liberals" as materialists, concerned solely with market processes, profits, and efficiency to the neglect of the human spirit, human values, and human rights.[3]

In the new economy of today, however, it is difficult to be a materialist, strictly understood. Consider your last purchase of a new disk or program for your computer. How much *material* do you actually have in your hand? About eighty cents worth of plastic. What you actually paid for is mostly composed of *mind,* the fruit of the human spirit, information in a design created by human intelligence. All around us, *matter* matters less and less, and *intelligence* (or spirit) matters more.

Conversely, as John Paul II explains, the cause of wealth *used to* be explained in largely material terms: At one time, the major form of wealth in most places was *land*. Later, especially for Marxist thought, wealth was *capital,* large inert investments in factories and huge machines. In our time, however, economists affirm that the chief cause of the wealth of nations is not material at all, but *knowledge, skill, know-how*—in short, those acts and habits of discovery, invention, organization, and forethought that economists now describe as "human capital," which is located in the human spirit and produced by the spiritual activities of education and training and mentoring.[4] Human capital also includes *moral* habits, such as hard work, cooperativeness, social trust, alertness, honesty, and *social* habits, such as respect for the rule of law.

The one factor that, more than any other, makes the rich countries rich is their investment in and development of human capital. A nation's greatest resource, economists say, is its people.[5] It is not material resources that make a nation rich. Some of the countries richest in natural resources are among the world's poorest nations. Some of the nations with virtually no natural resources are among the world's richest nations. The cause of wealth can no longer be said to be material. Today, as in biblical times, many confine their horizons to this earth as we sense it; they eat, drink, and make merry until they die. Not a few among the baptized are included in that number. In this sense, there will always be materialists. But in the world of theory, materialist doctrines have run aground. Marxist "dialectical materialism," for example, failed miserably in understanding economics and in generating humane societies. All the evidence of physics and the other sciences point beyond the reaches of materialism.

On the other hand, no principle is as basic to Catholic social thought as the primacy of spirit. Everywhere today that principle seems to be vindicated: in caring for physically and mentally ill people; in overcoming drug abuse and alcoholism; in turning from a life of crime; in forming morals; in developing economies; in nourishing among a people the rule of law and civic commitment; in encouraging people to act with unimpeachable honesty, even when no one is looking; and in engendering confidence in the future, even in the face of great obstacles. Empirical research seems to confirm the primacy of spirit and to disconfirm merely materialistic accounts of human behavior.[6]

Solidarity. When Leo XIII described in *Rerum Novarum* (1891) the tumultuous changes then churning through the former agrarian and feudal world of premodern Europe, he saw the need for a new sort of virtue (a reliable habit of soul) among Christian peoples, especially lay people; and he wavered between calling it *justice* or *charity*—*social justice* or *social charity*.[7] By the time of *Centesimus Annus* (1991), John Paul II had brought that nascent intuition into focus in the one term *solidarity*. By this term, he did not mean the great Polish labor union that contributed so much to the fall of communism—although the worldwide fame of the term *Solidarnosc* added helpful connotations to what he intended. He meant the special virtue of social charity that makes each person aware of belonging to the whole human race, of being brother or sister to all others, of living in *communio* with all humans in God.

Solidarity is another way of saying globalization, but in the dimension of communal interiority and personal responsibility. Solidarity is not a habit of impersonally losing oneself in groupthink, disappearing into collectivity. Solidarity is exactly the reverse of what socialists meant by "collectivization" because it points simultaneously to personal responsibility and initiative and to communion with others. Solidarity awakens the individual conscience. Solidarity evokes responsibility, enlarges personal vision, and connects the self to all others.[8]

In these days of "globalization," when it is described in merely economic terms, it is almost impossible for an intelligent human being to imagine the self as an unencumbered, solitary individual unlinked to others. Globalization involves a dramatic drop in transportation and communication costs; instantaneous communication; a single global market; worldwide Internet, satellite, cellular phone, and television availability; and a geometric increase in foreign direct investment and cross-border trade. Globalization also has an interior dimension. External, economic globalization has changed the way individuals *experience* themselves and the way they *think*.

People find it increasingly hard to think about local conditions only. Isn't this a major step toward the realities of solidarity? Aren't human beings planetary creatures, one another's brothers and sisters, members of one body with every part serving every other part?[9]

These are the best times for those committed to solidarity and pinching, painful times for those committed to a view of themselves as solitary individuals—pinching like shoes that do not fit. If a Catholic cannot feel confident in a time of globalization, what is the point in bearing the name "Catholic," which is another name for global? (The imperative for globalization began with the commission "Go and make disciples of all nations," which turned Christianity away from being the religion of only one tribe or one people and commanded it to see the human race as one people of God.) Globalization is the natural ecology of the Catholic faith.

On this ground, Pope John Paul II welcomes the "new thing" of globalization. All the streams that contribute to the definition of globalization, as mentioned above, point to good effects as well as bad. And, for the poor of the world, being included in the circle of exchange and development is better than being marginalized. There is at least a possibility that global procedures will heighten the transparency of local transactions and reduce local corruption. The pope urges international institutions and citizens everywhere to open their arms to the world's poor and to help bring about a springtime of worldwide development, excluding no one and embracing all. His call to solidarity offers a vision of genuine globalization, and works as a vantage point of criticism for those times when globalization falls short of its potential for human well-being.

The subjectivity of society. The theme of subjectivity in Pope John Paul II's writings has been overlooked in popular expositions of Catholic social thought. For example, anyone who has a pet in the house knows that animals *behave*; they cannot do other than follow the laws of their nature. Our own children, however, do not always "behave." They imagine new futures for themselves and invent new projects and new trajectories for their personal development. In part they invent themselves. In the long run, they must become provident over their own identity, responsible for choosing who they will become. Children must learn to reflect, deliberate, choose, take initiative, and accrue responsibility for their actions. Unlike other animals, they *can* choose against the laws of their nature, or they can choose to walk in those laws.

To summarize, whereas other animals *behave*, the human person *acts*. The human person is *the acting person* (Wojtyla 1979). Action flows from the interior life of insight, reflection, and decision—acts that only persons can perform, acts that humans have in common (analogously) with angels and with God but with no other known creatures.

By the time Pope John Paul II wrote *Centesimus Annus,* he had come to distinguish between "the subjectivity of society" and "the subjectivity of the individual," though both were held to be antipathetic to "real socialism" (Paul 1991, Sec. 13). He then pushed his earlier thought to the new insight that human beings' capacities for creative action are the cause of the wealth of nations and from an economic point of view the most important form of capital (Paul 1991, Secs. 31–32).

This concept enabled the Holy Father to talk about solidarity in terms of personal responsibility and initiative. Simultaneously, the concept of solidarity enabled him to talk about the individual in terms of universal *communio,* the communion of all human beings in the love and being of God.

Without the integrity of the human subject, there is no genuine communio without communio; there is no whole human subject. Without solidarity, subjectivity degenerates into unencumbered individualism. Without subjectivity, solidarity degenerates into mushy, mindless collectivism.

We can grasp the complementarity of these two conceptual tools because we have experienced the excesses of both collectivism and individualism. We have lived through the failures of both socialist and liberal materialism.

Subsidiarity. Simultaneous with the great rushing power of economic and legal globalization, there has also arisen powerful demands for greater local autonomy and for a stronger role for intermediate institutions and mediating associations. In other words, from outside and from within, the nation-state is under great pressures. These pressures are all the more acute, since, at least from the time of Hegel, the nation-state has been considered the mythical embodiment of the *Geist* of a whole people. We can read the history of the last two centuries as an enactment of the myth of the benevolent nation-state, caring for its people as the nanny for her children, rendering them secure and happy. From Lenin to Hitler, Mussolini to Perón, Mao Zedong to Castro, Kim Il Sung to Qaddafi, dictators have loved this myth. They have portrayed themselves as personifications of Popular Will.

Various forms of socialism, social democracy, and the liberal welfare state have embraced versions of the same mythic impulse. The twentieth century has predominately been the story of the nation-state, at the expense of every other social structure—family, church, and mediating institution. The nation-state has proved inadequate, however, to its own boasts. It has overpromised and underachieved. Great pressures from without and from within are bursting through its governing myths.

Catholic social thought has a great deal of its conceptual weight in a theory of the state, especially the welfare state, which has not met the tests of reality. A massive amount of rethinking is needed, and quickly.

The need for rethinking is obvious in the international dimension. The pope often calls for new international institutions to "guide" the new energies of globalization.[10] But much of the rethinking must attend to the intra-national dimension, the vitality of the smaller institutions *within* states that the hyperactive national governments of the last one hundred years have repressed and suppressed. Whole regions, ethnic groups, cities, townships, and villages have been neglected. Yet today many diverse local forces are stirring and coming again to life.

The defense of the civic association by the church is at least as old as Innocent IV's vindication of "corporations," such as cities, cathedral chapters, and guilds independent of the state (Collins 1986), and Thomas Aquinas's apologia for the human rights of the members of mendicant orders, such as the new Franciscans and Dominicans.[11] But the Catholic doctrine of "subsidiarity" appears to have been given a great boost by the Swiss and the American experiments in confederation and federalism, respectively. Lord Acton identified federalism—that is, one form of subsidiarity—as one of the great achievements in the history of liberty.[12]

The basic justification for subsidiarity is epistemic. Decisions taken closer to the concrete texture of reality and the immediate interests of the decision makers are likely to evince a higher degree of practical intelligence, not to say wisdom, than decisions taken at a higher, more abstract remove. Practical wisdom tends to demand hands-on, experimental knowledge, the sort of knowledge Jacques Maritain identified as "knowledge by connaturality," a kind of knowledge by "second nature" (See Maritain 1951, 1978).

Breaking the Chains of Poverty

Still, with all this discussion of doctrine, it is well to remind ourselves of our main task in this new century: to arrange our institutions so that all the poor of the world may exit from poverty. In the last 150 years we have made tremendous strides in that direction, but much work remains.

About three-quarters of the population in the hemisphere of the Americas, for instance, has escaped from dire poverty. Still, about 78 million persons in that hemisphere live on an income of less than one dollar per day, and 182 million live on less than two dollars per day.[13] The life expectancy of these poor peoples may have been substantially extended, but their living conditions are still unnecessarily harsh. Enough is known about how to create new wealth on a systematic basis that the poverty of these 182 million is unnecessary, even scandalous. It makes us ashamed. It fires our determination to alter their circumstances.

Our goal must be to eliminate the last large pockets of poverty in this world during the next two generations—by, say, 2040. We know that human capital is the most important form of capital. Therefore, education is the most crucial form of economic development, the sine qua non of all others. The good news is that adult literacy around the world has jumped from about 48 percent in 1970 to about 72 percent in 1997 (UNDP 1999, 25). That is a good gain in less than thirty years. In the next fifteen years, we ought to push this number above 90 percent. Nothing would better reduce poverty than this increase in human capital.

But job creation must be added to education.[14] There cannot be new employees if there are not new employers, that is to say, new businesses. The creation of an atmosphere, a legal system, and a banking system favorable to the creation of many new small businesses is an urgent matter for the liberation of the poor. Business formation depends on our exercising abilities the Creator has instilled in every person—the creativity and the desire to serve others with honest goods and useful services. As it happens, in Latin America and particularly in Africa, women excel in launching new small businesses.

Until now, theologians and bishops have not had to extend a great deal of thought to economic and business matters. If they must do so today, it is for the sake of the poor. Better than giving the poor bread is helping them launch bakeries and other firms, through which they might serve others, as a way of providing for their own families in an independent, honorable, and prideful way (Paul 1991, Sec. 32). In no other systemic and practical way can the poor be brought "into the circle of exchange" (Paul 1991, Sec. 34). Such progress will occur only within a market economy. Yet capitalism may be the most besieged liberal institution within Christian circles. The challenge to the morality of markets deserves to be addressed systematically.

Defenses of Capitalism

"The driving power of capitalism," writes the distinguished English Christian missionary to India, Leslie Newbigin, "is the desire of the individual to better his material condition. . . . The name that the New Testament gives to the force in question is covetousness. The capitalist system is powered by the unremitting stimulation of covetousness" (Newbigin 1986).

This is one justification (condemnation, rather) of capitalism. If it were accepted by a poor nation, such a theory would be its own punishment. Note, too, its image of wealth. Desiring to improve one's material condition is covetousness because whatever one needs for self-improvement already belongs to others—it is theirs, and one covets it. But this is to imagine wealth as a fixed sum, all of it previously assigned, and to overlook the dimension of invention, discovery, and the creation of new wealth. It is to imagine all gaining of wealth as "taking."

Leslie Newbigin's view of capitalism as covetousness is one example of a Christian interpretation of capitalism. Bishop Richard Harries of Oxford offers a far more sympathetic and nuanced view. His title asks, *Is There a Gospel for the Rich?* and his answer is his "conviction that God's liberation is for everyone. The rich need to be liberated no less than the poor. . . ." (Harries 1992, 72). Intelligently and with discrimination, the bishop discerns Christian potential in the social device of the free market, in private property, in innovation, in the business firm, in profit, and even in the transnational corporation. The bête noire and polemical foil for his book is the "New Right," to which he wishes to supply a sophisticated alternative. He describes Britain as a "post-socialist" society. His aim is to present a more humane and evangelical form of capitalism than any (he thinks) yet dreamed of on the "New Right." He is bigger on "affirmative government" than is the "New Right," for example.

In offering his argument on behalf of a market economy, Bishop Harries begins with a lead article from *The Guardian* in 1981, which accepted the market as an inescapable fact of life and an important source of much-needed knowledge: "It is the market which acts as an essential signal from consumers to firms telling them how much to produce, when to produce it, and what sort of quality to make."

Besides this information, "the profit of corporations (or cooperatives) is also the market's way of signaling success: it is an essential guide to, and source of, investment." Harries summarizes, to all except a small percentage of the Labour Party, that the free market is "essential, inescapable and, for all its flaws, to be valued" (Harries 1992, 88–89). This approval for markets, Harries notes, is "as robust as could come from any 'Thatcherite' economist." John Gray called such a defense of the market the epistemic argument for markets; he offers a brief and elegant statement of it in *The Moral Foundations of Market Institutions* (Gray 1992).

But Gray also offers a third fundamental and at least partly original defense—the defense from autonomy. More than any other system, he argues, a market system enhances the individual's scope for and frequency of acts of choice. Gray does not see this argument as necessarily universal. It may mean less to East Asian societies, for example, whose social and psychological structures are more communitarian and less individualist than those of the West. Nor does he think an emphasis on choice to be an unmixed blessing. On this as on other things, individuals and societies can go too far. *What* is chosen can matter greatly. Nonetheless, the argument from autonomy is difficult for any Western intellectual to dismiss, since Westerners value choice highly. The best rejoinder from the Left is to suggest that too few people actually possess autonomy in sufficient degree, so that much social (and governmental) effort must be expended in "equalizing people" through redistribution (Gray 1992, Chap. 4).

To his credit, Gray resists redistributionist policies. These are in practice doomed to failure and in principle unjust. But he does argue that any society that favors autonomy must, because of that very commitment, empower all its citizens to reach some basic level thereof. Gray thinks that he has found a way to define this basic desired level through a concept of "satiable needs" (Gray 1992). Yet since poverty is normally taken as a relative measure—by American standards, for example, more than a third of Western Europeans would be living in poverty (Rector 1990)—I doubt that Gray's efforts in this direction are sustainable. The human spirit is in principle insatiable.

"If only I could have that," we have often told ourselves, "I would be satisfied," only to find that we never are. Autonomy is always like that. We can never get enough of it. Whatever of it we have always runs into limits, often quickly, and we wish that we had no such limits; we wish to be like God. Even kings and princes rail against their too-narrow autonomy. Such is the stuff of the best English drama.

A fourth argument in defense of the market is based upon the growing immateriality of what people are actually willing to buy. Markets depend on people's choices. Kenneth Adams thinks that he has discerned an impending switch in consumers' preferences: "Suppose that our increasing demand is for entertainment, sport, music, theatre, literature and all other areas of human growth: in relationships, in intellectual and aesthetic delight—these will place much smaller demands on materials and energy. Furthermore, as desire grows in those wider, richer, higher areas of human need, it is likely that desire for increase in the material areas will stabilize or decline" (Adams 1990). This preference switch is represented by the information age. That is, an increasing proportion of production today lies in its *spiritual* rather than its *material* components. Industries are becoming cleaner; through miniaturization, physical products are becoming smaller, more powerful, and (usually) cheaper. The full implications of the term *information age* have barely begun to be absorbed by and articulated in theological thought.

The fifth argument for the market—admittedly an odd one—is that the economic plenty produced by market societies has proved conclusively that "man does not live by bread alone." The traditional Jewish and Christian predictions about the discontents inherent in materialism have been confirmed. The textual evidence for this lies in university bookstores in the sections devoted to astrology, witchcraft, and the occult—sections that are usually larger than those for traditional philosophy and theology. "When humans stop believing in God," Chesterton once wrote, "they don't believe in nothing; they believe anything." All around us we see signs of boredom, restlessness, and discontent.

None of these five arguments (except perhaps the first) is alien to Pope John Paul II, who, as the hundredth anniversary of *Rerum Novarum* approached, was asked again and again by bishops from Sri Lanka to Sao Paulo to Kiev, "What direction do you now recommend to us, after the collapse of socialism?" The pope was certain to issue an encyclical commemorating Leo XIII's 1891 encyclical *Rerum Novarum*; moreover, after the events of 1989, he had to provide an answer. He recommended "the free economy, the market economy," the economy of creativity and enterprise. He was even willing, although reluctant, to use the word *capitalism*, so long as the system intended by that word included both a worthy juridical system protecting human rights and a moral-religious system imposing ethical limits (Paul 1991). Yet his argument for this decision is different from the five preceding arguments.

Pope John Paul II's argument from creativity flows from his concept of "the acting person," worked out in his book by that title written before he became pope (Wojtyla 1979), though at the time, he had not seen its relevance for economics. What makes humans distinctive among the other animals, he held, is their capacity to initiate new projects (especially life projects): to imagine, to create, and to *act* as distinct from merely behaving. Throughout his pontificate, the pope has focused on this "creative subjectivity" of the human person (Paul 1981). In this he saw the *imago Dei:* humans are made in the image of the Creator in such a way that to be creative is the essential human vocation. In this, too, he saw the endowment of a fundamental human right to personal economic initiative.

This argument offers a different grounding for concepts such as "natural rights" from that offered by Hobbes, Locke, and other Enlightenment figures. The pope's argument is substantially philosophical and could perhaps be supported by philosophical analysis like that offered by Gabriel Marcel in *The Mystery of Being* and *Creative Fidelity* (Marcel 1960). The emphasis of certain phenomenologists and existentialists on human "becoming," on "creating oneself," and the like indicates what might be done. This argument also has much to commend it from the viewpoint of commonsense. It is far harder to predict the future of one's children, for example, than that of the household cat. The latter does not have to think about choosing a career at all, let alone choosing among self-invented possibilities. The exact way in which the pope deploys the argument, of course, depends on the doctrine of creation and a long-standing Christian interpretion associated with the Book of Genesis. Thus, the pope's argument is more properly theological than philosophical. Still, it is quite striking.

The pope sees that for much of Christian history the most important form of wealth was land, just as the term "capital" derived from counting the heads (*capita*) of sheep, oxen, cows, goats, horses, and other livestock that marked a farm's productivity, along with fruits, vegetables, and grains (Paul 1991, Sec. 32). Wealth in land belonged chiefly to the nobility, although in some places smaller freeholds were also conspicuous, especially in Britain and for unusually long and uninterrupted family tenure.

At a later period, the pope notes, wealth (like the term *Das Kapital*) came to be associated with ownership of the means of production—with machinery, factories, and other impersonal aspects. Indeed, in his first social encyclical, Pope John Paul himself used "capital" only for impersonal objects, reserving his use of "labor" to refer to human persons as factors in production, whatever their economic role (Paul 1981). In *Sollicitudo Rei Socialis,* he had already seen clearly enough that even common ownership of the means of production, and certainly state ownership, could not guarantee the humanity of an economic system—neither its capacity to produce wealth nor its capacity to respect "the fundamental right to personal economic initiative" (Paul 1988, Sec. 15). *That* right, he saw then, was grounded in the *imago Dei* imprinted on man's soul.

In *Centesimus Annus,* the pope carries this line of thought further. The new, deeper, and more telling referent for the word *capital* is neither land nor the impersonal means of production but, rather, "the possession of know-how, technology and skill." The chief cause of the wealth of nations is human wit—discovery, invention, the habit of enterprise, foresight, skill in organization. "The wealth of the industrialized nations is based much more on this kind of ownership than on natural resources." "Indeed, besides the earth, man's principal resource is *man himself.*" And again, "today the decisive factor is increasingly *man himself,* that is, his knowledge, especially his scientific knowledge, his capacity for interrelated and compact organization, as well as his ability to perceive the needs of others and to satisfy them" (Paul 1991, Sec. 32).

It seems to me, after countless re-readings, that the pope might be thinking in these passages of Japan—a tiny land, with hardly any natural resources, that is mostly dependent on overseas sources of energy. The cause of Japan's wealth cannot be an abundance of natural resources nor even proximity to its major markets. Instead, the Japanese have highly developed, and make exquisite use of, their human capital. Without even recognizing the Creator for whom Pope John Paul II speaks, the Japanese have shown remarkable capacities for creative action in world manufacturing markets. If John Paul II's theory about the *universal* human capacity for creativity is true, then this is as it should be. Creativity by any other name causes wealth, since natural resources alone do not.

But the powerful communitarian and centripetal structure of Japanese society brings to light the other argument for markets made by Pope John Paul II: where human creativity is at play, a new and highly interesting form of community is also at play. In the largest sense, the market of today is a world market; it interknits every part of the world within a single, complex web of contracts, transactions, and networks of supply and demand. Many of these transactions are instantaneous. World markets, for stocks and for commodities and above all for information (the newest, most vital form of capital), are open for simultaneously viewing television and computer screens linked to one another around the world in "real time."

Dostoevsky once described charity as an invisible filament linking the world in a network of impulses, along which a simple human smile or an aspiration of love could circle the globe in minutes to bring cheer to someone, even a stranger, faraway. A person who receives a smile, he noted, often feels impelled to pass it along by smiling to someone else in the next chance encounter, and so with the speed of light the smile circles the globe. The new television and computer images, like impulses bounced off cold and silent satellites in space to touch and vivify every part of earth, may only be metaphors for the nerves and tissues that have always tied together the Mystical Body spoken of by St. Paul, but such ligatures seem more visible now. Even in the fifth century AD, a great father of the Church, St. Gregory of Nyssa, observed that human trade—exchanging the wool of one place for the wine of another, the clay pots of one culture for the grain of another—is an image of the bonds uniting the one family of God. *Commercium et Pax* was once the motto of Amsterdam, whose scenes of commerce and shipping were often painted by Turner.

Even in the supposedly more individualistic West, the pope sees that the market is, above all, a social instrument. It has a centripetal force. It obliges sellers to find buyers (sometimes at great distances and across significant spans of time). It calls for sequences of action that involve many hands coordinated by remarkable capacities for foresight and organization. Indeed, most economic activities in the modern environment are too complex to be executed by one person alone; nearly all of them require the creation of a new type of community, not organic but artifactual, not natural (as the family is natural) but contractual, not coercive (as was "real existing socialism") but free and voluntary, not total like a monastery but task-oriented and open to cooperators, even ones of different belief systems and ultimate commitments. In short, the distinctive invention of capitalist societies is the business firm, independent of the state.

About the business firm, the pope is surprisingly eloquent. There has been a tendency in Roman Catholic thought—the document of Vatican II on "The Church in the World," Oswald von Nell-Breuning, S.J. has pointed out, is one example (von Nell-Breuning 1969, 299)—to notice only four economic roles: the owner, the manager, the employer, and the employee. The creative source of the firm, the practitioner of the virtue of enterprise, is entirely neglected. Pope John Paul II does not fall into this trap. Here is what he writes in *Centesimus Annus:* "It is [man's] disciplined work in close collaboration with others that makes possible the creation of ever more extensive *working communities* which can be relied upon to transform man's natural human environment. Important virtues are involved in this process, such as diligence, industriousness, prudence in undertaking reasonable risks, reliability and fidelity in interpersonal relationships, as well as courage in carrying out decisions which are difficult and painful but necessary, both for the overall working of a business and in meeting possible set-backs" (Paul 1991, Sec. 32).

Contemplating this modern economic process—this historically unique way of drawing upon the creative individual working within voluntary, cooperative community—the pope writes this stunning sentence: "This process, *which throws practical light on a truth about the human person which Christianity has constantly affirmed,* should be viewed carefully and favorably" (von Nell-Breuning 1969, Sec. 32). The modern business process—*business,* of all things!—"throws practical light on [Christian] truth." And then note: The pope urges theologians and other Christians to view this business process "carefully and favorably." The pope is only exercising here the classic Catholic habit of seeing in all things the signs of Providence at work, the hidden presence of that Logos "by whom and with whom and in whom were made all things that are made" (John 1:1–3). Sometimes referred to as the Catholic "sacramental sense" or "way of analogy," this mode of perception lies behind the tradition of blessing the fishing fleets, the fields to be sown, and the harvests. If humans are made in the image of God, then their actions (especially their creative actions) also reflect that image.

It is remarkable, of course, that things so scorned in theological literature, such as the business firm and the modern corporation, should be set before us by the Roman Pontiff to "be viewed carefully and favorably" for the "practical light" it sheds on Christian truth. (If I had written that line, I know writers who would have described it as excessive.) Yet such praise fits quite comfortably within an old tradition, in whose light grace was seen to be working even in tyrannical and amoral kings; in the thief who died beside Jesus on the cross; and in every neighbor a man meets. To see grace at work is not to see only beauty and light, but real things as they are in this messy, fleshly, and imperfect world. For the Creator looked on this world and proclaimed it "good," and for its redemption he gave his only Son. A Roman Catholic is taught to see grace in flawed and all-too-human popes, in the poor of Calcutta, and (sometimes hardest of all) in himself.

In summary, the pope has advanced two new arguments in support of his proposal that market systems shed practical light on Christian truth and advance human welfare. The first is that markets give expression to the creative subjectivity of the human person, who has been created in the image of the Creator of all things and called to help complete the work of creation through sustained historical effort. His second argument is that markets generate new and important kinds of community, while expressing the social nature of human beings in rich and complex ways.

There is another reason for proposing markets as a strategy for a Christian theology of liberation of the poor, a proposition for which the evidence of immigration patterns around the world offers prima facie support: market systems better allow the poor to rise out of poverty than any other known social system. Economic opportunity on this planet is as scarce as oil. Immigrants stream toward it by the millions.

Great Britain, Canada, Germany, Italy—most of the market systems on this planet receive steady streams of immigrants. The United States alone between 1970 and 1990 accepted some 16 million *legal* immigrants (nobody knows in addition the number of illegal ones). This is as if we had accepted during that time a new population four times larger than Switzerland's.

Most of these new citizens arrived in America poor. America is quite good at helping immigrants find opportunities, provided only that they are willing to seize them, as the vast majority are. Most of those new citizens were also non-white. Indeed, in America's largest state, California, English is now the *second* language of a plurality of households. This is why Americans rank "opportunity" quite high in evaluating economic systems. Bishop Harries does not quite get this point. He dismisses "the American dream," which is in fact more universal than he allows, in peremptory fashion: "It is not an ignoble [dream] but it is certainly limited. By its nature some fail to make it and are left behind, and when their numbers run into many million questions must be asked" (Harries 1992, 101). Questions must always be asked, yes, but it is good to have some perspective. Although virtually 100 percent of Americans arrived in America poor, today 87 percent are not poor. Only about 8 million of America's 30 million officially designated "poor" persons are able-bodied persons between the ages of 18 and 64; the rest are either 65 or older, 17 or younger, sick, or disabled. For the 8 million able-bodied, the work of the "opportunity society" is not yet complete.

America is also good at helping most of the American-born poor—the elderly, those under 18, the sick or disabled—for whom economic opportunity is not a saving option. Where private family-care is not available to them, where the many programs of civil society let them down, government medical aid, food stamps, housing assistance, and other programs have been supplied to fill the gap.

But for younger adults in good health, the "war on poverty" has actually done much damage (Murray 1984). Our government programs have failed our young. The fastest growing group among the poor has been single female householders with young children. This was not a relatively large group before, when people were far poorer than at present and when current government programs barely existed. Never before have so many males deserted females, with little or no sense of paternal responsibility. The results have been deplorable for children, young mothers, and the young males themselves.

Thus, the great moral and social challenge facing the United States today is to devise new ways to help this group of able-bodied poor adults, mostly young, without reducing them to a kind of serfdom or further depressing their morals. Concerning various ways to correct recent practices, I have written elsewhere at much greater length (Novak and Cogan 1987).

Here we should stress, rather, the crucial importance of dynamic market systems for raising up the poor of central and eastern Europe, Latin America, and throughout the "third world" (which is actually several different worlds). For these poor have in common not only a lack of opportunity but also a sustained, systematic repression of their right to personal economic initiative. Most of them find in their homelands no institutions that might nourish and support that right: constitutionally protected private property, open markets, cheap and easy legal incorporation of businesses, access to legal and low-cost credit, technical assistance, training, and the like. To gain access to such institutions, many millions must seek freedom of opportunity far from home.

The fact that market systems open opportunity for the poor is one of the most important arguments in their favor. This means, of course, the type of market economy that is not protective of the rich, but gives the able-bodied poor many opportunities. Such markets, regularly revolutionized by new inventions and new technologies, bring down many of the formerly rich (as old technologies and ossified firms become obsolete). But their greatest strength lies in the openness and dynamism of the small-business sector through which many millions rise out of poverty.

Open markets liberate the poor better than any known alternative. Open markets favor creativity and dynamism. They also narrow the perceived distance between personal action and personal fate. To narrow the gap is to strengthen human dignity. Nonetheless, like all things human, market systems are not without their ambiguities.

One of my favorite writers on social ethics is Ronald Preston of Scotland, a follower of the great American theologian of the last generation, Reinhold Niebuhr. While fussing about its residual problems, Preston concedes much of the historical argument to capitalism, including its stress on the importance of innovation, incentives, private ownership, flexibility (rather than central planning) with respect to the future, and the many utilities of markets. Preston writes more complacently: "I propose to argue that the issue is not between the free market and the central, planned economy, but how we can get the best of what the social market and democratic socialist models propose" (Preston 1991, 5).

Now, this proposal is remarkable in two ways. First, it turns out that Preston's discussion of the social market model and the democratic socialist model stresses the virtues of markets to a surprising degree. Second, Preston's own ideological commitments prevent him from even considering what many take to be a more humane, dynamic, progressive, and Christian alternative to social market and democratic socialist economies—the democratic capitalist model. He simply leaves it out of account.

More admirably, Preston qualifies his own "social Christianity" by taking on board some of the insights offered by writers to his right, such as Friedrich von Hayek and James Buchanan. Moreover, although he seems not to recognize it, many of the arguments that he makes concerning the "ambiguity" of markets are also consistent with the philosophy of democratic capitalism. There are, for example, some things that should never be bought or sold; in some domains, markets are illegitimate; neither democracy nor the market is a device suited for all purposes. On such matters, Preston and I are in agreement.

Yet there is one point on which Preston seems clearly to be incorrect, at least by omission: his treatment of inequalities of income. First, he praises markets for what they do well: "[O]ther things being equal, markets are a highly efficient way of getting economic decisions made in accordance with the freedom of choice expressed by consumers: that is, by dispersed exercise of political and economic power. They are incentive to thrift and innovation, so tending to maximize the productivity of relatively scarce economic resources." But then Preston adds a sentiment in need of vigorous challenge: "On the other hand, left to themselves market economics produce cumulative inequalities of income which distort the market by drawing the relatively scarce resources to what the wealthy want and away from the necessities of the poor" (Preston 1991, 74).

The assumption here seems to be that non-capitalist systems produce less income inequality. But this is clearly not true of the precapitalist third world regimes of present-day Latin America, Africa, and Asia, in which inequalities of income are of enormous proportions and opportunities for the poor scarcely exist. Nor was it true of communist societies, whose poor are now known to have lived in squalor and whose elites lived in closed circles of high privilege.

Furthermore, Preston omits another salient contrast. Neither precapitalist societies nor socialist societies have done much to lift large majorities of their population out of poverty, as democratic capitalist nations have done. The degree of upward mobility in capitalist societies has no precedent in history, and the array of opportunities that capitalist societies offer to the poor for advancement by way of talent and effort has had no equal. Moreover, it does not seem to be true that market economies produce "cumulative" inequalities of income or that they draw "relatively scarce resources" away from "the necessities of the poor."

To begin with the last assertion, the condition of the poor today is far improved over what it was, say, in 1892 (or 1932) so that the very word "necessities" now entails far higher standards than in centuries past—often we are not talking about mere survival or subsistence. The phrase "relatively scarce resources" is similarly problematic.

Moreover, Preston's accusation of "cumulative" inequalities of income seems doubly dubious. For one thing, during the life cycle of individuals, incomes tend to rise and then fall; for another, from one decade to another, there is immense churning among individuals moving up and down within income brackets. Fortunes are often quickly dissipated. Technologies on which a fortune may be based become speedily obsolete; heirs are seldom as talented or as highly motivated as the creators of the family fortune. Downward mobility is frequent. Elites circulate with rapidity. Preston seems to take the unilateral cumulative growth of wealth as a given; but the staggering fragility and the changeability of fortunes would seem far more prevalent.

Possibly, this difference in perception is due to the unique fluidity of American social structure as contrasted with that of Europe. To a remarkable degree, European societies still consist within aristocratic, feudal institutions; the United States is far more committed to universal opportunity and, in that respect, is a more "purely capitalist" society. Quite often in Europe today, dominant firms are run by the descendants of old aristocratic families (Buttiglione 1992). There really is a perception that wealth and power are stable and cumulative. In America, by contrast, the great families of the 1700s have nearly all died out or lost their prominence. With few exceptions, such as the Rockefellers, the same is true of the great families of the 1800s. Many of the great fortunes of today have been acquired by the living; a significant number, especially among the nouveaux riches of film and entertainment, have also been lost by the living. Great inequalities there may well be, but these are remarkably ephemeral. They are also lacking in moral seriousness: it is not position that counts but quality of performance.

Besides, the good Lord himself forbade covetousness five times in the Ten Commandments: envy is to be resisted. Equality of income is an ideal appropriate only to the unfree and the uniform. What matters far more than inequality is universal opportunity. As an ideal, universal opportunity is far better suited to creatures made in the image of God, who by God's providence are set in dissimilar circumstances. On this fundamental moral issue, Preston should face more squarely the ambiguities of socialism. He might in that confrontation begin to detect its moral and anthropological errors.

Democracy, capitalism, and pluralism (the three social systems whose combination constitutes democratic capitalism) are each ambiguous—all things human are. The relevant social question is not "Is this utopia?" but "Compared to what?" In comparing which system is more likely to bring about universal opportunity, prosperity from the bottom up, the *embourgeoisement* of the proletariat, and the raising up of the poor, the historical answer is clear: for the poor, market systems provide far better chances of improving income, conditions, and status. That is one reason so many of the world's poor migrate toward democratic and capitalist systems.

Market systems combined with democratic political systems offer better hope to the poor of the world than do socialist or traditionalist systems. Despite the inevitable ambiguities of market systems, that is one of their strongest claims to moral recognition—a recognition now clearly accorded by Catholic social teaching.

This chapter originally appeared in Bandow and Schindler, Wealth, Poverty and Human Destiny (2003). Reprinted with permission from ISI Books. Some footnotes in the original version that quoted large sections of the pope's writings were abbreviated to include only a reference to those writings.

Questions for Review

1. In your own words, how would you summarize the Catholic case in favor of democratic capitalism, as understood by Novak? Do you find it persuasive? Why or why not?

2. If, as Novak maintains, democratic capitalism is consistent with Catholic social teaching, then why do you think so many Catholics (not to mention Protestants) are suspicious of corporations and markets?

3. Novak sees markets as central to a Christian theology of liberation of the poor. Please explain.

Notes

[1] See, for example, John Paul II, *Centesimus Annus* (1991), especially sections 32–42 on the economic good, sections 44–48 on the political good, and sections 49–52 on the culture worthy of human beings.

[2] Professor Russell Hittinger of the University of Tulsa is currently working on a major historical study, drafts of which I have been privileged to study, documenting this history from an original and compelling viewpoint. His book is as yet untitled, but his theme is the animosity of many significant liberal regimes toward the Catholic Church (and sometimes other churches), from just before 1789 until about 1950. In this respect, his theme adjoins some of the writing on the struggle between liberalism and the churches undertaken by Pierre Manent, one of the more eminent political philosophers in France.

[3] See, for example, *Ecclesia in America* (Paul 1999, Sec. 56).

[4] See, for example, *Centesimus Annas* (Paul 1991, Sec. 32).

[5] Amartya Sen, for instance, and the other authors of the 1999 Human Development Report, http://www.undp.org/hdro/99.htm (accessed October 7, 1999). This report cites the 1990 development report:

> The real wealth of a nation is its people. And the purpose of development is to create an enabling environment for people to enjoy long, healthy and creative lives. This simple but powerful truth is too often forgotten in the pursuit of material and financial wealth.

See also Becker (1993).

[6] For an interesting survey, see Glynn (1999).

[7] See Leo 1891, *Rerum Novarum* (Secs. 11, 16, 17, 19, 27, and 45).

[8] See *Sollicitudo Rei Socialis* (Paul 1988, Sec. 38–39).

[9] See *Centesimus Annas* (Paul 1991, Sec. 10).

[10] *Centesimus Annus* (Paul 1991, Sec. 58):

> Today we are facing the so-called "globalization" of the economy, a phenomenon which is not to be dismissed, since it can create unusual opportunities for greater prosperity. There is a growing feeling, however, that this increasing internationalization of the economy ought to be accompanied by effective international agencies which will oversee and direct the economy to the common good, something which an individual state, even if it were the most powerful on earth, would not be in a position to do.

[11] St. Thomas Aquinas, *Contra Impugnantes Dei Cultum et Religionem* (1256). St. Thomas presents here the first known defense of association, cited by Leo XIII (1891) in *Rerum Novarum* (section 37) as the locus classicus on associations. Also Russell Hittinger's unpublished lecture at the Summer Institute, Krakow, Poland (July 1998).

[12] See especially The Influence of America (in Sec. II) and The Anglo-American Tradition of Liberty in *Essays in the History of Liberty: Selected Writings of Lord Acton*, edited by J. Rufus Fears (Indianapolis: Liberty Classics, 1985): 198–212.

[13] See http://www.worldbank.org/poverty/data/trends/income.htm (accessed October 7, 1999). The total population of Latin America and the Caribbean is estimated at 519 million people in 2000. See http://www.un.org/popin/wdtrends/popl999-00.pdf (accessed August 21, 2001).

[14] In the World Labor Report, unemployment was estimated for this area at about 59.6 million. See http://www.ilo.org/public/english/80relpro/publ/wlr/97/annex/tab8.htm (accessed October 7, 1999). Youth unemployment rates are usually double the national average, and women's unemployment rates are 60 percent higher than men's rates. Overall employment in Latin America increased on average 2.9 percent between 1990 and 1998, but this was not sufficient to absorb the annual 3.3 percent expansion of the labor force. See http://www.ilo.org/public/english/235press/pr/1999/26.htm (accessed October 6, 1999).

References

Adams, Kenneth. 1990. "Changing British Attitudes." *ASA Journal* 80 (November).

Becker, Gary S. 1993. *Human Capital: A Theoretical and Empirical Analysis, with Special Reference to Education.* Chicago: University of Chicago Press.

Buttiglione, R. 1992. "Christian Economics 101." *Crisis* 34 (July–August).

Collins, Randall. 1986. *Weberian Sociological Theory.* New York, NY: Cambridge University Press, 51–52.

Fears, J. Rufus, ed. 1985. *Essays in the History of Liberty: Selected Writings of Lord Acton.* Indianapolis: Liberty Classics.

Glynn, Patrick. 1999. *God, The Evidence: The Reconciliation of Faith and Reason in a Post Secular World.* Rocklin, CA: Prima Lifestyles.

Gray, John. 1992. *The Moral Foundations of Market Institutions.* No. 10 of *Choice in Welfare Series.* London: IEA Health and Welfare Unit, 5–17; 63–72.

Harries, Richard. 1992. *Is There a Gospel for the Rich?* London: Mowbray.

Leo XIII. 1891. Encyclical Letter *Rerum Novarum.* One of several places one can find it is: http://www.papalencyclicals.net/Leo13/l13rerum.htm.

Marcel, Gabriel. 1960. *The Mystery of Being.* Chicago: Gateway Edition.

Maritain, Jacques. 1951. *Man and State.* Chicago: University of Chicago Press.

———. 1978. *Approaches to God.* Westport, CT: Greenwood Publishing Group (reprint, June).

Murray, G. 1984. *Losing Ground.* New York: Basic Books.

von Nell-Breuning, S. J. Oswald. 1969. Socio-Economic Life. In Vol. 5 of *Commentary on the Documents of Vatican II,* edited by H. Vorgrimler. New York: Herder and Herder.

Newbigin, Lesslie. 1986. *Foolishness to the Greek.* Grand Rapids, MI: Eerdmans.

Novak, M., and John Cogan. 1987. *The New Consensus on Vanity and Welfare.* Washington, D.C.: AEI Press.

Paul, John II. 1981. *Encyclical Letter Laborern Exercens.* Washington, D.C.: St. Paul Publications.

———. 1988. *Encyclical Letter Sollicitudo Rei Socialis*. Washington, D.C.: St. Paul Publications.

———. 1991. *Encyclical Letter Centesimus Annus*. Washington, D.C.: St. Paul Publications.

———. 1999. *Ecclesia in America*. Washington, D.C.: St. Paul Publications.

Preston, Ronald. 1991. *Religion and the Ambiguities of Capitalism*. London: SGM Press.

Rector, R. 1990. "How Poor Are America's Poor?" *Heritage Foundation Backgrounder* 791 (September).

UNDP. 1999. *Human Development Report*. New York, NY: United Nations Development Program. http://www.undp.org/hdro/99.htm (accessed October 7, 1999).

Weigel, George. 1999. *Witness to Hope: The Biography of John Paul II*. New York: HarperCollins.

Wojtyla, Karol. 1979. *The Acting Person*. Translated by A. Potocki. Dordrecht, Boston and London: D. Reidel Publishing; originally published as Wojtyla, K., 1969. *Osoba i czyu*. Krakow: Polskie Towarzystwo Teologiczne.

CHAPTER 2

WHO IS MY NEIGHBOR?
A THEOLOGICAL APPROACH TO
GLOBALIZATION

A. Sue Russell

Globalization is often defined in terms of the growing integration of the world's economy, a process that has accelerated sharply over the last thirty years. The focus is often on the removal of barriers to free trade, the increased freedom in which capital can move around the world, and the increasing domination of national economies by global financial markets and multinational corporations. As Friedman (2005) explains, competition for customers, talent, and jobs is no longer confined by national boundaries. Instead, companies—and even individuals—are now competing head-to-head with companies and individuals from around the world. The division of labor is now global.

However, globalization is more than just economic integration; it also describes the growing interconnectedness of people to one another. Beyer (1994, 1) describes globalization as a new social reality, "one in which previously effective barriers to communication no longer exist." In this new reality, people are no longer isolated, and the increased ability to communicate has created what some have referred to as a global culture in which cultural ideas are exchanged through the flow of people, technology, finances, media, and ideologies. Anthropologists like Lewellen (2002) see the increasing flow of culture, ideas, and people as central to the definition of globalization. King (1997, 12) describes it perhaps most simply as "the process by which the world becomes a single place."

Many scholars are quick to point out that globalization is not entirely new. From the earliest of time there has been trade and other forms of economic interaction between people from different cultures and geographic locations. These trade relationships included many asymmetrical relationships, which caused social problems that are also common today. However, most agree that there is something fundamentally different about today's experience. As Lewellen (2002, 10) puts it, there has been a "deterritorialization of production and finance" caused by the rapid advances in technology and communication that has connected the world. Similarly, King (1997, 12) argues that the difference today is the way "that regionalism, localism and globalization now form a single, unified system, more closely integrated than ever before."

In this chapter, I argue that globalization has not only changed our economic relationships but it has also created a world in which we are connected and influence one another culturally, technologically, socially, and ecologically. Those in need are no longer only the poor across the street or the disadvantaged child in the inner city. Globalization has brought us face to face with famine in Africa, child prostitution in Thailand, and genocide in Darfur. For Christians, globalization has radically changed the answer to the question "Who is my neighbor?"

We begin by addressing the question of "Who is my neighbor?" in this world of radical interconnectedness. We will then examine biblical principles for being a good neighbor. Finally, we will consider how those principles can be worked out in the world in which we live.

Who Is My Neighbor?

Today we are bombarded with the needs of others around the world. We are even prone to what experts call "compassion fatigue," because we see so many needs, and we cannot begin to meet those needs. As followers of Jesus, we want to know whom we need to love: who should have the priority for our time, our energy, and our money. If the Lord requires us to love our neighbor then we must ask, "What does it mean to love someone?" and "Who is my neighbor?" Two thousand years ago a young Jewish lawyer raised these same questions with Jesus. Jesus answered with the parable of the good Samaritan. In order to understand Jesus' answer, we must first understand the context of the question and the cultural dynamics involved in Jesus' answer.

The Setting

> And behold, a lawyer stood up to put him to test, saying, "Teacher, what shall I do to inherit eternal life?" He said to him, "What is written in the Law? How do you read it?" And he answered, "You shall love the Lord your God with all your heart and with all you soul and with all your strength, and with all your mind, and your neighbor as yourself." And he said to him, "You have answered correctly; do this, and you will live." But he, desiring to justify himself, said to Jesus, "And who is my neighbor?" (Luke 10:25–29 ESV)

The context for the story of the good Samaritan is a conversation between Jesus and a lawyer, in some translations "an expert in the law" (Green 1997). Many view the lawyer's initial question as a challenge to Jesus—experts in the law continually tested his orthodoxy. Others see this encounter as a challenge to Jesus' authority as a teacher (Stein 1992; Green 1997). The question the lawyer asked, "What shall I do to inherit eternal life?" should be interpreted from within the orthodoxy of Jewish faith. As Bock (1996) explains, *eternal life* was the technical expression for the eschatological blessings of righteousness, so the question is probably best interpreted to mean "What must be done to participate in the future world of God's blessing?"

Jesus does not answer the lawyer's question. Instead Jesus asks the lawyer a counter-question, "What is written in the Law?" This confirms Jesus' own orthodoxy, since he defers to the authority of God reflected in the Torah. What does God require? The lawyer responds with two familiar passages from the Torah. The first is Deuteronomy 6:5, which is part of the Shema that is recited twice a day. The second is Leviticus 19:18, the context of several tangible ways in which people are to love their neighbor. The lawyer answered correctly that people are created in God's image and loving God means that we must also love man (Bock 1996). Green (1997, 428) notes the impact of this answer:

> So his answer reflects the Shema (Deut. 6:5)—a passage that was fundamental to Jewish life and worship in the home, the synagogue, and the temple. To the Shema the lawyer attaches, inexorably, the law of neighbor-love found in Lev. 19:18. In its co-text in Leviticus love of neighbor is a disposition of the heart expressed in tangible behaviors—related, for example, to a neighbor's honor and possession.

Jesus concurred with his answer. The lawyer's answer was in agreement with Jesus' teaching that love for God is reflected in how people treat others. Throughout the New Testament, love for one's neighbor is linked to devotion to God (Bock 1996). Jesus commends the lawyer to go and do what he has answered. The verb in the present in Greek translates as continuing action. He is not to love just once, but love is an action to be done on an on-going basis.

The Question

The lawyer then asks, "Who is my neighbor?" This question is not extraordinary. We are not given the reason he asked the question, but he, like many others, sought to exploit the ambiguity of the passage (Green 1997). The lawyer wants to justify himself by limiting the extent to which he had to love, or perhaps he wants to justify his past actions (Bock 1996). By quoting Leviticus 19:18 in his answer, he opens the door for carrying out the actions within its context. Among the tangible ways Leviticus 19 outlines to love neighbors are to not steal, cheat, lie, or rob. It also states people are not to take advantage of the weak; but they are to pay workers promptly, to treat the deaf and blind with respect, and to not show favoritism to the rich. Leviticus 19 also exhorts Israelites not to exploit foreigners in the land, since they too were considered neighbors.

In Leviticus 19, love for a neighbor is directed toward fellow Israelites and resident aliens living in the land. However, the situation in Israel had changed. During the time of Jesus' exchange with the lawyer, numerous foreigners lived within the boundaries of Israel because of Hellenistic and Roman conquests. Many of the foreigners who lived in the land were not there to embrace the covenant of God, but represented foreign oppressors, Roman officials, soldiers, tax collectors, and traders. Which of these foreigners did the lawyer have to love? Additionally there were parties and factions within Judaism, each promoting their own group as the true people of God. Green (1997, 429) notes, "Different attitudes toward these foreign intrusions developed into a fractured social context in which boundaries distinguished not only between Jew and Gentile but also between Jewish factions. How far should love reach?"

Many of us ask the same question when faced with the tremendous needs in the world. We ask if we should give priority to our family. We wonder if a Darfur refugee or an HIV/AIDS infected child in Asia is as much our neighbor as the person down the street. Our natural tendency is to limit the answer to our "in-group" of our family, our friends, and perhaps even our nation. Jesus' answer to the question was extraordinary.

The Answer

> Jesus replied, "A man was going down from Jerusalem to Jericho, and he fell among robbers, who stripped him and beat him and departed, leaving him half dead. Now by chance a priest was going down that road, and when he saw him he passed by on the other side. So likewise a Levite, when he came to the place and saw him, passed by on the other side. But a Samaritan, as he journeyed, came to where he was, and when he saw him, he had compassion. He went to him and bound up his wounds, pouring on oil and wine. Then he set him on his own animal and brought him to an inn and took care of him. And the next day he took out two denarii and gave them to the innkeeper, saying, 'Take care of him; and whatever more you spend, I will repay you when I come back.'" (Luke 10:30–35 ESV)

While Jesus' answer to the lawyer's question is perhaps one of the most well known parables, it is often misunderstood or allegorized. The parable, however, was set in a "real life" context. The audience would have understood the full impact of the story within their social and cultural setting. Jesus starts his parable with an ambiguous "certain man." The man is anonymous and cannot be identified in any particular category. The lawyer and Jesus' audience cannot automatically justify the actions of the priest and the Levite because they were just following a socially acceptable form of action. "The impossibility of classifying this person as either friend or foe immediately subverts any interest in a question of this nature" (Green 1997, 429).

The man was traveling a well known path from Jerusalem to Jericho. The purpose of his journey is vague; perhaps he is a priest or Levite on his way home from his temple duties, or he could be anyone who had just been to the Temple. We are not told anything about the man, his ethnicity, social class, or religion. He was just a man. The audience knew that the journey was dangerous. It was a rocky path that wound through the desert and was surrounded by caves where bandits often hid (Bock 1996). The unknown man is overwhelmed by bandits and is left for dead; his state is such that he cannot help himself. "Stripped of his clothes and left half-dead, the man's anonymity throughout the story is assured; he is simply a human being, a neighbor, in need" (Green 1997, 429).

The first two travelers to see the man in the road are representatives of the Temple elite. Both of these represented the emphasis of Judaism at the time on the Law and purity. Many have tried to justify the travelers' actions by noting that they would have made themselves impure for their Temple service. However, both the priest and Levite were heading *down* from Jerusalem, so they were finished with their Temple duty. Bock notes that identifying the two who passed by as officials of Judaism is a generalized condemnation of official Judaism that placed purity over compassion of those who saw the world as us-them (Bock 1996). Green (1997, 429) describes the issue:

> Priests and Levites shared high status in the community of God's people on account of ascription—that is not because they trained or were chosen to be priest but because they were born into priestly families. They participated in and were legitimated by the world of the temple, with its circumspect boundaries between clean and unclean, including clean and unclean people. They epitomize a worldview of tribal consciousness concerned with relative status and us-them cataloguing.

After a quick succession of Jewish leaders who saw but passed by, we are introduced to the Samaritan. Jesus introduces the Samaritan last. For the Jew, a "good" Samaritan is an oxymoron. A Samaritan was the last person that a Jew would consider a neighbor. The Samaritans were considered half-breeds because of their exile to Assyria and their intermarriage with non-Jewish people. After their return from exile, the Samaritans sought to help rebuild the Temple, but their help was refused. After that, they attempted to impede its progress. Then, the Jews destroyed the Samaritan temple on Mt. Gerizim, causing a mutual hatred between Jews and Samaritans. The Jews would have never considered the Samaritans to be neighbors. They were outsiders geographically, socially, religiously, and culturally; and they were considered unclean and therefore to be avoided. "For a Jew, a Samaritan was among the least respected of people" (Bock 1996, 1031).

Jesus does not briefly mention the Samaritan and then end his story. He elaborates and prolongs the story to reinforce his message. The Samaritan takes six concrete actions: (1) he comes up to the man on the road, (2) binds his wounds, (3) anoints him with oil and wine, (4) loads him on a mule, (5) takes him to an inn, and (6) provides for his care (Bock 1996, 1032). In contrast to the two Jews, the Samaritan gave generously and did everything he could to take care of this unknown man. Jesus continues:

> Which of these three, do you think, proved to be a neighbor to the man who fell among the robbers? He said, "The one who showed him mercy." And Jesus said to him, "You go, and do likewise." (Luke 10:36–37 ESV)

Jesus' counter-question is not who *is* my neighbor, but who *acted like* a neighbor, or in the Greek, "Who became the neighbor?" The implication is that neither geographic, nor social, nor familial ties define a neighbor; rather a neighbor is defined in terms of the one who has a need. The one who showed compassion and met the need became a neighbor. Jesus turned the discussion from the meaning of neighbor to the meaning of love (Blight 2007).

In the story, Jesus takes away the limits of our love and responsibility to our fellow man. We are no longer able to quibble over who is our neighbor or where does our responsibility lie. We can no longer say we are responsible only for our family, friends, and nation. Jesus does not give guidance on prioritizing to whom we should be a neighbor. The man in Jesus' parable did not have an identity. His ethnicity, his geographical hometown, and his religion all remain unknown in his anonymity. He simply was someone who needed a neighbor. Willard (1998, 111) notes, "We don't first define a class of people who will be our neighbors and then select only them as objects of our love—leaving the rest to lie where they fall. Jesus deftly rejects the question 'Who is my neighbor?' and substitutes the only question really relevant here: 'To whom will I be a neighbor?'" Bock (1996, 1035) also notes that love no longer has boundaries: "Neighborliness is not found in a racial bond, nationality, color, gender, proximity, or by living in a certain neighborhood. We become a neighbor by responding sensitively to the needs of others." Stein (1992, 319) notes that "Jesus sought to illustrate that the love of one's neighbor must transcend all natural or human boundaries such as race, nationality, religion, and economic or educational status."

For those of us living in the twenty-first century, it is increasingly more difficult to remain ignorant of the people in need around the world. Modern communication technology is bringing us face to face like never before with people in need in our new global community. Globalization has radically changed who is our neighbor. Although the scope of our awareness has changed, those in need have not changed since biblical times. Our neighbors are still the most vulnerable and powerless of society. In Leviticus 19 the most vulnerable and powerless are foreigners, hired workers, the poor, the elderly, the disabled; and Deuteronomy 24 adds widows and orphans. The key characteristic is that they cannot work and therefore need a social system to take care of them. According to Blomberg (1999, 78), "The poor here refers not to the majority of the people eking out a subsistence-level income, but those who were utterly destitute."

The same categories still apply today but to a greater degree. Our neighbors are those like the "certain man" in Jesus' parable. They are hopeless, anonymous, naked, and abandoned. They are the most vulnerable in society—the sick, refugees, orphans, and widows. They are those who no longer have a social safety net of kin or government to ensure their survival. They are

Poor: The 3 billion people who live on fewer than two dollars a day, and the 1 billion people who live on less than one dollar.

Children: The 130 million who do not read; the 250 million who go to work instead of school; the 2 million children kidnapped or sold to brothels in the global sex trade; the 200,000 boys who serve as soldiers; the 150 million children who live on the streets.

Orphans: The 15 million children who are orphaned because of AIDS.

Sick: The 11 million children who will die of preventable diseases; the 120 to 150 million children who suffer from disabilities; the 40 million people infected with HIV.

Women: The workers who comprise half the global work force but consistently work longer hours and receive lower pay.

Foreigners: The 6 million immigrants; the 15 million refugees; the 42 million labor migrants who often live and work in harsh conditions for little pay.[1]

How Do We Become a Neighbor?

Given this broadened definition of neighbor, what does it mean to be a neighbor? First, we must recognize that we are different—being a neighbor does not mean we will be the same economically, culturally, socially, or ideologically as those we help. The Scripture recognizes an unequal distribution of wealth. With wealth there is a greater responsibility to others, since wealth provides the resources that can meet the needs of others. Three principles can be drawn from Scripture for being a neighbor in today's global world.

Treat Every Human as a Person Made in the Image of God

The very foundation for loving others is based on the fact that God created us in his own image (Gen. 1:26). If we say that we love God, we must also love the one who is created in his image (1 John 4:19–21). Every human is a unique reflection of the image of God. In economic relationships we often reduce people to "consumers" or "laborers," making it easy to dehumanize individuals and no longer acknowledge our responsibility to our fellow humans. We tend to categorize people into statistics; the AIDS orphans, the refugees, the poor. It is much easier to ignore statistics. It is much easier to exploit labor. It is much easier to sell unneeded products to consumers. Every number in a statistic, however, has a face. Every person who works is part of a family. Every orphan has a story. When Jesus says to love our neighbor as ourselves, he is requiring us to treat others as people we know. We need to ask, "Would I want my daughter to buy my product?" "Would I want my son to work at my company for the wages I pay my workers?" "What would I do if it were my brother who was infected with HIV?" Until we personalize and humanize statistics, we will never be good neighbors.

A personal example may help illustrate this point. My husband and I recently contracted with our gardener to remove stumps from our backyard. We agreed on a price, but after a whole day of working, it was obvious the job was taking longer than our gardener had calculated. On the second day, my husband said, "Do you realize that if we pay the price we agreed to, we would be paying him less than minimum wage?" We talked with our gardener and adjusted the amount he would get paid. It was interesting how our choice to pay fair wages, and to look out for his interest as well as our own, changed our relationship with our gardener. We became friends that day. As individuals, it is often easy to make economic choices to look out for the interests of others.

Don't Exploit

The second principle is that the wealthy are not to use their power to exploit or dominant others. The Old Testament has much to say about labor relations and powerful people who exploit their position at the expense of their workers. The wealthy are to pay their workers promptly, and they are not to oppress their workers (Lev. 19:13). They are to neither rob the poor nor exploit them in court (Prov. 22). Using power to oppress the poor is a direct affront to God. Proverbs 14:31 (NLT) says, "Those who oppress the poor insult their Maker, but helping the poor honors him." Throughout the Scriptures, it is clear that we are not to exploit the poor just because they are poor.

One difference between Israel and other nations is that Jewish kings were to follow the same law as their subjects—they were not allowed to use their power to exploit people. There are two striking incidents in the Old Testament of kings using their power to exploit the less powerful. The first is David stealing Uriah's wife, Bathsheba. Many interpret David's sin as adultery; however, if Nathan's rebuke is examined closely, it is about the rich using power to exploit the poor.

> So the LORD sent Nathan the prophet to tell David this story: "There were two men in a certain town. One was rich, and one was poor. The rich man owned a great many sheep and cattle. The poor man owned nothing but one little lamb he had bought. He raised that little lamb, and it grew up with his children. It ate from the man's own plate and drank from his cup. He cuddled it in his arms like a baby daughter. One day a guest arrived at the home of the rich man. But instead of killing an animal from his own flock or herd, he took the poor man's lamb and killed it and prepared it for his guest."
> (2 Sam. 12:1–4 NLT)

When Nathan tells David this story, David immediately recognizes the injustice and abuse of power and wealth against the poor. Nathan responds that David is the one who did such a thing. David had despised the word of the Lord by using his power to exploit the less powerful.

Another instance of a king abusing his power is Ahab trying to acquire the field of Naboth. Naboth acts righteously by refusing to sell the land of his ancestors, which makes Ahab angry. When Ahab tells Jezebel why he is angry, her response is, "Are you the king of Israel or not?" Then she tells Ahab that she will get Naboth's field for him. Jezebel proceeds to send false witnesses against Naboth, and he is stoned. When Ahab learns that Naboth is dead, he immediately goes to possess the vineyard. Ahab not only knew what Jezebel was about to do, he also condoned it by taking possession of the field. Although Jezebel was the agent (1 Kings 21:7), it was Ahab's responsibility as king to protect the poor. The Lord responds by sending Elijah to tell Ahab, "Wasn't it enough that you killed Naboth? Must you rob him, too?" (1 Kings 21:19 NLT).

The Old Testament repeatedly warns the rich and powerful not to exploit the poor. There is an underlying assumption that there will always be some with more and some with less. However, the sin is the rich depriving the poor of what is rightfully theirs: basic subsistence (Blomberg 1999).

The New Testament writings also demonstrate that those in a position of wealth and power are not to exploit others. The Corinthians are rebuked when the rich eat dinner while the poor have nothing, thus humiliating the poor (1 Cor. 11:17–22). Men are not to dominate their wife and children, as was their right in Roman society (Eph. 5:25). The church is not to show favoritism to the rich over the poor. James 2:8–9 states, "If you really keep the royal law found in Scripture, 'Love your neighbor as yourself,' you are doing right. But if you show favoritism, you sin and are convicted by the law as law breakers" (NIV).

Wealthy and powerful nations can also violate this principle in the interest of looking after only their own national interest. As Stiglitz (2007) and others have pointed out, the rules of the global economy, made mostly by the more powerful and wealthy countries, provide maximum benefit to them. Stiglitz (2007, 4) argues:

> The rules of the game have been largely set by the advanced industrial countries—and particularly by special interests within those countries—and, not surprisingly, they have shaped globalization to further their own interests. They have not sought to create a fair set of rules, let alone a set of rules that would promote the well-being of those in the poorest countries of the world.

In some cases the asymmetry in trade agreements results in the poorest countries actually being worse off than before the agreement. As Finn argues in Chapter 3 of this book, a Christian perspective on negotiating the rules of trade seeks to balance self-interest, fairness, and justice.

Nations are not the only exploiters of power; large multinational firms often have an ability to exploit an imbalance of power. The income of many corporations exceeds that of entire developing nations. Of the one hundred largest economic entities, fifty-one are multinational corporations, and forty-nine are countries (Sernau 2006). Corporations have brought technology and investment into developing countries; however, because of their vast resources, corporations have also been known to promote their own interests at the expense of the countries they work in and over the social needs of the citizens of those countries.

Scripture is clear that those with wealth and power are to use it for others, not just for their own interests (Phil. 2:3–4). Those with resources are not to use them to dominate others, but to serve others. When Leviticus outlines the rules of buying and selling land in relation to the Year of Jubilee, the commands are summed up as "Do not take advantage of each other, but fear your God. I am the LORD your God" (Lev. 25:17 NIV). When articulating the rules governing the poor who may have to sell themselves as slaves, no less than three times, God concludes with "Do not rule over them ruthlessly" (Lev. 25:43, 46, 53).

Developed countries and large transnational companies are not to rule over or exploit the poor. The church should advocate for fair trade rules that look out for the interests of others, not just for a nation's narrowly defined self-interest. This may mean small developing countries should be allowed to play by a different set of rules than developed countries. Just as a poor man has little he can risk, smaller developing countries should be able to enter into trade agreements that limit their risk in proportion to what they can afford.

Do Good

The final principle is to not refrain from doing good or from doing what you want others to do for you. The wealthy and powerful are not only to refrain from exploiting the vulnerable but they are also expected to protect and do good to them. The utterly destitute are under special protection of the Lord. As the Psalmist says, the Lord himself is a father to the fatherless and a defender of widows, and he rescues the poor and helpless (Ps. 68:5; 72:12). In the Old Testament, wealth is considered a gift from the Lord, so those who are given the means are expected to act as God's agents in protecting the well-being of the vulnerable.

Landowners are instructed not to harvest along the edges of the fields nor pick up the gleanings that fall. Neither are they to pick every grape; and they are to leave the fallen fruit for the poor and the foreigner (Lev. 19:9–10). The landowner is not asked to give all of his profit away, but social concern is to outweigh maximization of profit. The wealthy are to be generous. Proverbs 11:24–25 states, "Give freely and become more wealthy; be stingy and lose everything. The generous will prosper" (NLT). We are not to withhold good from those who deserved it. We are, instead, to give when we have the power to do so (Prov. 3:27–28).

The powerful are not only to help the poor but they are also to defend them from others who would cause them harm. The righteous are to defend the cause of the fatherless, the rights of the poor and oppressed, and rescue the week and needy from the wicked (Ps. 82:3–4). The righteous are to care about justice for the poor (Prov. 29:7). Many times when God condemned the Israelites and other nations, part of his condemnation was that they failed to defend the poor and the fatherless (Jer. 5:28; Amos 4:1). Even though Sodom was notorious for other sins, often overlooked is that God condemned it not just for immorality but also that "she and her daughters were arrogant, overfed and unconcerned; they did not help the poor and needy" (Ezek. 16:49 NIV).

In the New Testament the same concern for the poor is found in the early church when it cared for widows and the poor (Acts 6). The wealthy contributed to the church by selling some of their possessions to be used by the church, and often they offered their house as a place for the church to meet (Acts 4:32–36). In the New Testament writings, loving people is the direct outcome of loving God. Doing good to someone in need is the outcome of someone's faith. James 2:14–17 (NIV) states the following:

> What good is it, my brothers, if a man claims to have faith but has no deeds? Can such faith save him? Suppose a brother or sister is without clothes and daily food. If one of you says to him, "Go, I wish you well; keep warm and well fed," but does nothing about his physical needs, what good is it? In the same way, faith by itself, if it is not accompanied by action, is dead."

These verses have often been interpreted as describing salvation as the result of works. However, James is not saying that doing good results in salvation. He is saying that salvation results in doing good.

The equation has not changed from the answer the lawyer gave Jesus. When we love God, this will be reflected in our love for people. In both the Old and the New Testament, love for God and love for people are never separated; you cannot do one without doing the other. The mandate is the same for Christians today. Blomberg (1999, 155) sums it up:

> So too, professing Christians today who have a surplus income (i.e. a considerable majority of believers in the Western world) who are aware of the desperate human needs locally and globally, not least within the Christian community (a situation almost impossible to be unaware of, given our barrage of media coverage), and who give none of their income, either through church or other Christian organizations, to help the materially destitute of the world, ought to ask themselves whether any claims of faith they might make could stand up before God's bar of judgment. This is not salvation by works any more than the examples of Abraham and Rahab in James 2:20–25, but it is the demonstration of a changed life, a heart begun to be transformed by the indwelling Spirit of God, which thereby produces an outpouring of compassion for those so much less well off than oneself.

We have a choice. Do we respond as did the priest and Levite, who saw but passed by on the other side of the road? Or do we respond to the person in need, generously out of compassion, and become a neighbor? The following suggests a few ways in which we as part of the wealthy minority might become a neighbor to those in need.

Being a good neighbor means that those policy makers and others in positions of influence in the global economy must value people, not just economic prosperity. Doing good means making sure the social needs and environmental concerns are given the same weight as economic issues. Doing good may mean that a corporation's success needs to be measured in terms of profit and by how they have improved the social, cultural, and environmental well-being of others. Policy makers should seek to ensure that the benefits of globalization reach all segments of society, particularly the most marginalized: the poor, the women, and the ill. The benefits should include increasing the income of the marginalized and providing access to education, technology, and health care so that they may rise from being merely recipients of the benefits to becoming full participants in globalization.

Globalization is often equated with the promotion of American culture and values, but care should be taken to respect and preserve the cultural practices and languages of others. Too often corporations bring in products that replace traditional goods, resulting in the loss of cultural knowledge. Many times people are too poor to continue their traditional practices; and only after the practices are lost does the next generation realize their loss of identity. The mass media, film, music, and television industries are motivated not by cultural diversity, but by monetary gain.

As participants in the global economy, we are individually responsible for not dominating, for doing good, and for being a good neighbor. Being a good neighbor involves more than making a deliberate effort to improve the economic situation of others. A good neighbor also values and respects the social, cultural, and environmental resources of others.

Conclusion

Globalization has changed the definition of who our neighbor is. It has also empowered us as individuals to treat as neighbors those we previously had little contact with or no knowledge of. Although few of us are in positions to make economic policy or manage a multinational corporation, we can all promote justice through our consumer choices and voting records, influencing those who are in such positions.

We now have the opportunity as never before to do great good by providing many people with access to goods, information, technology, services, education, and healthcare. However, we also have the opportunity to do great evil by increasing inequalities, assimilating cultures, and destroying the environment. As we learn in the parable of the good Samaritan, it is not enough to refrain from making things worse and from doing harm, as important as those things are. As good neighbors we should, as it says in Jeremiah 29, actively seek the welfare of the city, where "city" is now the globe.

We do not have to look far to make choices that will contribute to the common good. Many people have gardeners, domestic helpers, and child care workers in their employment; and many of us are served in restaurants by servers and in hotels by bellhops and house cleaners—usually low skilled, poorly educated immigrants vulnerable to exploitation. We can commit ourselves to pay fair wages and tip generously in order to look out for their welfare. We can also be good neighbors by buying products from and making investments in companies that demonstrate a commitment to treating their employees and suppliers justly.

Thanks to modern technologies, we can also increase people's awareness of issues such as conflict diamonds, invisible children, sweatshops, and child prostitution. With relatively minor changes in our lifestyle, we can donate money to organizations such as World Vision, Food for the Hungry, and many others that seek to help the most vulnerable in society. In our interconnected world one person really can make a difference.

Who is our neighbor? Sometimes the Lord surprises us with his answer. During the time I was writing this chapter, I stopped at a gas station, and a man approached me to ask for help. He and his girlfriend had run out of gas and were stranded. I helped push their car close to one of the pumps and paid for some gas. After filling their tank, we exchanged waves and smiles and went on our way. Will I ever see them again? Probably not. Why did I do it? Simply because it was the right thing to do. We do not get to choose who our neighbors are; we just need to respond when God brings them our way. Why? Simply because it is the right thing to do.

Questions for Review

1. The author claims that globalization has changed the definition of *neighbor*. Do you agree? Please explain.

2. How do you choose whom to help? Does Scripture give guidelines? What are some practical ways you can be a better neighbor?

3. In a world of 24/7 news cycles, how can we avoid compassion fatigue and remain sensitive to the needs of the world around us?

4. If, as Russell maintains, we are to "actively seek the welfare of the city, where 'city' is now the globe," what are the implications for U.S. trade policy? Immigration policy?

5. What do you think about Christians who argue against trade and/or immigration on nationalistic grounds? Are they being a good neighbor? Please explain.

Notes

¹ Statistics are from the World Bank, "Global Monitoring Report," and UNICEF.

References

Beyer, Peter. 1994. *Religion and Globalization*. London: Sage Publications.

Blight, Richard C. 2007. *An Exegetical Summary of Luke 1-11*. Dallas: SIL.

Blomberg, Craig L. 1999. *Neither Poverty nor Riches: A Biblical Theology of Possessions*. Leicester, U.K.: Apollos.

Bock, Darrell L. 1996. *Luke 9:51–24:53*. Grand Rapids, MI: Baker Books.

De Vries, Barend A. 1998. *Champions of the Poor*. Washington D.C.: Georgetown University Press.

Ferree, Myra Marx. 2006. Recognizing Transnational Feminism. In *Global Feminism*, edited by Myra Marx Ferree and Aili Mari Tripp. New York: New York University Press, 3–23.

Friedman, Thomas. 2005. *The World Is Flat*. New York: Picador.

Green, Joel. 1997. *The Gospel of Luke*. Grand Rapids, MI: Eerdmans.

King, Anthony. 1997. Introduction: Spaces of Culture, Spaces of Knowledge. In *Culture, Globalization, and the World System*, edited by Anthony King. Minneapolis: University of Minnesota Press.

Lewellen, Ted C. 2002. *The Anthropology of Globalization*. Westport, CT: Bergin and Garvey.

Sernau, Scott. 2006. *Global Problems*. Boston: Pearson.

Stein, Robert H. 1992. *Luke, The New American Commentary*. Vol. 24. Nashville: Boardman Press.

Stiglitz, Joseph. 2007. Making Globalization Work. New York: W. W. Norton & Company.

UNICEF. 1999. "The State of the World's Children." New York, NY: UNICEF.

Willard, Dallas. 1998. *The Divine Conspiracy*. San Francisco: HarperSanFrancisco.

World Bank. 2007. "Global Monitoring Report." Washington, D.C.: World Bank.

PART II

The International Flow of Goods, Services, Capital, and Labor

CHAPTER 3

MORAL VALUES AND THE RULES OF INTERNATIONAL TRADE

Daniel Finn

All human interaction requires rules of some sort—whether explicitly agreed upon or simply internalized unconsciously. International trade is no exception. Thus, the task of setting rules for international trade is exceedingly important, but it is remarkably difficult. The immense scale of trade is part of the problem—it affects so much of daily life around the globe. An equally important impediment, however, arises because each nation begins with the conviction that many of its trading partners don't "play the game" by the right rules. The diversity of cultures is a key feature here.

The role of culture is so subtle that people tend to be unaware of its power in shaping their lives until they have contact with others who live differently. The same act that in one culture is understood as an immoral bribe, for example, in another is interpreted as a gift of appreciation. A work schedule and intensity that in one culture indicates a commitment to excellence might be seen as nearly manic compulsive in another.

Different nations take for granted different rules by which daily life and commerce should occur. Thus, it is quite common that a nation believes it is disadvantaged because its international trading partners

75

play by different rules. U.S. firms point to the economic rewards of the Japanese *keiretsu* system of closely integrated industrial firms, a monopolistic advantage forbidden in the United States under antitrust laws. Canadian firms point to the economic advantage of their American competitors due to weaker (and less costly) protections for workers and the unemployed in the United States. The list of examples could be extended, but the principle is the same: We take for granted most of the ordinary ways of doing things at home (even if that puts outsiders at a disadvantage), and we are vividly aware of the advantages that others abroad enjoy, particularly those that we ourselves have eliminated at home due to moral conviction. As a result, an international agreement on "fair" rules of trade is critically important.

In fact, existing international agreements on a host of issues far beyond trade stand as a truly significant moral accomplishment of the modern world. Though limited and flawed in many ways, international agreements—concerning arms reduction, environmental standards, human rights, and a long list of other important moral issues—mark real moral progress.

Morality, Self-Interest, and the "Rules of the Game"

Christians throughout history have had to cope with the moral ambiguities of political and economic institutions. The problem, of course, is that the ethics of love and self-denial that Jesus preached and Christians endorse cannot easily be translated into political and economic rules, even in a nation comprising only Christians. It is far more complicated in a pluralistic society, where religious appeals have limited effect in public discourse. Although a full-blown investigation of the complexities of neighbor-love and self-interest cannot be undertaken here, two insights are critical for Christians thinking about the rules of trade.[1] First, those who would "play hardball" in trade negotiations and feel justified in asserting national self-interest in all settings misunderstand the necessary limits on self-interest. Second, those who would propose purely altruistic principles for international economic relations underestimate the complexities of political and economic organization and the effects of sin, finitude, and ignorance in human life more generally.

An adequate Christian response to modern economic life understands the assertion of self-interest in a nuanced way. Although there are indeed times when looking out for one's own interests is morally justifiable, the centrality for the Christian of love of neighbor means that any moral endorsement of self-interest must be limited and context-dependent. Whether and to what degree self-interested activity "works" in society depends immensely on "the rules of the game."

Markets can be thought of as "spaces" where people interact with one another through voluntary agreements (for example, buying and selling, agreeing to contracts, and so forth) and it is understood by all involved that participants are looking out for their own interests. As a result we do not and ought not feel guilty when we seek a promotion, for example, or look for the very best farm produce at the grocery store. Similarly, we expect that the local Ford dealer's "sale price" on a new car is an attempt to make a profit without losing customers to the Chevrolet dealer across town.

For nearly all of us, of course, self-interest is not all we will look out for—our moral commitments will lead us to be friendly to strangers, help coworkers, and so forth. The moral character of the people who make up any society is critical for the success of its markets and other institutional arrangements. These institutional arrangements are bounded by law, and a good deal of the law amounts to restrictions on activities in which self-interested individuals might otherwise engage, but that are now deemed as illegitimate market behavior.

Michael Walzer (1983) refers to some of these prohibitions as "blocked exchanges." Although most things are fair game for buying and selling, there is a long list of possible exchanges prevented or "blocked" by law. Thus, the laws of most industrialized nations today do not allow the buying or selling of human beings, cocaine, hand grenades, the votes of legislators, the votes of citizens, the obligation to serve in the armed forces, the judgment of the courts, and so on. Ways around some of these prohibitions certainly exist, but they stand blocked in principle, and society regularly attempts to strengthen the barrier to them by better law or more effective enforcement. The history of commerce shows that when laws against violence or exploitation eliminate the business advantage of "thugs" and exploitive practices, other moral characters take on leadership roles in economic life.

A host of other exchanges, while allowed in some circumstances, are regulated in one way or another. Although it has become popular in recent years to criticize the bureaucratic excesses of regulation, such criticism often clouds the underlying reality that most citizens, including a majority of economic conservatives, would support many of these basic restrictions on activity. Included here are regulations of "insider trading," the sale of prescription drugs, the disposal of hazardous waste, health standards for restaurant kitchens, safety standards for nursing homes and coal mines, and so on.

Envisioning markets as an arena bounded by laws, within which the assertion of self-interest is morally legitimate, does not solve the "real" problem of determining whether any current restrictions ought to be removed or whether any currently legal activities ought to be regulated or prohibited altogether. But this understanding of the relation of government and markets does eliminate much simplistic rhetoric on each side: it contradicts those who argue against government as if human life or even economic life would be better without any "government interference," and it calls to realism those Christians who reflexively criticize the activities of large economic actors, such as multinational firms or labor unions, simply on the grounds that they are acting out of their own self-interest. It does not resolve the issues of power in international trade—of the government, of transnational firms, of the wealthy—but it does provide a framework within which conflicting moral and empirical claims about power can be adjudicated.

Critical to all these discussions is the notion of justice in Christian social ethics. It is helpful to recall that justice has traditionally included three interrelated dimensions in Christian ethics. The first is that individuals have an obligation to other individuals with whom they have made contracts or agreements. This is the dimension of justice most self-evident in modern society. If I make an agreement with you, I am obliged in justice to fulfill it. The second dimension is an obligation all persons have to contribute to the well-being of the community. Rooted in the covenant of the Hebrew Scriptures, the Christian notion of obligation to the community entails a requirement that the able-bodied both contribute to the community's production and support shared institutions. The third dimension arises from God's abundant gift of creation to humanity. Justice requires that the prosperity of the well-to-do meet the needs of those unable to provide for themselves.

Moral Values and the Rules of Trade

In accord with this understanding of the relation of self-interest and the "rules of the game," Christians should advocate for rules of trade that prevent the worst abuses that the exertion of self-interest in trade would otherwise inevitably cause. The logistics of agreeing upon the rules of trade have become much more complicated as the number of members of the World Trade Organization (WTO) has risen. Under the WTO's predecessor, the General Agreement on Tariffs and Trade (GATT), the rules were made by consensus among wealthy nations. Developing countries generally went along with this because they often were not constrained by the agreements. However, under the WTO, all signatory nations are obliged to live by the agreements. The much larger number of members, most of them poor, means that the consensus process has broken down and agreements have been much harder to reach due to conflicting economic interests.

Identifying a Christian perspective on justice and the rules of trade is a challenging task, in part because one finds few specific references to international trade in the Bible or later Christian reflection. Still, it is possible to draw on general themes for ethical guidelines related to economic life. Thus an authentically Christian view of trade would require that the following moral concerns be integrated into the rules that structure trade.

The Economic Welfare of the World's Poor

The God revealed in the Hebrew Scriptures is a God who cares about the poor: the widow, the orphan, and the resident alien. This is a God who intends that creation meet the needs of all humanity, a God who knows that the powerful and prosperous can easily forget the poor, and those whose needs are left unmet.

Moral discourse today frequently employs the language of "rights"—including economic rights such as the right to food, clothing, and shelter. However, the Christian tradition before the modern period cast the argument somewhat differently. The focus there was on unmet needs, based on the universal conviction from the Bible, the early church, and the Middle Ages that God created the earth to meet the needs of all. In focusing on needs of the poor rather than on the gap between the wealthy and the poor, the tradition does not call for an economic egalitarianism. Rather, it leaves the definite impression that if the well-being of the world's poor were secure, *differences* in income and wealth between rich and poor would not be morally problematic (even though wealth would still threaten to harden the hearts of the wealthy).

Most Christian churches today have openly endorsed the notion of "economic rights" as adequately naming a claim of poor people, based on God's reign. Such rights must be implemented carefully to prevent the creation of dependency in the poor (itself a violation of their God-given dignity). But this Christian insight rejects the libertarian response, which denies the existence of both economic rights and our obligations to the poor.

The phrase "option for the poor" is often used today. As originally conceived by liberation theology, this option suggests as *epistemological* privilege of the poor, arguing that the economic and political situation can only be understood when the Christian self-consciously takes the experience of the poor and oppressed as normative (see, for example, Cormie 1992). Nearly everyone involved in Christian ethics openly acknowledges that the experience and perspectives of the world's poor and oppressed are essential for moral discourse and are too often ignored. However, most outside liberation theology would argue that it is excessive and, in this case, somewhat romantic to assign a hermeneutically privileged position to the view of any one group.

A fundamental moral argument in favor of international trade is the potential it has to increase the income and productivity of the world's poor. This implies that a free trade stance can be consistent with an explicit concern for the welfare of the world's poor. However, because developing nations are often at a disadvantage in trade negotiations, such a stance needs to be coupled with efforts to write remedies into the rules of trade that correct the imbalance.

A case in point is the "Generalized System of Preferences" (GSP), which grants preferential (duty-free) access to the markets of more than twenty industrialized countries for the exports of the developing world. These GSP schemes have benefited producers (both owners and workers) in more than 140 developing nations. In 2006, for example, the United States imported $310 billion worth of products from the 112 developing countries included in the U.S. GSP program (Jones 2007). Considering the issue worldwide, evidence indicates that GSP has increased exports from beneficiary countries by about 8 percent annually. Domestically, the effects in the US economy are small, mainly because imports are a relatively small share of the U.S. economy, and imports from developing countries are a small part of those U.S. imports. The loss of U.S. tariff revenue, for example, amounts to a tiny three one-hundredths of one percent (0.0003) of the $2.4 trillion dollars the government took in that year (Jones 2007).

A complete removal of developed nations' trade restrictions (including tariffs and non-tariff barriers) facing third world exports to the West would raise those exports by approximately 10 percent, resulting in about a 3 percent increase in the GDP of developing nations, a sizable annual benefit (Finger and Messerlin 1989; Salvatore 1992). In addition to the economic stimulus such reform would create, it would allow third world nations significantly greater flexibility in reaching their development goals. Other "exceptions" for the poorest of the developing nations—such as an exemption from the prohibition on export subsidies—have been built into the WTO, although these remain more controversial. While not sufficient, such systematic exemption to trade rules is morally important.

Another important exemption to trade rules was reached in August 2003, when WTO nations negotiated an agreement on the trade-related aspects of intellectual property rights (TRIPS). Sought by the industrialized nations, the TRIPS agreement aims to strengthen protections of intellectual property rights in developing nations. The agreement allows developing nations, in certain circumstances, to produce or import generic drugs without paying the high royalties usually required by pharmaceutical companies, particularly to address the AIDS epidemic. This intentional erosion of intellectual property rights is still being worked out around the world. It is definitely an advantage for poorer nations, but it is not clear whether this exception will lead to others.

Equally important has been the increased representation of third world nations in the administrative mechanisms for world trade. The councils overseeing global and regional trade agreements, as well as the dispute resolution committees established to adjudicate concrete allegations of trade rule violations, should include sizable representation from third world nations. The World Trade Organization is overseen by a council, comprising representatives of its 151 member nations, each casting a single, un-weighted vote (Subramanian 2004). As a result, there is clearly the potential for developing nations to have a greater influence over the WTO than over many other international economic institutions.

Sustainability

Because Christians understand that the world is God's creation, their relation to that world must respect the Creator's purposes for it. Discerning those purposes, of course, is a controverted process. And because we have only recently come to a general awareness of humanity's technological power to deform the biosphere, Christian theology and ethics are still working out an adequate analysis of environmental issues.

The biblical tradition has provided two fundamental moral warrants for humanity's use of the rest of nature. The first is the notion of God-given dominion: In the creation story God grants "dominion over the earth" to Adam and Eve and their descendants (Gen. 1:28). As we have seen, twentieth-century Christians have become vividly aware that this sense of dominion has in many ways been overextended, and recent theological attention has restricted this idea to a sense of stewardship, a standing in for the Creator for the household of creation. The second is the notion of humans created in "the image of God," endorsing a uniqueness of the human species on the planet and granting a kind of moral priority to humans, while at the same time requiring them to respect a creation that lived in vital splendor before humans appeared and, except for humanity's threat, would carry on if humans vanished.

The phrase "the integrity of creation" has come into frequent use in Christian ethics in an attempt to name that value, implicit in the biosphere, which humans have an obligation to respect. Some have preferred this language of the integrity of creation over that of human stewardship for creation out of fear that the latter can feed into the well-proven arrogance humanity has shown in its relation with the rest of the natural world (see, for example, Rasmussen 1995). Nonetheless, because humans pose a real threat to the integrity of the biosphere and alone have the rationality and ingenuity capable of controlling that threat, the language of active stewardship in pursuit of sustainability seems equally appropriate.

The rules of international trade must reflect this concern for the integrity of creation. International trade agreements have traditionally allowed for one important kind of restriction on trade for environmental reasons: the banning of particular products by any nation, as long as both domestic and foreign products fall under the same ban. Thus, for example, any nation concerned about ozone depletion could, if it wished, ban all sales of ozone-depleting chlorofluorocarbons (CFCs) without violating the standards of international trade rules. (In fact, the Montreal Protocol and related agreements have phased out numerous ozone-depleting substances.) An outright prohibition of some products is appropriate—for example, some particularly destructive chemicals.

Far more important in reducing environmental damage, however, are restrictions on manufacturing *processes*, that is, penalizing in one way or another processes that generate disproportionate environmental harm.[2] Thus, for example, efforts to reduce the amount of sulfur coming from the smokestacks of power plants or efforts to reduce the toxicity of wastes flowing into sewers and rivers have been fundamentally important methods of restricting environmental damage within any one nation. The problem in international trade arises, however, because the rules of trade have traditionally rejected "process standards." Nations are not free to discriminate among identical products, allowing the import of some but restricting the import of others based on how they were produced. Thus, while a nation is free to ban trade in CFCs, it is not free under international trade agreements to restrict trade in products simply because they were made with technologies that produce CFCs as a waste product. The original motive behind this policy was the concern that individual nations would, in a protectionist manner, simply assert that the dominant production processes used domestically were environmentally (or by some other standard) superior to those used abroad, thus protecting domestic producers by prohibiting the import of that product unless foreign producers switched technologies (a change that would increase costs, at least in the short run).

A multitude of environmental problems can be addressed only by process restrictions, such as mandating particular "clean" technologies or establishing a system of tradable pollution permits to reduce overall pollution levels. Every industrialized nation has used process restrictions domestically to reduce the polluting effects of production. A blanket rejection of process restrictions in international trade rules today is therefore simply indefensible. With an "environmental legitimacy" added to the agreements of the World Trade Organization, and with further efforts by the WTO to incorporate the trade-related sections of international environmental agreements, the rules of international trade could be shaped to encourage, rather than ignore, sustainability (see, for example, Sampson 2005; Esty 1994).

During the Uruguay round of GATT negotiations, the signatory nations agreed to establish the Committee on Trade and the Environment, within the World Trade Organization. The Committee is charged with examining WTO policies concerning the transparency of trade rules, the relation of the WTO to various international environmental agreements, and more concrete issues, such as process standards and the export of goods prohibited from domestic sale (Schott and Buurman 1994). However, to date the Committee has only acknowledged that trade sometimes worsens environmental problems and encouraged national governments to work together to address them. The Committee has made little progress toward making environmental standards a part of the WTO rules of trade.[3]

Labor Standards

Christians recognize that every human being has a dignity based on creation in the "image of God" and that this dignity sets standards for all human interaction, whether domestic or international. International agreements should recognize the right of workers to organize, the importance of child labor laws, and the need for fundamental workplace health and safety regulation. As a corollary, rules of trade should allow individual nations to discriminate against imports from other nations where such fundamental labor standards are disregarded. A number of large international retailers have begun to set labor standards for their third world suppliers because of consumer pressure, and while this effort is far from completely successful, it indicates a potential for stronger international agreements in this area that did not exist a decade or two ago.

Considerable discussion has occurred concerning whether labor standards should be left to the International Labor Organization (ILO) or incorporated directly into the WTO. The United States has pressed for an agreement to establish labor standards within the WTO. The nations of Europe were mildly supportive. But the proposal was strenuously opposed by many developing countries that fear producers in the industrialized world will allege abuse of workers' rights as an excuse for further protectionism. "Free market" trade proponents are opposed in principle to employing the WTO for this purpose, and even economists who are receptive to the idea are concerned about the negative effects of implementing labor standards as part of the rules of trade. There is greater openness to and possibility for labor standards that focus on basic human rights, such as eliminating forced labor, rather than on standards addressing working conditions and pay.

We should recognize, of course, that even concerning such basic issues, moral judgment is a difficult one when the debate moves beyond some fundamental level of labor standards. Different nations have taken different approaches to the powers and opportunities given to unions, the age and conditions under which children may work (particularly in developing nations without an adequate school system), and the degree of health and safety risks allowed. These issues are hotly debated within each nation, and though Christian ethics has much to contribute here, a single unified standard for all nations is unwise. Differences in both cultural meanings and political possibilities are too large.

Incorporating new concerns into WTO agreements is a slow process, and the availability of an international agreement on labor standards is uncertain. The moral case, however, is clearer than the political. Christian faith calls for all economic institutions to treat persons with dignity. Concretizing this call and marshalling the political will to accomplish it remain the challenge.

Cultural Identity

One of the most striking characteristics of the modern world is the frequent interaction between people of diverse cultural identities, and this has had both good and bad effects. In learning more about the stranger from another culture, humans are learning to allay the fear and hatred of others, reduce the disparagement of others' points of view, and make ethnic wars less likely. The viciousness and inhumanity apparent in the struggles in Bosnia in the 1990s and more recently among Iraqi Muslims stand as examples of some of the worst kinds of inter-ethnic hatred. Still, the fact that so many people around the world find such hatred morally repulsive stands as a tribute to a real, though limited, moral development in world history. International commerce has meant greater frequency of contact between peoples and a growing interdependence.

At the same time, economic forces have also had morally destructive effects on cultural identity. Consider the entertainment industry. It is morally discouraging when domestic entertainment firms act as a sort of pander, appealing to the baser elements of our culture. For those of other cultures, the problem is even more objectionable when such entertainment is available primarily through international trade. Particularly for "small" nations facing an onslaught of sophisticated entertainment products from "large" nations abroad, a simplistic "free trade" answer to such objections is morally inadequate.

Economists often underestimate the importance of institutional and cultural factors in national life. As a result, they tend to see entertainment, also referred to as "the culture industry," like the kitchen appliance or financial services industry—simply another part of the economy. In the Uruguay round of the GATT, for example, France insisted on the right to restrict the importation of (largely American) movies and television shows out of a combined concern for the future of French firms producing materials for the cinema and television and for French culture itself. France stood its ground and won, but the battle to preserve French culture continues to be difficult. In March 2000, for example, the French Ministry of Finance announced that it was banning many common business words in English, such as "start-up" and "e-mail." However, that same month, the French national airline, Air France, decided that its pilots must speak exclusively in English, even when talking with French air-traffic controllers at the Paris airport. Concerns for air safety in the face of the dominance of the English language in international business led to this very un-French concession (Gordon and Meunier 2001). Still, a moral case can be made that nations should be able to have some control over their language and culture.

At the same time, no complete ban on imports of cultural products is morally defensible. Fundamental human rights of individuals require access to different points of view from which governments and national elites might at times wish to isolate their population. Thus, any agreement on the rules of trade concerning culturally important products and services will have to be a careful compromise, one that will necessarily be a rough approximation rather than a precise definition of a just trading policy.

Human Rights

Although a number of the preceding elements include particular sorts of human rights, there are other more general and more generally recognized human rights that each nation should ensure for its own people. Rights of free speech, assembly, a free press, universal suffrage, and a variety of other more concrete political guarantees are morally critical for responsible public life. Although such human rights need to be recognized in international agreements, including trade agreements, it remains a debatable prudential judgment whether and to what extent they should become grounds for trade discrimination.

On the one hand, a moral argument can be made that, if a nation violates the rights of its citizens, then its exports should be open to restrictions if importing nations so wish. Thus, many critics of human rights violations in China have argued that the other industrialized nations of the world should reduce their international trade with China to penalize the Chinese government for its actions. On the other hand, there are two important moral arguments against such a policy. First, improving the human rights records of industrial democracies has come not simply from moral conviction but also from a rise in the economic welfare of the citizenry, something that has yet to occur in many parts of the world. Thus some critics of Chinese human rights policy argue that the most likely cause of a transformation in that policy will be the domestic pressure arising from citizens whose economic welfare has increased, in large part through international trade. Second, moral humility causes a responsible observer to recognize that there is likely no nation perfectly responsible in all matters of human rights. For example, many nations find the American practice of capital punishment and its conduct in Guantanamo Bay morally objectionable. Extreme caution should be exercised before restricting trade due to morally based disapproval of actions by another nation's government, because it could further impoverish needy citizens who are not responsible for their nation's activities.

Thus, while the internal logic of trade negotiations can support the inclusion of work-related human rights standards within the rules of trade, well-meaning people will likely continue to disagree about the use of trade policy to further more specifically political human rights. Strong efforts need to be made to further human rights throughout the globe, and these may include sanctions as strong as those implemented by the United Nations against South Africa in the 1980s. However, the temptation of protected industries to appeal to human rights arguments is so strong that relying on trade policy to further a general human rights agenda is inappropriate.

Moral Responsibility for Dislocations from Trade

The moral argument in favor of international trade is that, within the proper "rules of the game," trade does more good than harm. Similar to dislocations caused by changes in technology, which are widely recognized as good in the long run, dislocations caused by the movement of production facilities from one nation to another is both personally painful and economically costly to the workers harmed.[4]

Studies have found that losses to displaced workers are largest during the first year, averaging as much as 40 percent of their pre-displacement earnings. The initial loss is reduced after the first year, when those affected seek better jobs. Over time, losses drop, with the average earner's income being only 25 percent lower during the fifth year after separation (Jacobson, LaLonde, and Sullivan 1993). A 2007 study found that among workers dislocated by trade, those with more seniority experience a greater drop in wages in their next job. Part of the story is that they are older, so retraining and relocation may be more difficult. Another factor is that their seniority may not travel well to the next job, and their new wage is not much higher than their younger co-workers also moving to jobs in the new workplace (LaLonde 2007; Kletzer 2004).

Any morally founded national trade policy must anticipate such dislocations and assist affected workers in the transition to another job. Unemployment payments, retraining and relocation stipends, and employment counseling are critical to the process, even though they cannot guarantee an income as great as before dislocation. In fact, if a group of workers is currently working at the highest-paid job available to them, then any dislocation will leave them with only lower-income alternatives. Put more simply, although international trade will bring consumers lower prices and increase the demand for workers in export industries, those workers who produce products that now compete more directly with imports will be harmed. As a result, "trade adjustment assistance," as it is called, is critically important and must be seen as a morally integral part of a nation's trade policy. Unfortunately the U.S. Trade Adjustment Assistance (TAA) program, administered by the Department of Labor, is small and not well constructed. In 2006 it provided only $220 million for retraining workers displaced by trade.[5] The moral case for international trade hinges in part on the reform and expansion of the TAA program.

Regulating Unfair Trade

In recent decades, several rounds of trade talks under the aegis of the GATT and the WTO have slowly reduced tariffs, the fees that national governments charge on goods coming into their nation. The chart below depicts the reduction of average tariffs on goods entering the United States with each of these rounds of negotiation. Tariff levels are shown as percentage reductions from levels prior to 1945.

As these tariffs have fallen, there has been a simultaneous rise in the significance of nontariff barriers on trade, for two reasons. First, even if the nontariff barriers remain unchanged, they become relatively more important when significant tariff barriers have been reduced. Second, the international pressure to cut tariffs has pressed nations wishing to protect their domestic industries to use less visible, nontariff

U.S. Tariff Levels: 1945–2005
After Successive Rounds of Trade Negotiations

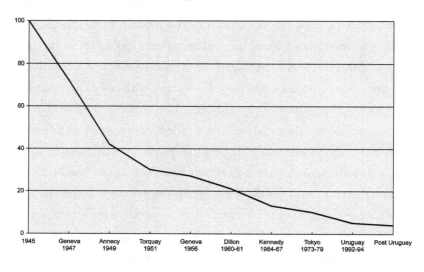

techniques. Included here are import quotas, national subsidies to particular industries, anti dumping rules, selective enforcement of antitrust laws, national product standards or government procurement standards that discriminate in favor of domestic firms, and a variety of other administrative procedures.

Because the U.S. and Canadian economies have on average been less protected by high tariffs than those of their competitor nations, there has been rising concern that too much may have been conceded in focusing so much on reducing tariffs across the globe, and that "unfair" trade is occurring through a panoply of nontariff barriers erected by "competitor" nations. This more recent sense of needing to combat unfair, nontariff barriers of other nations has added equity to the list of arguments proposed by threatened firms to support national policies aimed at protecting domestic industry. The difficulty in sorting through such claims is that although there can indeed be truth to assertions about unfair trade, such assertions can easily mask more self-interested, protectionist proposals that will in fact not benefit the nation as a whole. When appeals for governmental relief in the face of "unfair trade" are teamed with concerns about, for example, the family farm, the environment, or the loss of manufacturing jobs, the moral difficulty becomes even greater.

Thus, though space is insufficient for an exhaustive analysis, it may be helpful to review two of the most important elements in the debate over unfair trade: dumping and subsidies.

Dumping

Nearly everyone prefers to pay lower prices for goods and services than higher prices. Thus, it would seem that most people would be quite happy if a large manufacturing firm wanted to cut profits or perhaps even sell at a loss. The difficulty, of course, is that a large firm might do this to drive smaller competitors out of business, to be left free to raise prices after attaining a monopoly. For this reason, nations have antitrust laws preventing such "predatory pricing" practices.

The international equivalent of such destructive pricing is called "dumping." The most direct definition of this practice is the sale abroad of goods priced below the prices of comparable goods sold in the country of origin. The danger with dumping is that a large multi-national firm with a strong hold on its domestic market could use large profits at home to subsidize predatory pricing abroad in order to drive competitors from that foreign market. However, most economists discount this threat, since the process is remarkably risky. Dumping is not only costly, if it drives rivals into bankruptcy, their factories remain in existence; and if the foreign competitor eventually raises prices to take advantage of the monopoly, other domestic firms can buy up those factories and begin production again.

Nevertheless, many nations have established laws that prohibit and penalize dumping. The difficulty in enforcing both the domestic preda-tory pricing laws and the international dumping laws is that periodic discounting of prices is quite normal for firms that face a fluctuating demand and yet have high fixed costs. A prime example here is automobile companies, who face high demand for their product during a boom time but find consumer demand dropping severely during a recession when average consumer income falls. Such firms do adjust their production schedules by laying off some workers. But the high fixed costs of existing plant and machinery lead them to produce and sell automobiles below cost, if necessary during recessions, to help pay their "fixed" costs related to maintaining their plant and machinery in order to be available during the next boom.

The obvious problem here is that business cycles in different nations are not identical. The United States or Canada might be experiencing a recession when, say, Japan is still at a "boom" stage prior to a slowdown. In such a situation, it is quite problematic to use the standard that dumping occurs when a firm sells its product at lower prices abroad than at home. As a result of complications such as this and because of the pressure of domestic firms for protection, the operating definition of dumping has shifted, beginning with the Trade Act of 1974 passed by the United States Congress. In that statute a foreign company was considered to be dumping if the selling price abroad was equal to the selling price at home but both were below the production costs for the item. This and a number of more technical changes made it more likely that allegations of dumping in the United States would be upheld and that penalties would be enacted in response.

One recent example concerns accusations against Chinese firms for dumping wooden bedroom furniture in the United States. Initially, several U.S. producers started factories in China and benefited from the lower costs while still selling the products to furniture stores in the United States for a handsome profit. Eventually, Chinese manufacturers learned they could sell directly to furniture stores in the United States and undercut the prices offered by the U.S. manufacturers. In 2003 the manufacturers accused the Chinese firms of dumping, and in

2004 the U.S. International Trade Commission ruled in favor of the U.S. firms.[6]

Any ethical assessment of the economic issues underlying disputes over dumping must share the same concerns raised by domestic predatory pricing concerning monopoly and antitrust. There is the additional concern that in the case of some products, national security interests could conceivably be at stake. At the same time, recent allegations of dumping within the leading industrialized nations, and particularly within the United States, often seem to mask a more self-interested protectionism on the part of large firms. Adjudicating such claims and counterclaims is morally important, but it is complex and requires a case-by-case analysis. It may prove helpful here to note an important danger usually accompanying this process.

Critics of this process argue that the usual approach to allegations of dumping focuses attention almost exclusively on the domestic producers (the "frontline" competitors) who claim they have been damaged by dumping. From the viewpoint of a national moral assessment of economic welfare, authorities should also take into consideration any negative effects that remedies for alleged dumping might have. In our furniture example, U.S. manufacturers of furniture were hurt and some U.S. workers lost jobs. But furniture stores and consumers who buy furniture, including universities, churches, homeowners, and renters, were hurt when the anti-dumping ruling raised prices.

The technicalities involved in assessing such claims and counterclaims are immense. Here we may content ourselves with the moral standard that any damage done by unfair pricing of foreign goods should be assessed not simply for the costs imposed on domestic producers of similar goods; the benefits or damages caused to all domestic firms and consumers should also be assessed. Any administrative process designed to assess dumping complaints should recognize that the special-interest effect will leave frontline competitors more motivated to lodge and lobby for their complaints than consumers and other producers will be to present evidence against them.

Subsidies

If the problems surrounding the definition and assessment of dumping are difficult, those same issues concerning subsidies are even more complicated. At one level it would seem that every nation has the moral right to collect and spend the citizens' taxes in accord with citizens' wishes. For example, if the government of Canada chooses to spend tax dollars to further the nation's forests or farms or any other business enterprise, it would ordinarily have the right to do so. At the same time, however, nations have entered into trade agreements that have attempted to reduce the subsidies that national governments otherwise grant to domestic industries. Such limitations on the fiscal options open to national governments do indeed limit national sovereignty. We should begin our consideration of trade subsidies with the two central reasons why nations agree to trade rules that prohibit them.

The first reason is that nations are in a sort of "prisoner's dilemma" situation concerning the subsidy of exports. If only one nation chooses to subsidize its export industries, it can quite conceivably enhance them and reap additional gains from trade. This is often called "strategic trade policy." However, once one nation has begun the process, most other nations feel driven to create similar subsidies. Once this occurs, the aggregate expense of all national governments on subsidies is far greater than the aggregate benefits accruing to them. This amounts to a simple transfer of funds from taxpayers to owners and workers in those subsidized industries. This line of reasoning is quite similar to the well-founded argument against a system of tax breaks granted by local units of government to entice relocating firms from other parts of the nation to establish factories locally. If only one municipality does it, it can gain jobs and tax base because it offers the relocating firm lower costs than are available elsewhere. However, such policies predictably force nearly all other municipalities to do the same. The result is simply a system that transfers money from local taxpayers—both individuals and corporations—to relocating firms and has almost no effect on the overall number of jobs available in the economy.

The second reason nations agree to trade rules that limit subsidies is rooted in the "special-interest effect." Small producer groups—including both owners and employees—will often exert disproportionate pressure on national legislatures to fund subsidies, even if these may cost the nation more than they are worth. We might refer to such arguments in favor of subsidies as "national priority" arguments, where those advocating the subsidy argue that the nation's interests require this expenditure. Included here are arguments for strengthening the industrial base ("If war were to come we wouldn't want to be dependent upon our enemies for X"), or for cultivating "infant industries" ("We will never get industry X started in the face of international competition unless we subsidize it"), or for pursuing environmental priorities ("If we want a healthier environment we should not let free-trade agreements prevent us from investing in industry X").

Both kinds of subsidies—the national priority subsidy and the strategic trade subsidy—may violate trade agreements designed to prevent the waste involved in replicating export-subsidy industries throughout the world. From a moral perspective, the two kinds of subsidies need to be treated differently.

National priority subsidies need to be defended in principle even though in practice, among special interest groups, they often amount to an excuse rather than a principled stand. The complaints of U.S. lumber interests against the expenditure of Canadian tax dollars to subsidize Canadian reforestation is a case in point. From the U.S. perspective, this allows Canadian timber companies to lower their costs of production. At the same time, many Canadians defend the subsidy as an effort to invest in long-term environmental development. Without getting into the specifics of this case, the point here is that those who assert a national priority argument need to give evidence that it is not simply a fig leaf for protectionism. Thus in the Canadian forestry case, one would have to ask whether the subsidy leads toward a long-term net increase in forested acreage instead of simply a higher rate of annual timber harvesting or lower exploitation fees for timber companies cutting from public lands.

Any moral assessment of strategic trade subsidies depends heavily on an empirical assessment of their effectiveness. The classic case here is the leadership provided by Japan's Ministry of International Trade and Industry (MITI) after World War II. The prevailing perception in North America is that MITI's subsidies and protection of key high-tech industries explains Japan's remarkable economic success after the war. This perception led many in the United States and Canada to argue strongly for an analogous "industrial policy" or "strategic trade policy" that might promise similar economic success. Careful economic analyses of various episodes in this history, however, have shown a mixed record. MITI's Very Large-Scale Integrated Circuit Program was indeed successful, leading to Japanese dominance in computer memory chips in the 1980s. A number of notorious blunders are less often heard about, such as when MITI tried to consolidate automobile production in Japan, attempting to eliminate Honda Motors, and discouraged Sony after World War II from investing in transistor technologies (Nivola 1993, 39–41, 160). At stake here are critically important empirical presumptions about the effectiveness of subsidies and broader national strategic trade policies, but investigations of those lie beyond the scope of this study.

Most important, this very brief view of debates over regulating "unfair" trade has illustrated the recurring complexity of the issue. On the one hand, morally appropriate concerns about foreign firms dumping products or foreign governments unfairly subsidizing their own industries need to be dealt with both in the fundamental international rules of trade and in national laws designed to cope with violations of those international rules. On the other hand, domestic producers will predictably accuse foreign competitors of dumping and their governments of unfair subsidies, even in situations where a more broadly based moral assessment might find domestic producers' claims completely self-interested and the remedies they propose actually harmful to national welfare as a whole. Such assessments need to occur on a case-by-case basis.

Conclusion

From a moral perspective, the rules impinging on international trade are as important as the rules for purely domestic trade. In fact, international economic exchange must follow nearly all the domestic rules for commerce in both nations. Because this fact is so elementary, it is often overlooked in discussions about trade; advocates of increased trade are tempted to speak of "free" trade, by which they often mean no limitations on international trade that do not exist on domestic interaction. The problem caused by this oversight is that they then often come to think of such economic exchanges as simply not requiring a moral analysis to decide what aspects of these exchanges need to be regulated or even forbidden.

Once we recognize that a long list of restrictions on economic exchange, both domestic and international, must exist due to moral conviction, it becomes easier to see that the question is not whether trade can be "free," but rather what framework of limitations is needed to legitimate morally the assertion of self-interest on the part of individuals and firms in international trade.

As we have seen, a moral assessment of trade from the perspective of Christian faith requires that the framework within which trade occurs must attend to several fundamental moral concerns: the welfare of the world's poor, sustainability, the dignity of workers, cultural identity, and human rights more generally. Such concerns will influence the rules of trade in diverse ways. Concerns about labor standards would give signatory nations to trade agreements the right to discriminate against foreign imports produced under conditions that violate the fundamental human rights of workers. Concerns about cultural identity would give "small" nations the right to restrict the import of mass media entertainment products from "large" nations. Concerns about sustainability will require that international rules of trade incorporate not only product-based discriminations but also process-based discriminations, in order to discourage the environmentally irresponsible, but cheaper, production processes to which foreign competitors might otherwise resort. Concerns about the economic welfare of the world's poor endorse the generalized system of preferences already in place and call upon nations to develop more effective biases in favor of the exports from the world's developing nations, particularly the poorest in that group. Critically important here is the removal of tariffs and nontariff barriers in the industrialized world that currently discourage imports of agricultural products and textiles from the developing world.

Christians should also support a broadening of membership on the councils overseeing trade agreements, although one must guard against the temptation on the part of special interests to press their local and regional representatives for changes that may not be in the best interest of their nation as a whole. An important example of this phenomenon is the effort to regulate "unfair trade." Although unfair trade is a reality that needs to be dealt with, governmental responses to special-interest appeals for protection against dumping and foreign subsidies are often little more than thinly disguised protectionist self-interest. The moral values involved and the costs and benefits to all—both immediately affected "frontline" groups as well as less directly affected groups such as other producers and consumers—must be carefully discerned.

A moral trade policy will be, then, a complicated matter. It must begin with a list of core moral values to which nations are committed and out of which general rules for a framework of trade flow. Because the rules of trade are an international compromise, they will usually not meet the standards of the most morally responsible nations that are parties to the agreement. They can, however, increase global responsibility and, when well crafted, will substantively assist in accomplishing of the moral values on which they are founded.

This chapter is an updated and substantially revised version of work that originally appeared in Just Trading: On the Ethics and Economics of International Trade by Daniel Finn (Abingdon Press, 1996).

Questions for Review

1. Do you agree that the "moral character of the people who make up a society is critical to the success of its markets and other institutions"? Is it possible for people with strong moral character to have different understandings of right and wrong in economic affairs? Explain your answer.

2. Have you ever thought someone was wrong for doing something they thought was perfectly moral? Might that be parallel to international differences on the morality of trade?

3. Do you think there should be any mandatory labor standards for countries that export goods to the United States? If so, give two examples.

4. How might labor standards be used as a form or protectionism, as many developing countries fear? What standards are the most enforceable in your opinion? Do you agree that a single unified standard for all nations would be "unwise"? Please explain.

Notes

[1] For one perspective, see "Who Is My Neighbor? A Theological Approach to Globalization" by Sue Russell (Chap. 2 in this volume).

[2] Judith Dean refers to these as "techniques" in Chapter 12 of this volume.

[3] See for example, World Trade Organization, "Discussion Paper on the Environmental Effects of Services Trade Liberalization," WT/CTE/W/218 (October 3, 2002); World Trade Organization, "Environment: Issues Environmental Reviews," http://www.wto.org/english/tratoop_e/envir_e/reviews_e.htm.

[4] For a careful argument that Christian morality requires attention to and at times compensation for such harm, see Barrera (2005).

[5] For a thorough discussion of the effects and problems with this program, see GAO, "Trade Adjustment Assistance: Changes Needed to Improve States' Ability to Provide Benefits and Services to Trade-Affected Workers," GAO-07-995T (June 14, 2007).

[6] http://www.wto.org/english/thewto_e/minist_e/min01_e/mindecl_e.htm#tradeenvironment.

References

Barrera, Albino. 2005. *Economic Compulsion and Christian Ethics*. New York, NY: Cambridge University Press.

Cormie, Lee. 1992. "Vantage Points of the Historically Marginalized in North America: A Response to Gustavo Gutiérrez." *Proceedings of the Forty-Seventh Annual Convention*. Vol. 47. Santa Clara, CA: Catholic Theological Society of America, 35–38.

Esty, Daniel C. 1994. *Greening the GATT: Trade, Environment, and the Future*. Washington, D.C.: Institute for International Economics.

Finger, Michael J., and P. A. Messerlin. 1989. *The Effects of Industrial Countries' Policies on Developing Countries*. Washington, D.C.: World Bank.

Gordon, Philip H., and Sophie Meunier. 2001. "Globalization and French Cultural Identity." *French Culture and Society* 19, no. 1 (Spring), 35–36.

Kletzer, Lori G. 2004. "Trade-related Job Loss and Wage Insurance: A Synthetic Review." *Review of International Economics* 12, no. 5 (November).

Jacobson, Louis, Robert LaLonde, and Daniel Sullivan. 1993. *The Cost of Worker Dislocation*. Kalamazoo, MI: W. E. Upjohn Institute for Employment Research.

Jones, Vivian C. 2007. "Generalized System of Preferences: Background and Renewal Debate." CSR Report for Congress RL33663 (May 22). Congressional Research Service.

LaLonde, Robert J. 2007. *The Case for Wage Insurance*. Council Special Report 30 (September). New York: Council on Foreign Relations Press.

Nivola, Pietro S. 1993. *Regulating Unfair Trade*. Washington, D.C.: Brookings Institute.

Rasmussen, Larry. 1995. The Integrity of Creation: What Can It Mean for Christian Ethics? In *The Annual of the Society of Christian Ethics*, edited by Harlan Beckley. Society of Christian Ethics. Boston: The Society, 262–75.

Salvatore, Dominick, ed. 1992. *National Trade Policies*. New York: Greenwood Press.

Sampson, Gary P. 2005. *The WTO and Sustainable Development*. New York: United Nations University.

Schott, Jeffrey J., and Johanna W. Buurman. 1994. *The Uruguay Round: An Assessment*. Washington D.C.: Institute for International Economics, 34–37.

Subramanian, Arvind. 2004. "Trips." *Finance and Development* (March), 138–39.

Walzer, Michael. 1983. *The Spheres of Justice: A Defense of Pluralism and Equality*. New York: Basic Books.

CHAPTER 4

FOREIGN DIRECT INVESTMENT —THE "MONSTER" REVISITED

Stephen L. S. Smith

Foreign direct investment (FDI) is one of the most enduringly controversial topics in economic development. Inextricably linked to the multinational firms (MNCs) that by definition make cross-border investments, FDI and MNCs have long been regarded with suspicion and animosity. In 1977, when global FDI inflows were $27 billion per year, Raymond Vernon could title his famous book, *Storm over the Multinationals*. In 1993, when global FDI inflows had exploded to the previously unimaginable height of $224 billion, *The Economist* magazine could refer to multinationals as "everybody's favorite monster." By 2006, global FDI inflows had surged to $1,306 billion—near their 2000 peak of $1,411 billion—and it was routine to hear pleas for "worldwide resistance to corporate globalization," to cite the title of a recent Zed Books primer.[1] Clearly, even as FDI has grown more prominent in the global economy, it has not become less contentious.

Policymakers in both developed and less-developed countries now regard FDI more positively than in the first few decades after World War II. Much else has changed, too, in terms of the sources, destinations, and characteristics of FDI over the past fifty years. But it remains difficult to find development advocates and NGOs willing to say anything positive about FDI. This is also true about those who approach economic development from a specifically Christian point of view. One must look long and hard for positive statements about MNCs or FDI. Christian commentary on development is cool, if not outright hostile, toward FDI.

In high-income countries some of the concern about FDI centers on national security. Foreign ownership of defense firms, or firms in strategic minerals and infrastructure, can draw intense scrutiny, such as the firestorm in 2005 over China National Offshore Oil Company (CNOOC) attempting to acquire Unocal. Additionally, FDI outflows can prompt concerns about job losses.

We begin with a survey of recent trends in the nature, direction, and composition of FDI flows over the past twenty-five years. Facts are essential for understanding FDI, and the empirical record is instructive. The rapid run-up in overall FDI inflows since the late 1970s masks disparate trends. All FDI is definitely *not* alike. The type of industry represented by FDI inflows has a large influence on its likely effects. Furthermore, "developing countries" are a wildly heterogeneous group. It does not make sense to think about such countries' relation to FDI in purely generic terms: the differences among host countries matter.

Following a review of the trends, we will survey the theoretical arguments and evidence about FDI's effects. Basic economic theory has much to say about FDI's costs, benefits, and likely consequences in host countries—and so do FDI's critics.[2] This part of the FDI debate most animates anti-globalization activists and Christian thinkers.

The final section considers Christian ethical thinking on FDI. Christian scholars in the social sciences, and policy advocates and practitioners in the NGO community, should regard FDI as a mostly positive phenomenon, though with some caveats. Christian activists tend to think about FDI in simple redistributive justice terms. FDI is better thought of in terms of the Christian virtue of practical wisdom (or prudence). In that light, FDI offers strong potential to assist poor countries' growth by providing capital and skills that would not otherwise be available. The problems commonly associated with FDI are better understood as originating in features of domestic political economy in developing economies—in weaknesses in capital markets, the financial system, and in governance in general—rather than in foreign ownership of capital per se.

Empirical Trends

FDI occurs when any cross-border investment includes a significant measure of ownership control. This definition spans a wide range of investments, from new factories built in Thailand by the Ford-Mazda joint venture there to the purchase of the Land Rover brand and factories by the India-based Tata Automotive Group. It also spans from transactions that are truly gargantuan—multibillion-dollar investments in Papua New Guinea mining, say—to tiny ones, such as a small Indonesian firm buying used equipment from a Korean-owned factory in China to make shoes in Cambodia.

Amounts and Destinations—An Instructive Empirical Record

Table 1 reports data on FDI inflows, in billions of U.S. dollars, on an annual average basis over the five five-year periods from 1982 through 2006. Annual FDI flows bounce around significantly, so viewing them as annual averages over a longer period is helpful in identifying long-term trends.

The rapid growth in FDI inflows since the early 1980s is readily apparent. World inflows, listed at the bottom of the table, averaged $63 billion per year over 1982–1986—already dramatically higher than levels of the 1970s—and then surged to $908 billion per year in 1997–2001. While falling slightly during 2002–2006, they remain substantially higher than in the 1980s and 1990s. FDI inflows to

Table 1. Trends in FDI Inflows

Average annual inflows, $ billions

	1982-1986	1987-1991	1992-1996	1997-2001	2002-2006
Developed economies	47.4	146.8	190.4	738.6	598.3
United States	21.5	51.7	51.6	206.9	108.0
United Kingdom	4.8	21.8	16.8	73.4	86.0
France	2.1	8.3	16.9	38.9	57.2
Belgium & Luxembourg	1.0	6.4	10.3	66.3	49.7
Germany	1.2	3.6	4.8	63.5	31.1
Developing economies	15.7	24.1	82.7	159.0	200.0
Top 15 destinations...					
China	1.4	3.4	30.3	43.7	61.8
Mexico	2.0	3.2	7.7	16.8	19.2
Brazil	1.5	1.4	4.1	26.3	15.7
Chile	0.3	0.9	2.6	5.5	5.8
Turkey	0.1	0.5	0.7	1.4	7.1
South Africa	0.1	0.0	0.5	2.7	1.6
Korea, Republic of	0.2	0.8	1.0	6.1	5.8
Thailand	0.3	1.6	1.9	5.2	6.6
Argentina	0.4	1.3	4.7	10.6	3.6
Malaysia	0.9	1.9	5.7	3.5	4.1
Saudi Arabia	4.5	-0.3	0.4	0.2	6.7
India	0.1	0.2	1.3	3.5	7.9
Taiwan	0.2	1.2	1.3	2.9	2.6
Venezuela	-0.1	0.6	1.3	4.5	1.3
Colombia	0.7	0.4	1.4	3.0	4.7
Other destinations...					
Nigeria	0.33	1.00	1.76	1.32	3.04
Vietnam	0.00	0.12	1.39	1.67	1.72
Indonesia	0.26	0.84	3.28	-0.99	3.07
Pakistan	0.06	0.20	0.50	0.49	1.79
Costa Rica	0.06	0.13	0.31	0.50	0.87
Tanzania	0.00	0.00	0.08	0.29	0.37
Guatemala	0.06	0.14	0.09	0.32	0.20
Bangladesh	0.00	0.00	0.07	0.48	0.49
Ethiopia	0.00	0.00	0.01	0.22	0.37
Honduras	0.02	0.05	0.06	0.19	0.30
Ghana	0.01	0.01	0.12	0.13	0.18
Kenya	0.01	0.04	0.01	0.04	0.05
World	63.1	171.0	276.8	908.3	836.0

Source: author's calculations based on UNCTAD data. "Developing" category excludes, and "developed" category includes, Hong Kong, Singapore, Russia, the Bahamas, and the Cayman Islands. Full data at http://www.unctad.org/Templates/StartPage. asp?intItemID=2921&lang=1

developing countries have also exploded since the early 1980s, from an average of $16 billion per year (1982–1986) to $200 billion per year over 2002–2006. Those FDI inflows are the particular focus of this chapter—but it must be noted that they are small compared to FDI inflows into developed economies, never rising above 25 percent of the latter. Data on FDI outflows (not reported here) confirms what Table 1 hints at: most FDI flows are from developed economies to other developed economies. FDI is, first and foremost, an intra-rich country phenomenon.

One crucial difference between developed and developing countries lies in the *balance* of FDI flows. For the United States, for instance, over the 2004–2006 period inflows averaged $137 billion per year while outflows averaged $149 billion per year. This kind of rough balance between inflows and outflows is characteristic of FDI in developed economies and helps explain why FDI is not as highly politicized in developed economy politics as it is for developing countries. Large capital outflows are simply less problematic when matched by large inflows, and vice versa. Textile firms may have left the Carolinas for China, but it is harder to make a political issue of that when BMW and Haier are investing heavily in those same states. In contrast, FDI inflows into developing countries have, historically, far exceeded outflows. Over 2004–2006, FDI outflows from developing countries reached an all-time peak of $131 billion dollars but still were less than 30 percent of inflows.[3] This asymmetry, the one-way inward direction of FDI when viewed from many developing countries, stokes political concerns about dependence and vulnerability.

This asymmetry should not be exaggerated. FDI outflows from developing countries represented 14 percent of the total outflow and appear likely to rise dramatically in absolute and relative terms over the next quarter century. Large developing country-based MNCs are quickly becoming household names in the United States (LG, Samsung, Hyundai, and Embraer). Chinese and Indian MNCs in particular are beginning to locate some of their marketing and production operations in the United States (Haier and Infosys are prominent examples). There is no reason to expect a slowdown in these trends.

FDI flows into developing economies cluster in a small number of countries. Table 1 lists the top fifteen developing-country recipients (ranked not by the size of recent inflows, but by their total stock of FDI). These countries, led by China, Mexico and Brazil, accounted for more than 75 percent of all inflows. Inflows to selected other developing countries are also listed in Table 1. Stark contrasts are evident—the absolute size of FDI inflows varies dramatically between countries. Thailand (among the top fifteen) received $6.6 billion per year on average during 2002–2006; Ethiopia received a mere $0.4 billion per year. Indonesia received $3.1 billion, Bangladesh just $0.5 billion. In short, FDI inflows in developing countries cluster within certain large and/or fast-growing Latin American and East Asian nations. With the exception of India, South Asia is not a major FDI destination. Sub-Saharan Africa is a particularly small recipient of FDI, with the exception of oil FDIs in Nigeria, Equatorial Guinea, and Chad.[4]

The simple descriptive data in Table 1 is consistent with empirical research findings on the 1980s and 1990s that per capita FDI inflows rise with the size (total income) and per capita income of the host economy.[5] Inflows do not congregate in the smallest, poorest nations. The patterns of developing-country FDI inflows are not consistent with the view that FDI is primarily motivated by MNCs' search for low wages. Sub-Saharan African wages are a fraction of Chinese wages but are not able to induce much FDI. (Whatever the ills that beset the poor nations of sub-Saharan Africa, too much FDI is not one of them.) Neither does FDI gravitate to the countries with the least stringent environmental protections. Environmental regulations may matter to some extent and in some cases, but, manifestly, other considerations appear to dominate decisions of location.[6]

Types of FDI—Instructive Differences

There are three basic kinds of FDI inflows into developing countries. They are substantially different from one another economically and in terms of their political economy implications. One problem with much of the popular literature on FDI, and some of the academic literature, is that it often treats FDI as an undifferentiated, uniform activity when it is not.

Extractive Industries. First, there are natural resource-based or extractive industries. The high capital demands of mining and drilling mean that multinationals in these industries are among the most capital intensive firms. Their expensive assets, distributed around the globe strictly based on geologic accident, regularly place these firms toward the top of the MNC size rankings (such as ExxonMobil in oil or Freeport-McKenna in mining). FDI, associated with a single project in these industries, can run hundreds of millions of dollars or more—vastly large fixed costs compared to the relatively low marginal costs of extracting the resource after the investment is made. When commodity prices are high, large rents are made. Furthermore, MNCs often are the key source of technological knowledge and expertise necessary to run the operation.   All of these features set the stage for potentially severe problems for both the MNC and the host country. Corrupt governments vie to capture the rent, often in collusion with the military (which can be paid off handsomely with the rent). Endemic intra-national distributional issues arise. Regions where the natural resource is produced tend to believe, often with cause, that they do not get a fair share of the revenue. When commodity prices boom, governments can borrow far more than is prudent, and the influx of rent and borrowed capital can appreciate the domestic currency, cause local inflation, and squeeze all the other sectors of the economy. When commodity prices fall, the resulting recessions can be severe. These problems are so well known and commonplace that they are called the "resource curse."[7]

In absolute terms, extractive-industry FDI in developing countries has risen sharply since the early 1980s. But as a *share* of FDI in developing countries, it has fallen from 11 percent in 1989–1991 to 9 percent in 2004–2006 (Table 2). In Africa it remains by far the preponderant form of FDI inflow, where the countries with oil, diamonds, gold, and other valuable minerals receive the most FDI, and for those countries, it accounts for most of their FDI. For instance, 75 percent of Nigeria's FDI stock is in the oil industry.[8]

Table 2. Sectoral Distribution of FDI Inflows, 1989-1991 and 2003-2005.

Shares (percent) by sector for each destination.

Sector	1989-1991			2003-2005		
	Developed Countries	Developing Countries	World	Developed Countries	Developing Countries	World
Primary	6.1	10.7	7.0	13.7	9.1	12.2
Manufacturing	32.1	45.6	34.8	16.6	37.5	23.4
Services	56.3	31.6	51.4	62.8	49.7	58.6
Unspecified	5.4	12.2	6.8	6.9	3.7	5.8
	100.0	100.0	100.0	100.0	100.0	100.0

Source: Author's calculations based on *World Investment Report 2007*, Annex table A.I.11; excludes "private buying and selling of property" category, and combines CIS/Southeast Europe with developing country data for 2003-2005 for comparability with 1989-1991.

Manufacturing. Manufacturing represents a larger share of FDI inflows into developing countries than extractive industries—though contrary to popular perception, perhaps, its share has fallen since 1989. To host any kind of manufacturing FDI, a strong transport infrastructure, access to inputs, and policy stability—closely linked to political stability—are crucial. In their absence, FDI simply may not occur.

Beyond that, it is essential to distinguish between manufacturing that is physical capital-intensive or human capital-intensive on the one hand, and labor-intensive manufacturing on the other hand.

Automobile and steel firms, for instance, are typically capital-intensive, using relatively high amounts of physical capital per worker. They might also be human-capital intensive, using relatively high levels of high-skilled labor per unit of low-skilled labor. Advanced technology manufacturing of products such as aircraft, machine tools, and pharmaceuticals also tends to be human capital-intensive.

Plants in these kinds of industries are not easy to move—they are not "footloose." They typically require years to build and years to recruit and train workers before they reach their highest quality output and lowest feasible unit costs. They often exhibit substantial economies of scale because their specialized capital and well-educated workforce, particularly high-skilled management teams, are fixed costs.

What motivates FDI in these cases, from the MNC point of view? In principle, firms could serve developing-country markets with exports from home plants. But the developing country may block exports to it by tariffs and other trade barriers. In this case the firm will need to "jump" the protective barrier and produce locally to serve that country's market. Much of the FDI into Latin America in the 1960s and 1970s was of this sort. "Tariff-jumping" FDI is less common now—developing-countries' tariffs are much lower today—but it still occurs and poses distinctive challenges.

There are other important reasons why capital and human capital-intensive firms invest in developing countries. Manufactured goods sold directly to consumers must have desirable attributes—in style and function they must "work" with the often distinctive tastes and needs of host-country consumers. Whirlpool in India, for instance, makes entirely different lines of washing machines and dryers, suited to the tastes and small apartments of India's burgeoning middle class, than it sells in the United States. Achieving success requires communication among design teams, research and development engineers, marketers, and market researchers—something often done best by locating in the host market.

Local production also may confer external benefits. If an MNC with multiple product lines produces one of its products in the host country, it can earn a reputation for being a good corporate citizen and a reliable large employer, and it can build political capital and better local networks for selling its other products. Presence is voice—in retail networks, in customer service, and in regulatory matters.

Whatever the motivation, FDI in human capital- or capital-intensive industries requires a large host-country consumer market to sell to, or rock-solid open trade policies so that output can be exported and vital inputs obtained cheaply. In practice this means it is generally not attracted to small, poor countries, and in particular, it is not attracted by low wages.

Labor-intensive manufacturing, characteristic of low-technology consumer goods such as textiles, apparel, footwear, and simple consumer electronics, uses much less capital per worker. The technologies may be new to a particular country, but they tend to be well-known, widely-used, and not dependent on proprietary engineering knowledge. While some labor-intensive manufacturing plants are large, scale tends to be much less important than in capital-intensive manufacturing. Plants with twenty or fifty workers can be profitable. Total capital requirements are modest and generic used machinery may be widely available. Thus plants can be footloose, moving relatively often to find low labor costs, low taxes, good transport infrastructure, and policy stability.

Services. FDI inflows are largest in services. They have grown from a 32 percent share in 1989–1991 to a 50 percent share in 2004–2006.[9] Some of the largest categories within services are financial services (banking, insurance, and investment management), travel and tourism, food, retail, transport, construction, and utilities.[10] McDonalds in China, where franchises are among the world's largest, is perhaps the most famous example of service sector FDI. Most are more prosaic—the Philippine fast-food chain Jollybees expanding in Thailand, Canadian insurance giant Manulife selling policies in Indonesia, or a Chinese construction company buying a firm in Tanzania.

One important feature of most service sector businesses is that firms need to locate in markets with enough income to sustain demand for their services. Firms are not drawn by low wages, but by customers. And for their employees, firms are not necessarily looking for low-skilled labor, but for literate and numerate labor skilled enough to interact with customers and prepare products (such as a meal or a financial transaction) reliably with good attitudes. Service sector work may be grueling—say, spending all day checking out customers at a Carrefour in Kuala Lumpur—but it is not "sweatshop" labor. In this respect, service FDI is comparable to human capital-intensive and capital-intensive FDI.

Host-Country FDI Policies

Since the late 1970s, when China made its decisive turn toward economic liberalization by creating special economic zones, developing-country policies toward FDI have become more welcoming. Nationalizations and expropriations of installed plant—not uncommon in the 1960s and 1970s—have become infrequent today.

But in other respects it is hard to make generalizations about trends in developing-country policies. Performance requirements on FDI are the norm. These include rules on minimum export shares, local input content, employment, technology-sharing, foreign exchange balancing, and, above all, joint ventures, which are required in many manufacturing and service sectors. Performance requirements, all else equal, make any particular destination less attractive to MNCs. But they are often matched with tax incentives—multiyear "holidays" from corporate income taxes are common—and reduced taxes on inputs.

Not only is there considerable cross-country variation in performance requirements, but there is usually within-country variation by FDI sector as well. For instance, China allows 100 percent foreign ownership in low-wage manufacturing FDI but requires majority domestic ownership (via joint ventures) in advanced-technology manufacturing and, crucially, services. McDonald's in China is majority Chinese-owned. Thailand allows 100 percent foreign ownership in any manufacturing sector, but it only offers tax holidays in favored sectors. India for many years banned foreign retailers and now allows only limited, minority foreign ownership in the retail sector.

Unlike trade and the WTO, there is no multilateral treaty or treaty organization to govern the treatment of FDI in host countries. Instead, policies have evolved bilaterally, often codified in bilateral investment treaties and bilateral tax treaties (BITs and BTTs). Experts consider China's FDI policies, in their totality, to be mildly discriminatory against foreign ownership relative to domestic ownership, but drifting towards neutrality over the past decade. In contrast, sub-Saharan Africa maintains relatively discriminatory rules against foreign ownership despite some recent liberalization.[11]

Effects of FDI in Developing Countries— Theory and Evidence

The discussion so far has identified several reasons why MNCs may decide to locate in developing economies. Now we turn to the question of whether and how those countries benefit.

Economic Theory and FDI Critics

Standard economic theory suggests three fundamental rationales for FDI and a range of caveats. First and arguably foremost, FDI increases the size of a poor country's capital stock. This has several direct welfare-improving effects. Everything else being equal, more capital means faster economic growth. More investment means more capital per worker, raising productivity and wages—first in the industry with the FDI and in the long run in the economy as a whole. This suggests that FDI may have a long-term, poverty-reducing effect.

Nations with well-functioning financial systems and high savings rates may not need FDI. For example, Japan, Korea, and Taiwan did not allow much FDI in their periods of rapid economic growth, but they expanded their capital base internally from their large pools of domestic savings. So economic theory does not suggest that FDI is required for development.

But when FDI adds fresh capital to an economy it is unambiguously welfare-improving because of the rise in the country's capital stock. The size of the gain will be reduced if FDI squeezes out some domestically-owned capital ("crowding out"). The extra capital can leave a country better off even if no taxes are paid (the country was not collecting taxes from this investment to begin with), though the size of the gain will be reduced if there is crowding out. And FDI can leave a country better off even if all profits are repatriated, because the gains to labor are large enough to more than offset the lower profits earned by domestic owners of capital who compete with FDI.

Profit repatriation and tax breaks are frequently mentioned as features of FDI that, on their face, harm a poor country. Theory's clear insight on these points is important. While collecting taxes on corporate profits is of course reasonable and just, the gains from capital stock-increasing FDI can be large enough to leave a country better off overall even if profits are not taxed and all profits are repatriated.

The second major source of gain from FDI is the technological learning and enhanced skills that workers obtain. Developing countries rightly covet the more advanced technologies with which MNCs equip their factories and plants. On-the-job training, learning-by-doing, and experience with world-class standards of operation all build workers' skills. Because these human capital gains are spread around the economy when workers move jobs, these are genuine positive externalities. One particular form in which this externality occurs is when an MNC uses local firms as suppliers. Working closely with MNCs helps local firms meet higher standards, gain familiarity with state-of-the-art technology, gain skills to work with other major international firms, and possibly become exporters themselves.

The third major benefit of FDI is the efficiency and variety gains that arise when MNCs enter markets and compete with domestic producers. This is a particularly pronounced phenomenon in services, where foreign firms are known for bringing new health and sanitary standards to food retailing or bundling new kinds of services together in banking or retailing. So, for instance, as Watson (2006) documents, when McDonald's opened in Hong Kong in 1975, it set new standards for restaurant toilet cleanliness that helped raise standards across the territory. Likewise, when foreign banks compete with domestically-owned banks, domestic banks are forced to raise customer service standards. Consumers' welfare gains are likely to exceed the transition costs imposed on some owners and employees of displaced domestic firms.

The benefits of competition and skills-development often run together. Foreign firms' demonstration of new kinds of services and products—that domestic firms want to imitate—spurs learning that results in higher human capital for all workers and less expensive, better quality services for consumers.

What are the problems with FDI? Economic theory suggests several possibilities. The gains that FDI brings are not unlimited, so host-country governments may offer enough costly inducements to FDI to end up with a net loss. This can occur if out-of-pocket government expenditures on subsidies and infrastructure development are large. Large negative externalities from the FDI—such as, say, pollution—can also in principle leave a country worse off overall than if the FDI had not been made.

Furthermore, if there is significant crowding out—FDI replacing domestically owned investment that would otherwise occur—then there really does need to be sufficient taxation of MNCs' profits for FDI to be welfare improving. That is, if crowding out is significant, the country loses tax revenue on domestically owned capital (and loses income earned by domestic capital owners), which may perhaps exceed the gains from FDI.

"Tariff-jumping" FDI may not be welfare-improving. Such FDI—induced to enter a country because trade barriers make exports to the market uncompetitive—can result in small, inefficient plants unable to prosper if the trade barriers are removed. Ironically, the foreign owners of such FDIs have an incentive to join protectionist voices in the host economy to the detriment of the overall national economic welfare. Similarly, performance requirements designed to force linkages between FDI and the domestic economy may reduce FDI's external benefits. For instance, requiring joint ventures, especially ones with technology-sharing rules, reduces MNCs willingness to use advanced technologies in FDIs.[12] Anecdotally, this has been a major concern in China where weak commercial law appears to have left MNCs vulnerable to patent stealing and other intellectual property theft even inside of joint ventures.

The catalog of complaints leveled against FDI is much larger than the problems suggested by economic theory. Among the most salient charges made—perhaps most strongly by anti-globalization intellectuals but also by others—is that FDI embodies the "race to the bottom" in wages and environmental damage. In this view, firms seek to move to locations with low wages and lax environmental standards; and the desire for FDI tempts host-country governments to *keep* wages low and environmental standards lax.

Another salient charge made by critics is that MNCs exercise undue political influence in developing countries. The large amounts of capital that they invest, combined with the implicit backing they receive from their (wealthy and strong) home country governments, gives them the ear of the host government. They can meddle, this argument asserts, and they can twist policies in directions that favor corporate welfare at the expense of the wider population. In making this argument, critics will often compare MNCs' economic size—total sales, often—with country GDPs, suggesting that their sheer size as economic actors makes them more powerful than many country governments.[13] In a related argument, MNCs are frequently asserted to exercise "control" over market access and to practice socially harmful oligopolistic pricing.[14]

The third salient charge brought against FDI and MNCs is that the brands and advertising they promote create a harmful, materialistic consumer culture. Traditional cultural values are undercut, while unhealthy new consumption habits are encouraged. This line of argument is most recently associated with Naomi Klein's book, *No Logo* (2000), though cultural issues have been of concern for decades—as evidenced, for example, in India's banishment of Coke and Pepsi in the 1960s.

Evidence and Assessment

The disparate theoretical arguments outlined above cry out for empirical resolution—or at least empirical investigation.

Consider wages first. The evidence is overwhelming—across countries, across decades, and across types of FDI—that workers at foreign-owned firms earn more than workers in comparable jobs in domestically owned firms. In the mid-1990s in low-income host countries, compensation paid by foreign affiliates was on average twice the domestic manufacturing wage (Graham 2000, 94). In southern China, annual earnings of low-skilled workers in footwear manufacturing exceed national average income (Frenkel and Scott 2002). In Ghana in the late 1990s foreign-owned firms' wages were on average 49 percent higher than domestic firms (Gorg, Strobl, and Walsh 2007). Moran, Graham, and Blömstrom (2005) and Brown, Deardorff, and Stern

(2004) survey the empirical literature on wages and working conditions. The conclusions could not be starker. As Brown put it,

> There is virtually no careful and systematic evidence demonstrating that, as a generality, multinational firms adversely affect their workers, provide incentives to worsen working conditions, pay lower wages than in alternative employment, or repress worker rights (Brown, Deardorff, and Stern 2004, 322).

The precise reasons for this are not well understood. Some firms are high-profile employers that want to be seen as good employers. Spar (1998) has termed this the "spotlight" effect. Higher wages also could be linked to higher labor productivity due to either technological advantages or better worker training. Foreign-owned firms tend to have less turnover than domestic firms, so the wage differential appears to be part of a cluster of management- and technology-related factors that encourage firms to favor tenure over turnover.

Another focus of empirical work is whether FDI raises countries' growth rates. If the economic theory sketched out above is correct, the additional capital and skill-development that FDI brings to a country should result in higher growth, all else equal. By studying the FDI-growth link, researchers sidestep the notoriously difficult problem of measuring the value of externalities (such as labor skill development through linkages).

Studies of the manufacturing and service sectors' FDI find generally positive, and sometimes neutral, effects of FDI on aggregate growth and per capita growth.[15] There appear perhaps to be "threshold effects" as well. That is, in some cases FDI has a positive effect on growth only when a host country's average labor skills and income level have reached a high enough level. Extractive FDI has ambiguous growth effects related to the resource curse described above.

But the statistical issues involved in identifying the effect of FDI per se on growth are daunting. Blonigen and Wang (2005) argue that many studies inappropriately combine developed and developing country observations, biasing results towards finding little effect. Studies may not adequately control for industry type or for performance requirements. Single-measure indices of performance requirements are inadequate to capture the cross-cutting incentives host countries offer and their variation across sectors. Neither do studies typically control for situations in which FDI moves into highly protected environments where it would not be expected to raise growth (Moran, Graham, and Blömstrom 2005). Cross-sectional analysis across groups of countries may be misleading when there are FDI regime shifts over time, so longitudinal case studies may be best. For all these reasons the definitive work on FDI and growth remains to be done. The best that can be said at present is that there is no evidence that, overall, FDI harms growth.

In light of this mixed record, Dani Rodrik has famously argued that FDI is the same as domestic investment: "One dollar of FDI is worth no more (and no less) than a dollar of any other kind of investment."[16] But that is not quite right. If it is easier to obtain FDI than it is to obtain equivalent additional investment from the domestic financial system, the FDI will in fact be helpful and, in a real sense, superior to domestic investment. The domestic financial sector, and its strengths and weaknesses in generating capital for investment and growth in developing countries, is a key but often underappreciated element in analyzing the effects of FDI.

Another important issue for evaluating FDI is crowding out. As argued above, if crowding out is substantial, FDI can reduce a host-country's welfare. The empirical evidence suggests more crowding in than crowding out; the few studies that find evidence of crowding out find it in Latin America, not in the rest of the world.[17] As with the question of growth, however, it is hard to draw a straight line between a finding of crowding out and a policy recommendation about FDI. Crowding out, when it occurs, does not identify an inherent difficulty with FDI as much as a weakness in domestic financial markets. Crowding out means, by definition, that funds flowing into a host country have the effect of pushing domestic funds out of investment. This would not be possible if the domestic capital market functioned well—in developing countries' capital-scarce environments there is no reason why capital inflows from abroad should close off profitable investment opportunities for domestic funds. In short, the existence of crowding out suggests that complementary reform of financial markets might be helpful, not that FDI is inherently problematic.

Another major strand of empirical work has attempted to find evidence of an environmental race to the bottom in FDI inflows. This has proven quite elusive. In part this is because pollution abatement costs tend to have relatively little bearing on firms' rate of return on capital, so environmental factors appear not to have induced much capital movement. At the same time, trade and market-induced FDI flows have worked to increase the output of relatively clean industries in developing countries.[18]

Finally, regarding MNC power, it is logically incorrect to compare an MNC's sales with a poor country's national income.[19] Such a comparison confuses national income, a value-added statistic, with sales, which is not a value-added statistic. This has the effect of greatly overstating firms' sizes relative to poor nations. Even more fundamental, such comparisons vastly overstate the long-term power and influence of even the largest market firms, because none possess the full tools of coercive power that states possess. Though they can plead with home and host-country governments for economic and political help, actually obtaining such help is a different matter.

Service sector MNCs and manufacturing sector MNCs of all kinds for the most part inhabit competitive or monopolistically competitive industries rather than oligopolistic industries. Thus their bargaining power relative to host-country governments will not be large, especially in large host economies. This lack of bargaining power helps explain Google's complete capitulation to the Chinese government on user-privacy policy in China.

One might think that extractive industries would offer the most fertile ground for MNCs to exercise undue political influence inside host countries. This does of course occur, the classic example being the Nixon administration's interference in Chile in the early 1970s at the behest, in part, of International Telephone and Telegraph. In light of thirty-five additional years of experience with FDI, it is clear just how unusual that case was. In practice, extractive MNCs appear to be highly status quo-oriented, desiring to make profits in peace and quiet and—rightly or wrongly—willing to work with whatever regime is in power. Sitting on expensive and immobile installed operations, their bargaining position relative to host-country governments is not strong. Royal Dutch Shell has been unable to influence Nigeria's government, for instance, despite considerable economic incentives to do so.

It is instructive to think of what the realistic alternatives are, for poor countries, to foreign MNCs in extractive industries. That would be, usually, a state-owned extractive firm. A U.S. MNC would operate under the strictures of the Foreign Corrupt Practices Act, while a state-owned firm would be a political agent of the ruling party. A U.S. MNC would be required to report full financial and production details for its operations; a state-owned firm would not. A U.S. MNC would be sensitive to public opinion in the United States and Europe about its environmental record and its distribution of the revenues paid to the host government; a state-owned MNC, much less so. On balance, it is not at all clear that developing-country welfare is well-served by avoiding the potential problem of domestic political influence from foreign firms by inviting the necessarily political influence and reduced transparency of a state-owned firm.

In summary: FDI is a multifaceted phenomenon with genuine potential for good and considerable evidence that it has been a force for good. The problems with FDI, where they exist, relate in part to adjusting regulations in prudent ways—say, in fine-tuning performance requirements or reducing subsidies so that FDI yields net positive welfare gains. Other problems with FDI relate to problems in domestic financial markets, if, say, crowding-out occurs, where a thoughtful mix of domestic financial sector regulation and liberalization can allow FDI to deliver gains. The exact details of appropriate regulatory regimes will vary from country to country and from sector to sector and defy categorization; though a general presumption that FDI will be welfare improving does not seem unwarranted. This is not to say that FDI is perfect or even that it is necessary for economic development. It is not. But at the very least, there can be no presumption that it is uniquely problematic because of its foreign origin.

FDI in Christian Ethical Perspective

Christian thinking about FDI is split. Christian economists tend to view it positively. They find the theory and evidence, as addressed above, more or less compelling (without necessarily signing on to every position I have taken).[20] By contrast, theologians, church leaders, and other more popular-level Christian thinkers and writers view FDI with deep suspicion and frequent hostility.[21] Much of this latter literature addresses FDI only tangentially, as part of wider critiques of capitalism, corporations, and neoliberalism. The thinking about FDI in these sources is often cast with little nuance in stark class-warfare terms.

For instance, consider Ron Sider, whose deservedly influential and admired book *Rich Christians in an Age of Hunger* has inspired two generations of evangelicals to care for the poor, to strive for generous giving, and to work for justice—and to do so not as an afterthought but as a central part of faithful Christian obedience. Sider paints a harsh picture of FDI and MNCs as lynchpins of global structural injustice: "Anyone concerned with the dangers of centralized power should be concerned with the way huge MNCs have concentrated economic and political power" (172). He portrays MNCs as moving FDI in and out of countries at will in order to exploit them:

MNCs have built up a strong bargaining position both because of their size and the fact that over the years developing countries have become increasingly dependent on their presence. By threatening to leave and thereby throwing a dependent economy into chaos, MNCs can some-times extort one-sided agreements on such issues as tax concessions . . . and so on (173–74).

Mainline denominations' economic statements are also highly critical of FDI and MNCs. The United Church of Christ's 2003 statement, "A Faithful Response: Calling for a More Just, Humane Direction for Economic Globalization," argues that global economic liberalization is focused on little but the fortunes of MNCs:

> Neo-liberal policies tend to advance and protect the interests of multinational corporations and elites around the world more than the interests of individuals, workers, local communities, or the environment (2). . . .The elite in the global north who largely run the governments and the international institutions, own the corporations, and manage the multinational subsidiaries are also focused on making the whole system work to the benefit of the multinational firms (10).

In this view, FDI is little more than a manifestation of a relentless corporate power for ill. Wendell Berry (2002, 2003) explicitly endorses that sentiment, offering an ultra-anti-corporatist vision of economic life that rejects FDI root and branch.

This is hardly a comprehensive survey of Christian thinking on MNCs and FDI. But it does convey the gist of much that is written and worried about among Christians who are not economists. Economists' views and the view of other Christian commentators seem starkly at odds.

Is there a way to square the disparate views? Perhaps not entirely. But there is surely common ethical ground that can be staked out. It is not unreasonable to think of FDI in terms of economic justice, which is of course a Christian virtue. The problem for Christians in developed countries, I believe, is that we are too quick to think of FDI in terms of distributive justice, and we are too slow to think of FDI in terms of practical wisdom, or prudence, which in fact is also a Christian virtue despite its ungainly name.[22]

To put this point differently, Christian writing on FDI plays the prophet and neglects to play the king. Prophets speak judgment on sin and structural evil. As long as humans are fallen, there will be need for prophets. But "kings" are necessary also—to exercise the dominion granted to humankind in creation. Best exercised through democratic governance, the dominion "function," so to speak, is vital for making actual policy choices and balancing competing goods against one another when resources are scarce. Therefore dominion requires practical wisdom, the virtue the ancient church called prudence. Only when directed by practical wisdom can humanity make sustained progress toward justice over the long haul.

So how does FDI look when considered through the eyes of practical wisdom? Better than its critics are willing to admit so far. Scarcities of physical and human capital are in fact real barriers to physical well-being in poor countries. Wages cannot simply be legislated higher or people wished into high-skilled jobs. So, there is something fundamentally just about capital flowing from regions where it is abundant to regions where it is scarce. There is something fundamentally just about poor regions getting access to skills development and competition for their business and the extra variety that FDI can bring. There is something fundamentally just about increased wages driven by access to capital.

There are at least two important FDI-related questions that Christian economists (as well as other Christian social scientists) would be wise to tackle. First is the difficult question of how to structure extractive investments in poor countries—FDI or nationally owned—in ways that minimize resource-curse problems. Progress in thinking about workable institutions and governance in this area would be directly welfare-improving in Africa. Second, Christian scholars could helpfully give some thought to the best means of improving labor conditions in developing countries. Labor abuses, where they occur, are associated with both foreign and domestic capital ownership and tend to be in low-skilled manufacturing sectors. They usually involve violations of a country's own domestic labor law. Market-friendly policy responses—such as product labeling standards, which promote labor's well-being without punishing successful developing country exporters—have not been adequately explored. In both of these areas for future research, the problems are not inherent in FDI. But the presence of FDI links rich-country consumers and firms to poor-country issues in ways that may allow leverage for improvements.

Christian economists have a special burden at this moment. Clear thinking about FDI requires cultivating our colleagues' moral imaginations so that the virtues inherent in FDI can be appreciated and recognized as such. This is not a call to endorse FDI uncritically, which is not and never will be a magic bullet for development. It is a call, though, to encourage the well-informed and holistic Christian ethical concerns in this area that are necessary to craft wise, welfare-promoting FDI policies.

Questions for Review

1. What are the different kinds of FDI? Why do differences between them matter?

2. In your local area, what firms or plants are foreign-owned? Are people generally aware of the ownership? Has their participation in the local economy generally been perceived favorably or unfavorably? Put differently, has the (foreign) management of those firms ever become a local issue of concern? Please explain.

3. The author argues that, from an employee point of view,

transnational or multinational employers are not intrinsically any worse, and may sometimes be better, than domestically owned employers. Why does he think this?

4. The author argues that some problems attributed to FDI in poor countries (such as poor working conditions) relate not to FDI's foreign-ness per se but to underlying problems in governance and law enforcement in poor countries themselves. Do you agree? Are there counter-examples?

5. What kinds of incentives can localities offer for new investment? What kind of governance and rules on government spending might help prevent excessive spending on attracting firms? In general, are there some kinds of government spending that might directly help the population as well as make a locality more attractive for foreign investment?

Notes

[1] Bennholdt-Thomsen (2001).

[2] Graham and Marchick (2006) analyze FDI and security.

[3] The figures cited in this and the previous paragraph are author calculations based on data in UNCTAD (2007) Annex Table B.1, excluding Hong Kong from the "developing" category.

[4] Clustering is also apparent when FDI is measured in per capita terms. Inflows averaged $36 per person per year (2002–2006) in all developing countries. Latin America is at $126; sub-Saharan Africa and South Asia are dramatically lower at $16 and $7, respectively; East Asia and China are at $70 and $47, respectively.

[5] See Carr (2004).

[6] See Judith Dean's discussion of "pollution havens" in Chapter 12 of this volume.

[7] Collier (2007) and Karl (1999) offer non-technical analyses of the political economy of resource curses.

[8] UNCTAF, *World Investment Report 2007* (Fig. IV.3, 104).

[9] Part of this growth is attributable to surging commercial services in Hong Kong.

[10] Note that countries can liberalize financial services FDI without adopting full capital mobility or complete financial liberalization. They simply allow foreign banks into the domestic market, without approving large volume, short-term international portfolio transactions.

[11] See Moss (2005); Long (2005); Moran (2005); Lawrence (2005).

[12] Moran (2005) offers case studies.

[13] See, for one example, Spero and Hart (2003, 120).

[14] See Spero and Hart (2003, Chap. 8); and Todaro and Smith (2008).

[15] Sumner (2005) offers a good summary of recent research in Tables 5 and 6.

[16] Quoted in Moran (2005, 281).

[17] Sumner (2005) provides a summary of recent work; Agosin and Mayer (2000) find crowding in Asia, crowding out in Latin America; Wang (2006) finds evidence of crowding in.

[18] Dean and Lovely (2008) document this effect for FDI in China; see Grether and de Melo (2004) for a survey of empirical results in this area.

[19] Wolfe (2004) skewers this notion with great élan.

[20] See, for instance, Claar and Klay (2007). Donald Hay (1989) is something of an exception among economists.

[21] This is a large generalization, and it is important to note that there are some exceptions, such as Max Stackhouse (2007).

[22] I have written about this more extensively in Smith (2007).

References

Agosin, Manuel R., and Ricardo Mayer. 2000. "Foreign Direct Investment in Developing Countries: Does It Crowd in Domestic Investment?" UNCTAD Discussion Paper 146 (February). Geneva: United Nations Conference on Trade and Development.

Berry, Wendell. 2002. "The Idea of a Local Economy." *Harper's Magazine* 304 (April).

———. 2003. The Total Economy. In *Wealth, Poverty and Human Destiny*, edited by Doug Bandow and David L. Schindler. Wilmington, DE: ISI Books.

Bennholdt-Thomsen, Veronika, Nicholas Faraclas, and Caudia Von Werlhof, eds. 2001. *There Is an Alternative: Subsistence and Worldwide Resistance to Corporate Globalization*. London: Zed Books.

Blonigen, Bruce A., and Miao Grace Wang. 2005. Inappropriate Pooling of Wealthy and Poor Countries in Empirical FDI Studies. In *Does Foreign Direct Investment Promote Development?* edited by Theodore H. Moran, Edward H. Graham, and Magnus Blömstrom. Washington, D.C.: Institute for International Economics.

Brown, Drusilla K., Alan V. Deardorff, and Robert M. Stern. 2004. The Effects of Multinational Production on Wages and Working Conditions in Developing Countries. In *Challenges to Globalization: Analyzing the Economics*, edited by Robert E. Baldwin and L. Alan Winters. Chicago and London: University of Chicago Press.

Carr, David L., James R. Markusen, and Keith E. Maskus. 2004. Competition for Multinational Investment in Developing Countries: Human Capital, Infrastructure, and Market Size. In *Challenges to Globalization: Analyzing the Economics*, edited by Robert E. Baldwin and L. Alan Winters. Chicago and London: University of Chicago Press.

Claar, Victor V., and Robin J. Klay. 2007. *Economics in Christian Perspective: Theory, Policy and Life Choices*. Downers Grove, IL: IVP Academic.

Collier, Paul. 2007. *The Bottom Billion*. New York, NY: Oxford University Press.

Dean, Judith M., and Mary E. Lovely. 2008. "Trade, Growth, Production Fragmentation, and China's Environment." National Bureau of Economic Research Working Paper 13860 (March). Cambridge, MA: National Bureau of Economic Research.

"Everybody's Favorite Monster: A Survey of Multinationals." 1993. *The Economist* (March 27).

Frenkel, Stephen J., and Duncan Scott. 2002. "Compliance, Collaboration, and Codes of Labor Practice: The ADIDAS Connection." *California Management Review* 45, no. 1 (Fall).

Gorg, Holger, Eric Strobl, and Frank Walsh. 2007. "Why Do Foreign-Owned Firms Pay More? The Role of On-the-Job Training." *Review of World Economics* 143, no. 3.

Graham, Edward M. 2000. *Fighting the Wrong Enemy: Antiglobal Activists and Multinational Enterprises*. Washington, D.C.: Institute for International Economics.

Graham, Edward M., and David M. Marchick. 2006. *U.S. National Security and Foreign Direct Investment*. Washington, D.C.: Peterson Institute for International Economics.

Grether, Jean-Marie, and Jaime de Melo. 2004. "Globalization and Dirty Industries: Do Pollution Havens Matter?" In *Challenges to Globalization: Analyzing the Economics*, edited by Robert E. Baldwin and L. Alan Winters. Chicago and London: University of Chicago Press.

Hay, Donald. 1989. *Economics Today: A Christian Critique*. London: Apollos.

Karl, Terry Lynn. 1999. "The Perils of the Petro-State: Reflections on the Paradox of Plenty." *Journal of International Affairs* 53, no. 1.

Klein, Naomi. 2000. *No Logo*. New York: Picador.

Lawrence, Robert Z. 2005. Comment in *Does Foreign Direct Investment Promote Development?* edited by Theodore H. Moran, Edward H. Graham, and Magnus Blömstrom. Washington, D.C.: Institute for International Economics.

Long, Guoqiang. 2005. China's Policy on FDI: Review and Evaluation. In *Does Foreign Direct Investment Promote Development?* edited by Theodore H. Moran, Edward H. Graham, and Magnus Blömstrom. Washington, D.C.: Institute for International Economics.

Moran, Theodore H., Edward H. Graham, and Magnus Blömstrom, eds. 2005. *Does Foreign Direct Investment Promote Development?* Washington, D.C.: Institute for International Economics.

Moran, Theodore H. 2005. How Does FDI Affect Host Country Development? Using Industry Case Studies to Make Reliable Generalizations. In *Does Foreign Direct Investment Promote Development?* edited by Theodore H. Moran, Edward H. Graham, and Magnus Blömstrom. Washington, D.C.: Institute for International Economics.

———. 1998. *Foreign Direct Investment and Development*. Washington, D.C.: Institute for International Economics.

Moss, Todd J., Vijaya Ramachandran, and Manju Kedia Shah. 2005. Is Africa's Skepticism of Foreign Capital Justified? Evidence from East African Firm Survey Data. In *Does Foreign Direct Investment Promote Development?* edited by Theodore H. Moran, Edward H. Graham, and Magnus Blömstrom. Washington, D.C.: Institute for International Economics.

Sider, Ronald J. 1997. *Rich Christians in an Age of Hunger*, 4th edition. Nashville: Word Publishing.

Smith, Stephen L. S. 2007. "Zadok the Priest and Nathan the Prophet Annointed Solomon King." Convocation address at Gordon College (September). View at http://www.gordon.edu/page.cfm?iPageID=1452&iCategoryID=79&Economics_and_Business&Stephen_L.S._Smith.

Spar, Debora L. 1998. "The Spotlight and the Bottom Line: How Multinationals Export Human Rights." *Foreign Affairs* (March/April), 7–12.

Spero, Joan, and Jeffrey A. Hart. 2003. *The Politics of International Economic Relations.* Belmont, CA: Wadsworth-Thomson Learning.

Stackhouse, Max L. 2007. "Social Graces: Christianity and Globalization." *The Review of Faith & International Affairs* 5, no. 3 (Fall).

Sumner, Andrew. 2005. "Is Foreign Direct Investment Good for the Poor? A Review and a Stocktake." *Development in Practice* 15, nos. 3 and 4 (June).

Todaro, Michael P., and Stephen C. Smith. 2008. *Economic Development*, 10th edition. Boston: Addison-Wesley.

United Church of Christ. 2003. "A Faithful Response: Calling for a More Just, Humane Direction for Economic Globalization." Adopted by the Twenty-fourth General Synod of the United Church of Christ, meeting in Minneapolis, Minnesota, July 2003. Submitted by Justice and Witness Ministries, a Covenanted Ministry of the United Church of Christ. Available at http://www.ucc.org/justice/pdfs-1/A-Faithful-Response-Calling-for-a-More-Just-Humane-Direction-for-Economic-Globalization.pdf.

UNCTAD. 2007. *World Investment Report 2007.* Geneva: United Nations Conference on Trade and Development.

Vernon, Raymond. 1977. *Storm over the Multinationals.* Cambridge, MA: Harvard University Press.

Wang, Miao. 2006. "FDI and Domestic Investment: Cross Country Evidence." Processed; presented at the Southern Economics Association meetings (November).

Watson, James L., ed. 2006. *Golden Arches East*, 2d edition. Palo Alto, CA: Stanford University Press.

Wolfe, Martin. 2004. *Why Globalization Works.* New Haven, CT: Yale University Press.

CHAPTER 5

WELCOMING THE STRANGER?

IMMIGRATION AND JUSTICE IN
A GLOBAL ECONOMY

Brad Christerson

Immigration represents one of the most controversial and emotional issues related to globalization. On May 1, 2006 the city of Los Angeles experienced its largest public protest ever—over 500,000 people, mostly immigrants, flooded the streets to protest a bill that would have made being in the United States illegally a felony. This protest, which was matched in cities across the country, was followed by a backlash of sentiment and counter protests among native-born Americans demanding stricter control of the border and the deportation of illegal immigrants.

Likewise, in western Europe, immigration is at an all-time high, and the issue routinely tops public opinion polls as the most serious problem western Europe faces. In 2005, rioting in the largely Arab and African working-class suburbs of Paris led to a strong reaction by both the French public and the French government, which subsequently passed a number of laws restricting immigration from non-EU nations. Other European nations have seen the resurgence of nativist groups, and politicians are pressing for sharp reductions in immigration.

Only a small fraction (roughly 3 percent) of the world's population emigrates in any given year (UN 2006). In some locations, however, the cumulative effect can be quite large. For example, in immigration hotspots such as the United States and parts of western Europe, the percentage of the population that is foreign born is at or near historic highs. In 1990, 7.5 percent of the U.S. population was foreign born. By 2005, that percentage had risen to 12.5 percent. This is well below the 14.5 percent of foreign born at the peak of the last wave of immigration in 1905, but it represents a significant influx over the last two decades (UN 2006). Similarly, in Ireland, 10 percent of the population is now foreign born, and in Spain, the percentage is 11 percent, both historic highs (UN 2006).

Not all immigrants set out for the rich countries of the West, however. Approximately one-third of all migrants move from one developing country to another. Still, North America and Europe absorb the lion's share of international migrants, and the percentage of migrants received by North America and Europe is rising. Over the last fifteen years, North America and Europe together received nearly 60 percent of all migrants (UN 2006).

This chapter begins by putting these trends into historical perspective and examining their causes and economic consequences. It will also explore issues of justice related to immigration. Most importantly, the chapter fills a void in the Christian literature by asking how God would have us think about and act toward immigrants and the policies that are designed to control immigration.

The Current Wave of Immigration in Historical Perspective

There is nothing new about immigration. Humans are a migratory species, and a study of human history reveals an almost constant geographic movement of ethnic groups. God's command to Adam and Eve to "fill the earth" may be the only one that humans have consistently obeyed. While migration has taken place throughout human history, the number of people migrating increased sharply after 1500. Massey (et al. 1998) document three large waves of world migration since 1500:

The Mercantile Period (1500–1800). European colonization gave rise to European migration throughout Africa, Asia, and the Western Hemisphere as well as the movement of African slaves to the Western Hemisphere. Estimates of migrants worldwide during this time range in the tens of millions, changing the racial/ethnic composition of much of the world, most dramatically in North and South America where Europeans grew to dominate these continents numerically and politically.

The Industrial Period (1800–1925). During this period, an estimated 48 million people emigrated from rapidly industrializing and urbanizing Europe to sparsely populated former colonies. Of these, 85 percent immigrated to just five nations, the United States, Australia, Canada, New Zealand, and Argentina, further expanding European dominance of these areas.

The Post Industrial Period (1960–present). While Europe was the engine of the previous two waves of migration, the present wave is truly global as non-European nations have become major sending countries. Before 1925, Europe experienced a large net outflow of immigrants, as 85 percent of all international migrants came from Europe. By the 1980s this changed to a net inflow as Africa, Asia, and Latin America became the primary sources of immigrants and Europe became a major destination.

During the last fifteen years alone, the number of people migrating yearly rose from 155 million to 190 million, an increase of 23 percent

(UN 2006). Approximately one-third migrated from a developing nation to another developing nation, many to higher-income developing nations. For example, Saudi Arabia, India, Pakistan, the UAE, and Hong Kong were major recipients, together accounting for 12 percent of all international migrants (UN 2006). Another third came from developing nations to Europe and North America. The final third emigrated from high-income developed nations (Europe, North America, Oceania, and Japan) to both high and low-income nations around the world (UN 2006).

In the United States, the post-industrial period has produced an influx of immigrants. The sheer number of immigrants in this period, compared to other periods in American history, is much larger, although as a percentage of the population the current wave is still below the industrial period. What is different about the current wave is not the numbers in proportion to the native-born population, but rather the nations of origin of the immigrants. While the first waves came from northern Europe and the second from southern Europe, the third wave of immigrants is predominantly from Asia and Latin America. Like earlier waves, the current influx has set off anti-immigrant reactions from the native-born population.

The Forces Driving the Current Wave of Immigration

Economists and sociologists from a number of theoretical perspectives have identified powerful forces driving the current rise in international migration. While the following is not an exhaustive review of the debates surrounding why people migrate, most scholars agree that six factors are driving the current influx of immigrants to the United States and Europe.[1] Debates on immigration typically focus on the relative importance of each factor rather than on whether these factors exist.

Wage Differentials. Many experts emphasize that economic incentives are a reason individuals migrate. In particular, different nations have widely divergent wage rates, making immigration from a low-wage to a high-wage nation attractive for individuals. According to this theory, the greater the difference between real wages in the receiving country and those in the home country, minus the cost of emigrating, multiplied by the probability of securing employment, the more likely a person will immigrate (see Borjas 1989, 1994). Thus, large wage differentials between rich and poor countries, lower transportation and communications costs, and expanded job opportunities in developed nations drive much of the influx of immigrants in today's globalized economy.

Risk Management Among Households. New theories of the economics of migration emphasize households rather than individuals as the key unit deciding to immigrate (see Stark 1991; Portes and Rumbaut 2006). These scholars have discovered that households in poor and middle-income nations often send one or more family members to a high-income nation, not simply to maximize the income of the individual who emigrates, but to insure against bad outcomes such as crop failure, unexpected unemployment, or the inability to care for elderly household members. Many developing nations do not offer unemployment insurance, crop insurance, or retirement plans. In the absence of these benefits, households diversify their economic resources by sending certain members abroad to send cash home to supplement the family income, offsetting these risks.

Relative Deprivation. Other scholars theorize that households send workers abroad not only to minimize risk but also to gain income relative to those around them (Stark 1991;

Massey et al. 1998). If a household is located in a town where most neighbors own a car, a TV, and a DVD player, then a family may send a member to work in another country so that his or her remittances enable the family to keep up with the consumption patterns of their neighbors. This partially explains why immigrants are more likely to originate from middle-income developing nations, or more prosperous areas within sending nations, than from extremely impoverished areas, as the wage-gap theory would predict.

Demand for Labor in Developed Nations. The "global political economy" literature maintains that the globalization of capitalism has restructured economic activity in such a way that creates demand for immigrants in developed nations (see Sassen 1988). Advances in transportation and communication technologies, combined with liberalized trade and investment laws, allow for freer flow of goods, services, and people across national boundaries. As a result, businesses can locate different stages of their production process or "value chain" wherever the work can be done most cheaply and efficiently (Gereffi 1994; Porter 1998). This relative ease of organizing production on a global scale leads to the growth of high-skill, high-value operations (banking, finance, administration, business services, design, engineering) in rich countries with a highly educated workforce. Low-skill, low-paying and routine jobs are outsourced to developing countries with large pools of cheap, unskilled labor (Reich 1992). However, some unskilled services jobs have to be done on site in rich countries, such as dishwashers, cashiers, waiters, janitors, and construction workers. As a result of the economic growth created by the expanding global economy, demand has been created in rich-country economies for both highly educated specialists and low-skilled service workers that cannot be met by the native-born labor force. This explains the tight labor markets and relatively low unemployment rates that have existed alongside large-scale immigration to the United States in the past two decades.

Dislocation of Rural Laborers in Developing Nations. Globalization creates social forces that in turn create both international migration and internal migration in developing countries. Reduced trade barriers coupled with government farm subsidies in rich countries have put many small-scale farmers in developing nations out of business, leading to migration from rural areas to cities. Farmers and sharecroppers, displaced by import competition or capital-intensive agricultural production for global markets, move internally to cities to look for work (Zabin and Hughes 1995). Many find work in factories and "export processing zones" set up by multinational corporations. In cities, migrant workers are exposed to people and information that open opportunities to migrate internationally (Zabin and Hughes 1995; Delgado-Wise and Covarrubias 2007). As migrants already, they are often ready to move again for more promising opportunities in other nations. Thus, the process of globalization creates migration both internally and internationally.

Government Policies. For the economic forces mentioned above to actually produce large-scale immigration, states must institute policies that facilitate it. Most Western nations have liberalized their immigration laws in the past few decades, making it possible for more immigrants from developing nations to become legal residents. In the United States, for example, immigration patterns shifted dramatically in 1965 when key amendments to the Immigration and Nationality Act removed quotas favoring European immigrants and removed caps on the number of immediate relatives of U.S. citizens to immigrate. This has led to a steady stream of immigrants from Latin America and Asia seeking higher wages and unification with their families. The end of the Cold War and the creation of the European Union brought waves of immigrants from eastern Europe to western Europe. Historically, increases and decreases in immigration follow shifts in government policy.

The Consequences of Immigration

Discussions of immigration set off waves of anger and emotion, which tops the list of concerns for many immigrants and native-born people in the United States and western Europe. This raw emotion is tied to claims of injustice on both sides of the immigration equation. Many native-born residents feel they are being "invaded" by poor people from other countries who take jobs away from native-born residents, who refuse to assimilate or speak the native language, and who "drain the economy" by bringing down wages; overwhelming schools, hospitals, jails, and public services; and by using up government welfare benefits—without paying taxes. Some make no distinction between documented and undocumented immigrants, assuming that most are in the country illegally and therefore are law-breakers who have no right to be in this country. Immigrants, on the other hand, have their own claims of injustice. Many claim to be exploited in the workplace because of their immigrant status. They claim to be given the lowest-paying jobs in the harshest working conditions. And they sometimes claim to be abused by their employers. This section addresses each of these concerns. We will analyze the U.S. case, recognizing that the effects of immigration in other countries may not be the same. The U.S. case is instructive, however, because it is the nation that receives the largest number of immigrants, and the economic and fiscal effects of immigration have been researched more thoroughly in the United States than in other nations.[2]

Economic Effects in the Host Country

In host countries, native-born residents often claim negative economic effects as the primary reason to limit immigration. In particular, they cite effects on employment ("taking away our jobs"), wage competition, and the use of government services as negative outcomes of immigration. Others, particularly the business community, claim that immigration benefits the nation as the need for workers has increased with our expanding economy. What does empirical research tell us about the effects?

Most economists agree that the net economic impact of immigration is positive for the host economy. In an open letter to the U.S. Congress in 2006, five hundred American economists signed a statement that read, "Overall, immigration has been a net gain for American citizens, though a modest one in proportion to the size of our $13-trillion economy" (cited in Streitfeld 2006). This net economic gain is due to the fact that immigrants increase the supply of labor but are paid less as a group than native-born workers, thus moderating inflation and creating a net gain for consumers of the goods and services immigrants produce. For example, fruit and vegetable prices are held constant or even reduced because of immigrant field workers, and construction costs are moderated because of immigrant laborers. Lower wages and prices suggest that businesses that rely heavily on unskilled labor (for example, the agriculture, restaurant, hotel, and construction businesses) also benefit from immigration.

Immigrants also consume goods and services and thus have a stimulative effect on the demand side of the economy, which in turn leads to job growth and higher profits for businesses. Those hurt most directly by immigration are the less-educated, less-skilled workers who compete directly with unskilled immigrants in the labor market.

Native-born high school dropouts (about 10 percent of the population) are the most affected group. According to one study, the earnings of high school dropouts have declined as much as 5 percent from 1979 to 1995 as a direct result of immigration (Borjas 2003). Other studies estimate the drop in wages of high school dropouts to be between 1 and 2 percent (Smith and Edmonston 1997; Hamermesh 1996). For those with at least a high school education, however, the reduction in prices has resulted in an overall increase in real (inflation adjusted) incomes on average (Smith and Edmonston 1997).

There is also no evidence that large-scale immigration increases unemployment rates in the host society, even for unskilled workers. One study found that a 10 percent increase in the immigrant population in a local labor market reduces the number of weeks worked per year by unskilled native workers by a relatively insignificant 0.6 percent, or two days per year (Altonji and Card 1991). Other studies show an actual increase in employment for native unskilled laborers as immigration increased (Smith and Edmonston 1997). A comparison of unemployment rates between immigration hot spots—such as southern California and south Florida and areas without large immigrant populations—shows no significant difference in unemployment rates. In sum, if immigration has an effect on employment rates among natives, it is negligible.

Critics often identify the fiscal consequences (a net loss of tax revenue) of large-scale immigration as the most significant. However, it is important to distinguish between short- and long-run consequences and between states with high concentrations of immigrants and those with relatively fewer immigrants.

One comprehensive study found that if the yearly net fiscal impact of all immigrant-headed households in the United States were averaged across all native households in the United States, it would result in a tax burden of between $166 and $226 per year per native household (Smith and Edmonston 1997). This study cited three reasons why, on a year-to-year basis, immigrants use more in government resources than they pay in taxes. First, immigrant-headed households have more school-aged children than native households and therefore consume more educational services. Second, immigrant-headed households are poorer on average than native households and therefore receive more government income transfers. And third, immigrant-headed households have lower incomes and own less property than natives on average and thus pay lower state and local taxes.

Based on accounting in a single year, therefore, it appears that each immigrant household imposes an overall tax burden on native residents. However, the same study reaches a different conclusion when examining the long-term fiscal effects of each immigrant household. Smith and Edmonston (1997) concluded that the net fiscal impact of each immigrant household is positive over that immigrant's lifetime, because most immigrants arrive relatively young, when they have or are about to have school-aged children. The taxes they pay when they arrive are less than the government services they use, mostly due to the costs of educating their children. When these children enter the workforce, however, they will pay taxes, contributing a net fiscal gain to government over the lifetime of that immigrant family.

In states with high concentrations of immigrants, such as California, Texas, and New York, both the short-run and long-run fiscal impact is negative since state and local revenues pay for much of the education and health care of immigrants, therefore concentrating the costs of educating immigrant children in just a few states. Thus, taxpayers in states such as California and New York pay to educate immigrant children while the entire nation benefits from the taxes they pay when they enter the workforce. So while the long-term fiscal effects of each immigrant are on average positive for native-born residents (immigrants end up paying more in taxes than the services they use over their lifetime), they impose a negative tax burden on native residents in certain high immigration states (Smith and Edmonston 1997).

145

In sum, immigration does not impose a long-term fiscal burden on native-born residents overall, in fact it leads to an overall fiscal net gain for native residents. However, for certain native-born residents in certain high-immigration states, immigration does impose a fiscal burden. But, the overall net economic effect is still positive for native-born residents in those high-immigration states, since those residents are more likely to benefit from the economic stimulus and lower costs for goods and services that immigrants provide.

Overall, most claims by native-born residents of negative economic effects related to immigration have no empirical basis. Only two negative economic effects of immigration are empirically founded and, therefore, could qualify as an unjust outcome of immigration for native-born residents of the host society: (1) Native-born high school dropouts have seen their wages decline by as much as 5 percent as a result of immigration, and (2) native households in a small number of high immigration states experience a tax burden as a result of immigration. These problems can be addressed, however, without restricting immigration, which will be discussed in a later section.

Injustices Claimed by Immigrants

Many immigrants claim to be treated unjustly by their employers. This is particularly true of undocumented workers, many of whom claim to be paid less than minimum wage. A recent report in the *Los Angeles Times*, for example, found that undocumented workers at local car washes are often paid tips only (March 23, 2008). Similarly, an investigation of the garment industry in Los Angeles, conducted by the U.S. Department of Labor, found that 48 percent of the factories violated minimum-wage laws, and 51 percent did not pay overtime (U.S. Department of Labor 1998). This study did not include unlicensed factories, which comprise close to a third of all garment factories in the Los Angeles region and whose conditions are typically worse.

Other studies have found unsafe working conditions and physical abuse of immigrants. Bonacich and Appelbaum (2000), in their study of garment workers in Los Angeles, found unsafe working conditions and occasional physical abuse of immigrant garment workers, who were afraid to complain because their feared being fired or deported. Studies of agricultural, janitorial, and housekeeping workers found similar abuses (Cranford 2005; Loucky, Hamilton, and Chinchilla 1989; Mines and Avina 1992). Some studies have found that undocumented immigrant farm workers are routinely exposed to dangerous levels of pesticides, which leads to high rates of leukemia and stomach, uterine, and brain cancer (Mills and Kwong 2001) as well as neurological disorders and birth defects (Claren 2003; Rothlein et al. 2006). Because of their undocumented status, these workers fear speaking out about their conditions because of the prospect of deportation.

Clearly, these claims by immigrants of injustice do have empirical support. Those affected most by workplace injustice are at the bottom of the economic scale—undocumented workers in low-paying, low-skill jobs such as garment making, janitorial services, and agricultural labor.

Many highly educated, highly skilled legal immigrants face injustices as well. Often their education credentials obtained in their home country are not recognized or valued as highly, so they receive lower pay and lower status as a result. They are also often routed to technical jobs and face obstacles to moving into higher-paying management and executive positions (Aguirre and Turner 1998; Nguyen 1993; Chiu 1994).

In addition to workplace abuses, migrants are exposed to abuse by smugglers and traffickers (UN 2006), as well as racism, xenophobia, and discrimination in their host society because of tensions over the issue of immigration. In many places, these tensions can result in hate crimes and other forms of violence and intimidation (UN 2006).

Sending-Country Effects

Immigration has significant effects on the economies of sending nations as well. The largest effect is remittances from emigrants— money sent back to family members in the sending nation. According to World Bank estimates, remittances doubled from $102 billion in 1995 to $232 billion in 2005 (UN 2006; World Bank 2006). The percentage of worldwide remittances going to developing countries (as opposed to developed countries) has increased from 57 percent in 1995 to 72 percent in 2005. In twenty developing countries, remittances accounted for at least 10 percent of their total GDP. Overall, *remittances from migrants are now much larger than all forms of international aid to developing countries combined* (UN 2006).

Remittances raise the income of citizens in developing nations and often provide health care and education, thus improving the overall level of productivity and human capital in those nations. Because of multiplier effects, remittances also improve the lives of community members who do not have a family member sending back money. The UN estimates that every dollar an emigrant sends to a family member at home may add two or three dollars of income in that local community when the money is spent on goods and services supplied by local businesses (UN 2006). Migration is therefore a powerful engine of economic growth to develop nations, raise incomes, improve health care and education, and create jobs in local economies.

More problematic is the so-called "brain-drain" that occurs when highly skilled workers emigrate from developing to developed nations (Freeman 2006). One study estimates that in 2001, approximately 10 percent of all college-educated citizens of developing nations were living in North America, Australia, or Europe (Lowell, Findlay, and Stewart 2004). Another study found that over half of university-educated adults from the Caribbean live in the United States; and in some African countries, more than 35 percent of citizens with a college education live overseas (Kapur and McHale 2005). While this benefits the host country, it represents a decrease in human capital for the sending country. The cost is compounded if these nations invest in the education of their citizens, only to lose their services to other nations. Remittances can offset this loss to a degree, since the income of these skilled professionals is significantly higher in developed nations, thus freeing up more income to provide for family members left behind. In addition, highly educated emigrants in developed nations often help increase trade and investment flows between the home country and receiving country (Beine and Rapoport 2003). By emigrating, educated professionals can also benefit their home country by encouraging others at home to pursue a higher education, which will raise overall levels of education in those nations (Stark and Wang 2001).

The offsetting gains and losses described above make it difficult to assess the net impact of a brain drain. One study suggests that when more than 20 percent of a country's skilled professionals leave the country, the losses will exceed the benefits (Beine and Rapoport 2003). Overall, however, economists agree that emigration has had an overwhelmingly positive net economic effect on developing nations as a whole (UN 2006).

Toward a Christian View of Immigration

Several biblical principles are relevant to the current debate over immigration. This is not to say, of course, that Christians agree on the topic. However, stating these principles should bring some clarity to the debate.

The Kingdom of God Should Be Our Primary Goal

The New Testament writers constantly reinforce that we are citizens of a new kingdom that knows no geographic boundaries, and we are to go and "make disciples of all nations." Adding people in this new kingdom is the primary goal of God's people. Thus, people from other nation-states coming to our territory can be an opportunity to expand the new kingdom as we welcome them and make disciples.

Thus, we should see immigration as an opportunity to expand the transnational kingdom of God by making disciples of those who come to us from around the world. It is interesting that many evangelicals support sending missionaries to other nations to make disciples but demand policies to keep these same people out of their nation and their neighborhood. This contradicts the thinking of the New Testament writers, for whom reinforcing national boundaries was of no concern. Instead, they call us to overcome those boundaries in order to expand the kingdom of God.

Our Duty Toward Strangers and People in Need

In the Old Testament, God gave this command to his people: "When a stranger resides with you in your land, you shall not do him wrong. *The stranger who resides with you shall be to you as the native among you, and you shall love him as yourself, for you were aliens in the land of Egypt; I am the LORD your God* (Lev. 19:33–34 NASB, emphasis added). In his command to treat the alien as a native-born person, it is interesting that God reminds the Israelites that they too were once immigrants and that he is God. Indeed most of us, or our recent ancestors, are immigrants from current or earlier periods of migration. This reinforces the theme that we are all immigrants in a land that ultimately belongs to God.

In the New Testament, this theme of welcoming the stranger and the person in need is even stronger. The strongest example is Jesus' iteration that one who welcomes a stranger—or cares for one who is hungry, sick, or in need—does these things to God himself, and those who do not do these things are actively rejecting him (Matt. 25:31–46). Jesus so identifies himself with the poor, the marginalized, *and the alien* that to serve them is to serve him, and to reject them is to reject him. He calls each of us to welcome the foreigner, care for the needy, and speak up for the oppressed. All of this suggests that welcoming strangers and aliens in our midst and serving and loving them are central to our role as God's people in this world.

The Role of Government in a Fallen World

Throughout both Old and New Testaments, Scripture affirms that God is in control of the rulers of this earth and uses them for his purposes, even though they are fallen and corrupt. Romans 13 is the clearest depiction of every government being appointed by God, including the power of the sword (violence) to punish evildoers. How does this apply to controlling the borders of nation-states? Romans 13 affirms the right and responsibility of governments to regulate immigration as a fulfillment of their God-given task of promoting order, rewarding good, and punishing evil. Having no process in place for orderly immigration or having a policy that punishes good and rewards evil would be a violation of God's role of government.

If a government punishes people for doing good or allows evil to go unpunished, then it is the duty of God's people to point this out and call the government back to its proper role. The Old Testament prophets and the New Testament disciples often engaged in the civil protest of "speaking truth to power" in order that they may have a chance to reform.

This theme is relevant to undocumented or "illegal" immigrants. Some claim, including many Christians, that current immigration policy is rewarding law breakers by having no consequences for being in the country illegally. Some also criticize businesses for knowingly hiring undocumented immigrants to keep labor costs low, thus benefiting from breaking the law. As such, critics claim that government is not carrying out its task of securing our borders and is therefore failing to punish bad behavior. Some see undocumented workers as "stealing" jobs and resources by not going through the proper channels to immigrate legally.

The God-ordained role of government must lead us to two key questions: (1) Do our current laws reflect the God-ordained tasks of government to bring order, reward good, and punish evil? and (2) Are these laws properly and justly enforced? Question one must be answered first, because if our current laws are unjust, then God's people must raise this concern and call government to its God-ordained role rather than push to have those unjust laws enforced more rigorously.

Given the benefits of immigration, both economic and for the growth of God's kingdom, one could argue that current laws are unnecessarily restrictive, are criminalizing immigration, and therefore are unjust—a form of punishing good behavior. If a person simply wants to work hard in order to care for his/her family and his/her work, a blessing to those in both the sending and the receiving country, it is difficult to argue that this behavior should be criminalized. Given current levels of immigration and its economic effects, there is no evidence that the behavior of most immigrants is harmful to society as a whole. In fact, as we have seen, their behavior is on balance an economic benefit to both the host and the sending society. Thus, laws that criminalize this behavior could be seen as unjust. It could be, however, that much higher levels of immigration, because of open borders, would create disorder and harm to the host society, thus necessitating some level of control over borders.

The question of justice, therefore, in immigration laws and policies asks what level of immigration should be allowed and what procedures should facilitate and limit immigration—rather than asking if a government has the right to regulate its borders. It clearly does. Moving toward more just immigration laws and enforcement of those laws, based on the aforementioned Christian principles, will be the focus of the concluding section.

Conclusion: The Need for Reform

Globalization unleashes forces that increase both the demand for and the supply of immigrants in wealthy nations. In this context, immigration produces net economic gains for the immigrants themselves and for the sending and receiving nations. When thinking through government policies that would facilitate justice in the global situation, however, three questions must be addressed: Who benefits from immigration? Who is harmed by immigration? How are the poorest and weakest people affected by immigration policies?

In evaluating current policies with regard to these questions, there is a clear need for reform in order to facilitate a more just situation for both immigrants and citizens of host societies.

As shown above, not everyone benefits. In particular, those at the bottom of the economic ladder (high school dropouts), comprising 10 percent of the population, are negatively affected by wage competition and reduced wages from immigration. They are *not*, however, put out of work by immigrants as some suggest. Biblical principles command that care for and protection of those in need must be a priority for a just society. As such, the negative effects of immigration policy on high-school dropouts must be addressed. These concerns can be addressed, however, without limiting immigration levels. For example, some of the fiscal gains from immigration could be used to expand earned income tax credits for working, high school dropouts to offset wage losses due to immigration.

In addition, high immigration states, such as California and New York, that carry a disproportionate share of the fiscal burden from immigration should be reimbursed through a national benefit-redistribution scheme, something like the Trade Adjustment Assistance program. As we have discussed, undocumented immigrants often suffer exploitation and abuse as a result of their vulnerable status and lack of rights. This vulnerability could be reduced by expanding guest-worker visa programs for workers in industries that need more workers than can be found in the native-born labor force. Most economists agree that the number of work visas granted to people wishing to immigrate to the United States is too low to meet the demands of our expanding economy. Guest workers would have all the rights of native workers, including the right to join unions and to file complaints against their employer for workplace safety violations. Giving guest workers legal status would reduce the abuse of undocumented immigrants, since employers would be forced to comply with existing workplace law. Legal status would also reduce the abuses from the illegal human-trafficking industry.

Finally, the government has an obligation to guarantee an orderly process in facilitating and managing the flow of immigrants. Building walls and high-tech fences will ultimately fail to keep people from entering a country illegally. In fact, most undocumented workers simply overstay a tourist visa, which walls and fences have no power to restrict. A more effective way to control the flow of immigrants is to focus on workplace enforcement. Employers required to check work documents with a government database for verification, and punished if they knowingly hired an undocumented worker, would reduce the flow of immigrants greatly, since most immigrants come for employment. *However, this measure would have to be accompanied by a large increase in legal immigration to avoid the negative economic effects of reducing overall immigration levels.* In other words, reducing the flow of illegal immigrants must be combined with significant increases in the flow of legal immigrants in order to maximize the economic gains of immigration for the host country, the sending country, and the immigrants themselves.

In conclusion, despite alarmist rhetoric and fear among many native-born North Americans and western Europeans of being "invaded" and economically harmed by immigrants, immigration is generally beneficial to a nation. In addition to economic gains, God's people can rejoice in the enrichment that comes from experiencing new cultures and in the opportunities to make disciples of all nations—without leaving our own neighborhood and city. The downsides of immigration can be addressed through policy reforms, without halting immigration and its positive benefits. In fact, legal immigration can and should expand while addressing these injustices so that everyone benefits from immigration.

As it turns out, welcoming the stranger is not only a moral imperative for believers but it is also economically prudent.

Questions for Review

1. What were your views about immigration before reading this chapter? Did you find anything in this chapter surprising? Have your views changed at all? Please explain.

2. What are the economic costs and benefits of immigration to the host country? To the sending country?

3. What can the government do to reduce the costs and/or increase the benefits of immigration? What can it do to more effectively prevent or prosecute immigration-related injustices?

4. Do you agree that believers have a responsibility as the people of God to welcome immigrants to our country? Should the church push for policies that allow more immigrants to come legally? Please explain.

Notes

[1] I have excluded refugees and others fleeing conflicts and natural disasters as primary causes. These are an important source of immigration from one developing country to another. However, only 1.2 percent of all migrants to North America and 3.1 percent of migrants to Europe are refugees fleeing conflicts, famines, or natural disasters (UN 2006).

[2] The evidence cited below includes both legal and undocumented immigrants in examining economic and fiscal effects. It is difficult to separate the two using census and economic data, because the legal status of an immigrant is not included in this data; therefore, attempts to separate the economic impact of the two groups is difficult. On one hand, an argument can be made that undocumented workers are willing to work for less than documented workers and therefore could bring unskilled wages down further. On the other hand, they often use false documents and therefore do pay taxes, although they are ineligible for benefits that lead to a positive fiscal effect. In sum, it is difficult to distinguish documented and undocumented workers and ascertain whether the economic and fiscal effects of each are different. The evidence suggests that the economic effects are similar regardless of legal status.

References

Aguirre, Adalberto, and Jonathan Turner. 1998. *American Ethnicity: The Dynamics and Consequences of Discrimination.* Boston: McGraw Hill.

Altonji, J. G., and D. Card. 1991. The Effects of Immigration on the Labor Market Outcomes of Less-Skilled Natives. In *Immigration, Trade, and the Labor Market*, edited by J. Abowd and R. Freeman. Chicago: University of Chicago Press, 201–34.

Beine, Michel Frederic Docquier, and Hillel Rapoport. 2003. "Brain Drain and LDC's Growth: Winners and Losers." Institute for the Study of Labor Discussion Paper 819. Bonn: Institute for the Study of Labor.

Bonacich, Edna, and Richard P. Appelbaum. 2000. *Behind the Label: Inequality in the Los Angeles Apparel Industry.* Berkeley: University of California Press.

Borjas, George. 1999. *Heaven's Door: Immigration and the American Economy.* Princeton: Princeton University Press.

———. 1994. "The Economics of Immigration." *Journal of Economic Literature* 32, 1667–717.

———. 1989. "Economic Theory and International Migration." *International Migration Review* 23, 457–85.

———. 2003. "The Labor Demand Curve *Is* Downward Sloping: Reexamining the Impact of Immigration on the Labor Market," *Quarterly Journal of Economics* 118: 1335-74.

Chiu, Daina. 1994. "The Cultural Defense: Beyond Exclusion, Assimilation, and Guilty Liberalism." *California Law Review* 82, 1053–125.

Claren, Rebecca. 2003. "Fields of Poison." *Nation* 277, no. 22, 23–25.

Cranford, Cynthia. 2005. "Networks of Exploitation: Immigrant Labor and the Restructuring of the Los Angeles Janitorial Industry." *Social Problems* 52, no. 3, 379–97.

Delgado-Wise, Raúl, and Humberto Márquez Covarrubias. 2007 "The Reshaping of Mexican Labor Exports under NAFTA: Paradoxes and Challenges." *International Migration Review* 41, no. 3, 656–79.

Freeman, Richard. 2006. "People Flows in Globalization." *Journal of Economic Perspectives* 20, no. 2, 145–70.

Gereffi, Gary. 1994. The Organization of Buyer-Driven Global Commodity Chains: How U.S. Retailers Shape Overseas Production Networks. In *Commodity Chains and Global Capitalism*, edited by Gereffi and Korzeniewicz. Westport, CT: Greenwood Press, 165–87.

Hamermesh, D. S. 1996. *Labor Demand*. Princeton: Princeton University Press.

Hanson, Gordon. 2005. Challenges for U.S. Immigration Policy. In *The United States and the World Economy: Foreign Economic Policy for the Next Decade,* edited by C. Fred Bergsten. Washington, D.C.: Institute for International Economics, 343–72.

Kapur, Devesh, and John McHale. 2005. *Give Us Your Best and Brightest: A Global Hunt for Talent and Its Impact on the Developing World.* Washington, D.C.: Center for Global Development.

Loucky, James, Nora Hamilton, and Norma Chinchilla. 1989. "The Effects of Irca on Selected Industries in Los Angeles: A Preliminary Report." Bellingham, WA: Western Washington University (unpublished manuscript).

Lowell, B. Lindsay, Allan Findlay, and Emma Stewart. 2004. "Brain Strain: Optimizing Highly Skilled Migration from Developing Countries." Institute for Public Policy Research Working Paper 3, no. 40. London: Institute for Public Policy Research, 5.

Massey, Douglas, Joaquin Arango, Graeme Hugo, Ali Kovaouci, Adela Pellegrino, and J. Edward Taylor. 1998. *Worlds in Motion: Understanding International Migration at the End of the Millennium.* New York, NY: Oxford University Press.

Mills, Paul, and Sandy Kwong. 2001. "Cancer Incidence in the United Farmworkers of America 1987–1997." *American Journal of Industrial Medicine* 40, no. 5, 596–603.

Mines, Richard, and Jeffrey Avina. 1992. Immigration and Labor Standards: The Case of California Janitors. In *U.S.-Mexico Relations: Labor Market Interdependence,* edited by J. Bustamante, C. Reynolds, and R. Hinojosa-Ojeda. Palo Alto: Stanford University Press.

Nguyen, Beatrice Bich-Dao. 1993. "Accent Discrimination and the Test of Spoken English: A Call for an Objective Assessment of the Comprehensibility of Nonnative Speakers." *California Law Review* 81, 1325–6.

Porter, Eduardo. 2005. "Illegal Immigrants Are Bolstering Social Security with Billions." *New York Times* (April 5).

Porter, Michael. 1998. *The Competitive Advantage of Nations.* New York: Free Press.

Portes, Alejandro, and Ruben Rumbaut. 2006. *Immigrant America: A Portrait.* Berkeley: University of California Press.

Reich, Robert. 1992. *The Work of Nations: Preparing Ourselves for Twenty-First Century Capitalism.* New York: Vintage.

Rothlein, J., D. Rohlman, M. Lasarev, J. Phillips, J. Muniz, and L. McCauley. 2006. "Organophosphate Pesticide Exposure and Neurobehavioral Performance in Agricultural and Nonagricultural Hispanic Workers." *Environmental Health Perspectives* 114, no. 5, 691–6.

Sassen, Saskia. 1988. *The Mobility of Capital and Labor: A Study in International Investment and Labor Flow.* New York, NY: Cambridge University Press.

Smith, J. P., and Barry Edmonston, eds. 1997. *The New Americans: Economic, Demographic, and Fiscal Effects of Immigration.* Washington, D.C.: National Academy Press.

Stark, Oded. 1991. Relative Deprivation and Migration: Theory, Evidence, and Policy Implications. In *Determinants of Emigration from Mexico, Central America, and the Caribbean,* edited by Sergio Diaz-Briquets and Sidney Weintraub. Boulder, CO: Westview.

———, and Yong Wang. 2001. "Inducing Human capital Formation: Migration as a Substitute for Subsidies." IHS Working Paper 100. Vienna: Institute for Advanced Studies.

Streitfeld, David. 2006. "Illegal—But Essential." *Los Angeles Times* (September 30).

UN. 2006. *International Migration and Development.* UN Publication A.60.871. New York, NY: United Nations.

U.S. Department of Labor. 1998. "Survey of Compliance." Reported in *California Apparel News* (June). Washington, D.C.: U.S. Department of Labor.

World Bank. 2006. *Global Economic Prospects 2006: Economic Implications of Remittances and Migration.* Washington, D.C.: World Bank.

Zabin, Carol, and Sallie Hughes. 1995. "Economic Integration and Labor Flows: Stage Migration in Farm Labor Markets in Mexico and the United States." *International Migration Review* 29, no. 2, 395–422.

CHAPTER 6

OFFSHORING AND WORKER MIGRATION:

CHRISTIAN CONCERNS AND OPPORTUNITIES

J. David Richardson

This chapter is devoted to the concerns and opportunities raised by the growth of offshoring and worker migration. Discussions by Christians of these two phenomena are missing some important, below-the-surface shifts that could leave us unprepared and unable to effectively engage the opportunities offered.

We begin with a summary of the distinctive features of offshoring and worker migration and then move on to longer accounts of their recent growth, national impacts, and global implications. Their more specific implications for the "business-as-mission" movement are the focus of the last section of this chapter, using a conception of mission-driven firms that places them somewhere between pure for-profit firms and pure not-for-profits. The conclusion drawn is that the business-as-mission movement, which has pioneered creative offshoring to meet its objectives, should also explore ways to use legal guest-worker visas to accomplish its purposes. The business-as-mission movement might also help rich-country publics understand that expanding access for "imports" of temporary mid-skill-worker services is not only in their own narrow economic interest but are also extremely effective pro-poor policies for development.

A Brief Comparison of Offshoring and Worker Migration

Offshoring and worker migration are both similar and different in unappreciated ways.[1] Offshoring is a type of specialization and trade; worker migration is a type of "factor mobility," to use economists' language. Offshoring is the global integration of input markets, including services inputs, of which the most promising is worker services.

Both offshoring and worker migration can heighten economic opportunity, opportunity that is aimed squarely and effectively at the global poor. Research described below reveals that the wage gaps across countries for comparably skilled workers are enormous and much, much larger than price gaps for those goods and services traded in conventional output markets. We will see below that offshoring brings the world's employers to low-wage locations and that worker-migration opportunities bring the world's workers to high-wage locations. The obvious result is higher wages for low-wage workers, their families, and their home countries. Much less obvious, but equally apparent in the research, is that many high-wage workers in rich countries are *not necessarily* victims. They, too, have opportunities to gain from both offshoring and worker migration, and those opportunities are enhanced by modern innovations in traditional trade adjustment-assistance policies.

Both offshoring and worker migration blur traditional *national* boundaries of firm and family. This blurring forces a reconception and a redefinition of social justice and of important traditional principles by which global exchange is governed. Traditional nondiscrimination principles such as *national* treatment and most-favored-*nation* treatment must be reshaped. Even traditional language distinctions between domestic and foreign, or internal and external, prove inadequate in a blurry world of multinational firms and multiethnic families with dual workplaces and citizenship. Important new social-justice challenges include how to innovate new insurance arrangements (including social insurance) and how to negotiate the human, political, and labor-relations rights of temporary residents.[2]

Another important and unappreciated aspect of offshoring and worker migration is that they are interchangeable—"close substitutes" in economists' language. The same underlying innovation in information, design, and data-processing technologies, and the same decline in cross-border transport and communication costs, even for migrants, have caused both phenomena to mushroom. Reactive policies aimed at decelerating offshoring, in the name of some patriotic good (preventing "Benedict Arnold CEOs," for example), often undermine themselves by heightening the attractiveness of time-limited worker immigration, whether legal or not. Policies that "just say no" to unwanted immigration by "securing our borders and workplaces" often accelerate offshoring.

The key to appreciating the high interchangeability of offshoring and worker migration is to understand how much offshoring involves trade in "tasks." Tasks are observable worker activities, such as software development and testing, payroll processing, and customer-call service. Obviously, some task is what a given worker specializes in.[3] To a human-resource manager, as long as a vital task is completed well, it matters little whether the task is done by an employee working remotely (and electronically) or by a person sitting "just-across-the-partition-from-me." The *same* South Asian person could be the task-exporter or the temporary migrant-worker delivering the task in person.

Taken together, multinationality and interchangeability create an extremely broad and flexible input-and-cost environment for firms. Tasks may be sourced and sold globally; workers themselves can be hired and positioned globally. Input markets are becoming as globalized as output markets, and firms that take full advantage of both are said to be pursuing the global-business model.

Interchangeability presents Christians both opportunity and concern. One opportunity is to improve earnings prospects dramatically for the working poor and the middle class in poor countries—far more dramatically than traditional channels of foreign aid, merchandise trade, and microfinance. A second opportunity is to co-labor at home with managers and workers from abroad on temporary work visas. These opportunities are, to my knowledge, yet-to-be-explored frontiers in the business-as-mission movement.

Shift #1. Offshore Outsourcing

The global, *bidirectional* character of offshoring is rarely recognized in the recent cascades of fevered commentary. The reality is that *everybody* is doing it—offshoring is *not* a distinctively American practice or issue.[4] Indeed, many foreign firms now outsource some of their work to the United States. This aspect of the reigning business model truly is global.

Around the world, for-profit and not-for-profit firms are discovering they can often provide better service at a lower cost by engaging foreign partners as input suppliers. Technological change has already fragmented the vertically integrated firm (and its conglomerate family) through outsourcing; globalization allows the outsourcing to include foreigners (offshore outsourcing) on a non-discriminatory basis.

Grossman and Rossi-Hansberg (2006) explain how offshoring should be seen as a common-sense extension of familiar categories and conceptions, with a central role for "tasks." Tasks are what workers do and what employers coordinate and combine to produce output. Tasks can be marketed and traded across borders. In fact goods and services are just embodied tasks. From this perspective, it is no surprise that firms around the world have incentives to outsource some of their inputs (tasks), sometimes offshore, and to specialize in producing (and marketing, sometimes offshore) other inputs (tasks) that they describe as their core competency. It is equally no surprise that the world's workers have incentives to specialize in tasks in which they are comparatively advantaged. Finally it is no surprise if high-skill, technologically sophisticated countries have comparative advantage in tasks requiring high skills and technological sophistication, whereas other countries have comparative advantage in established, familiar, standardized tasks. This conceptualization of offshoring is confirmed in several studies that show how the "task content" of tradable service jobs in rich countries tracks this pattern quite tightly (Jensen and Kletzer 2008; van Welsum and Reif 2006; van Welsum and Vickrey 2005 a, b).[5]

The Impact of Offshoring in Developed Countries

Who's good, exactly, is served by offshoring? The obvious answer is that the offshoring firm itself gains. Improved precision, customization, and quality of inputs improve both process and output productivity (that is, process and product innovation). Reduced input costs allow high-productivity firms to expand market share and serve customers with greater diversity and quality at lower prices.[6] For-profit firms reward shareholders with higher profits. Not-for-profit firms benefit trustee-visionaries with superior satisfaction of their mission.

Less appreciated is that many workers benefit, too. Workers at globally integrated firms—those that export, import, offshore to suppliers and distributors, and cooperate with (share equity in) multinational joint-venture partners—earn about 10 percent higher wages in secure jobs that grow 2 percent per year faster than in local firms of comparable size, sector, and location (Bernard et al. 2005).

Not all workers benefit. When a company turns elsewhere for its suppliers, previous suppliers can be left out. Given the ubiquity of offshoring, any given worker (or community) could as easily gain as lose, depending on the tasks they perform and the identity of their employer. There is no obvious imbalance in it, no large *net* loss (or gain) of jobs from offshoring. But there is a pattern. In rich countries, skilled workers gain from offshoring by foreign firms, and the mid- to less-skilled come under pressure; in poor countries, the pattern is opposite.

Jensen and Kletzer (2008), for example, demonstrate that skilled American service workers in skill-intensive tradable service activities (for example, software and systems design, satellite telecommunications) earn a 20 percent premium over comparable service workers in non-tradable service activities. These skilled American service activities have maintained strong export performance and employment growth since the mid-1990s. Jensen and Kletzer further show that only one-third of American service workers in tradable-service activities are at risk of offshoring imports from poor countries, and those most at risk have fewer occupational skill sets compared to other tradable-services workers. By implication, skill upgrading would benefit such workers who could then transition to higher-skill occupations in American service sectors with comparative advantage. The vaunted loss of white-collar jobs to offshoring is concentrated on the least attractive, least demanding white-collar positions. The rest of the story—two-thirds of tradable-services jobs—is *better* white-collar jobs in service sectors benefiting from offshoring of firms abroad *to* American suppliers and their workers (sometimes called "in-sourcing").

National Approaches toward Trade Adjustment Assistance

Because of this, offshoring has naturally rekindled the rich-country debate over trade adjustment-assistance policies that help workers upgrade from import-sensitive tasks and skills to export-competitive tasks and skills.

In the European Union (EU), the European Globalization Adjustment Fund (EGF) has, since 2007, offered EU-level cofunding for large-scale worker displacement linked to trade, covering job-search and mobility assistance and training in entrepreneurship and information technology. Up to half of the expense is borne by the EU, up to one-half billion euros per year, which is roughly equivalent to the current U.S. budget for its comparable trade adjustment-assistance programs. (The remaining expenses are borne by national governments.) Both France and Germany have complemented traditional unemployment insurance in the past few years with wage insurance, in which a displaced worker receives payouts of up to half of any earnings-loss in a new job (with caps and limits on age and time duration). And Denmark's flexicurity system (Zhou 2007) has become famous as a kind of gold standard for effective, if expensive, active labor-market policies to help workers upgrade skills and adapt to change.

Not all European adjustment-assistance programs are linked to trade; some are designed to address broader structural change in labor markets. When they are linked to trade, as in the case of the EGF, they can in principle-aid, service-sector workers affected by offshoring (though in practice none of the 2007 or early-2008 EGF cases covered service-sector workers).

Indeed, the growth of offshoring helps explain the promising evolution of adjustment-assistance policies in rich countries toward broad, no-fault support for displaced-worker mobility and skill building in *every* sector and for *every* reason. Rapidly vanishing are limitations such as the need for displacement to be trade related, to be direct as opposed to indirect-through-supply-chains, or to be in manufacturing and merchandising sectors. The United States illustrates this evolution well. As of this writing, there is bipartisan congressional support to expand U.S. adjustment assistance to cover service-sector workers (though the contingent link to trade displacement and offshoring is maintained) and to maintain, even expand, the experimental wage-insurance program initiated in 2002. Budget calculations suggest a tripling of U.S. funding to roughly $3 billion per year. This funding is small by European standards, but it is coupled with creative private-sector initiatives in the United States, such as worker contracts within firms (for example,

Ford and United Technologies) for on-payroll job retraining and college tuition support, and such as union-managed insurance initiatives to maintain retiree pensions and benefits.

Offshoring helps explain this evolutionary expansion of worker adjustment-assistance because it is essentially outsourcing across borders, and the "borders" part is not the main problem for workers. Outsourcing itself, even within a firm within a country, causes similar worker displacement and pressure to retrain for new tasks. The same innovation in design, information, and communication technology—and in the market-based ways that firms with core competencies have become leaner and more interdependent—has driven *both* the ICT (information-and-communication-technology) revolution *and* globalization. Researchers and policymakers are recognizing that it is fruitless to try to decompose worker challenges into separate pieces due to technology and trade.

The Effect of Offshoring in Developing Countries

Research into the effects of global offshoring on poor-country workers is still in a formative stage.[7] The theoretical and empirical literature flagged above suggests quantitatively large mid- and low-skill gains in wages and job prospects. That, too, is no surprise. Globalization of tasks markets improves the world's sorting of high-skill workers into even higher-productivity tasks requiring their high skills, and sorting of mid- to low-skill workers into *higher*-productivity tasks that depend intensively on standard skills. It follows that *all* workers gain from shifting toward tasks in which they have comparative advantage.

More importantly, the worker-level gains will not depend on the vehicle by which the globalization of tasks markets is accomplished, whether offshoring or its inter-changeable substitute, worker migration across borders, discussed below.

Finally, one consequence of offshoring is neither purely good nor bad. Offshoring firms lose their national origins—they are increasingly *not* American or French or any other national "us" *anywhere* in the world.[8] Or, in a more sinister rendering, they are everywhere an "us-unto-ourselves," an affinity group called global business, with a corporate flag but no national flag and with a business model that views nation-state and other borders largely as nuisances (unless they can be manipulated to raise profits or to advance the mission of a not-for-profit). Much research and policy refinement lie ahead on these issues, all related to the global-business model.

Shift #2. Worker Migration and Global Services Trade

There is little doubt that world migration is mushrooming. The Organization for Economic Cooperation and Development (OECD 2007) reports that the yearly inflow of immigrants to OECD-members (which includes the United States, South Korea, Mexico, and most other developed countries) is growing by nearly 10 percent per year. If that rate were applied globally, the worldwide foreign-born population stock, which in 2005 was roughly 200 million (or 3 percent of world population), would be expected to increase to 322 million (or 4.5 percent of world population) by the year 2010. Put differently, the worldwide foreign-born population stock would increase by 61 percent in just half a decade, far outpacing the 6 percent increase in the world's population over that same period.

Most sense that this surge is a worldwide phenomenon—and often illegal. What many do not realize, however, is that the surge is motivated by employment opportunities rather than a desire to settle permanently. Even fewer (in rich countries) realize how selective emigration has been embraced as a strategic development policy for a large group of populous-developing countries, led by India and the Philippines, and as their negotiating strategy in the Doha or subsequent rounds of global-market liberalization under the World Trade Organization (WTO).[9] From their perspective, time-limited work opportunities for their citizens abroad are even more development-friendly than opening their own labor markets to foreign employers—interchangeability again. Emigrant workers predictably send large remittances back home and then return with skills and experience that boost the resources and productivity of the sending country. So much the better if such emigration limits the sending country's import of unwanted foreign-employer culture and the resulting need to send a portion of locally generated profits back to rich-country shareholders.[10]

Though most rich-country commentators understand that the next frontier of economic globalization is services, they often forget that paid employment is itself a type of service. Since the mid-1990s, services trade has been governed by explicit treaties between rich and poor members of the WTO that provide for time-limited cross-border movements of workers.

There are four modes of service trading. The first mode is virtual-services trade (for example, electronic diagnostics or tutorial services) that does not require the cross-border movement of buyers or sellers. Mode two involves the movement of services buyers (for example, tourists) and mode three the seller (for example, foreign direct investment by retailers). Worker migration with temporary work permits (for example, poor-country nurses filling guest-worker jobs in rich-country medical facilities) is often referred to as mode four.

At present, mode four worker-services trade accounts for less than 2 percent of overall world-services trade. But it is almost certain that rich countries will have little choice but to make concessions that allow mid- and low-skill, poor-country workers access into their market in order for their own rich-country retailers, banks, insurers, and consultants to increase their access to poor-country service markets. If no such concessions materialize, globalization of services will stagnate indefinitely at its present modest intensity.[11]

How will rich countries respond? The answer almost surely is very reluctantly, very marginally. Pritchett (2006, Chap. 4) goes further, predicting that any new worker-migration arrangements will be bilateral, not regional or global; by selected occupation, not across the board; with temporary work visas that have no promise of permanent residence; and initially with tight caps (quotas), presumably adjustable and contingent on internal labor-market trends.[12] Singapore has already created an intriguing model with exactly these features (see Yeoh 2007).

Almost all rich countries will respond if deeper-services globalization itself is truly at stake. And respond they should if they conclude, however grudgingly, that mid- and low-skill, worker-services trade is truly the most promising, highest-payoff type of development-inclusive trade.

The estimated benefits of worker-services trade are enormous to both poor and rich countries. Freeman (2006), for example, shows that cross-country, occupational-earnings gaps range from ratios of 3 to 7, whereas comparable cross-country, price-ratio gaps for goods are around 2, and gaps for the cost of capital are less than 1.5.[13] Because economists find such gaps to be reliable indicators of the standard-of-living gains from deeper global integration, it is clear that occupational-services trade has immense global promise. Both Winters (2003) and the World Bank (2006) in fact calculate that an across-the-skills-board increase of 3 percent in rich countries' labor forces, due to successive waves of temporary worker-services migrants, would generate in the global standard of living an increase nearly twice as large as moving to *completely* free trade, and many more times larger than current levels of foreign aid.

Even more interesting is the division of these large estimated standard-of-living gains. Contrary to what some might suspect, poor countries do not get all the gains. And rich countries do not concede gains to poor countries. They are mutual gains. Roughly half go to rich countries and half to poor, counting the temporary worker migrants—properly—as permanent residents of poor countries (Winters 2003,

Table 4.3). Interestingly, the source of these gains is not really remittances.[14] The source is more familiar: poor-country workers gain the chance to work in a higher-productivity, rich country; rich countries, and even their workers on average, gain from the import of complementary labor inputs. The complementarities and gains are highest for high-skill, rich-country workers, creating general-worker incentives for skill upgrading.[15] The more differentiated the tasks done by temporary immigrants, the larger the rich-country gains, even to the point of eclipsing the negative impact on rich-country workers doing closely substitutable tasks.[16]

But negative effects on at least some rich-country workers will clearly remain. On the distant frontier of worker adjustment-assistance programs discussed above is expanding those programs that maintain a contingent link to globalization to cover displacement from time-limited worker immigration as well as its near-perfect equivalent, offshoring.

Shift #3. Mission Businesses as Potential "People Movers"

A shift not unrelated to the previous two is the recent surge of interest in businesses that have non-financial as well as financial objectives. Often referred to as social enterprises, Christian circles use the term "business-as-mission" instead.[17] The Christian business-as-mission movement has surged in recent years, along with the worldwide acceleration of purposive not-for-profit (NFP) enterprise, including objective-driven philanthropy, so-called social entrepreneurship, and Islamic commerce.

Business-as-mission firms are best conceived and located somewhere on a continuum between pure for-profit (FP) firms and purpose-driven NFPs.[18] Glaeser (2003) and other NFP scholars show that the quantities and qualities that NFPs produce will be larger, and the price that they charge will be lower, than those associated with pure, commercial FPs. The exact location of a business-as-mission firm on the continuum depends on their board's tradeoff between business (profit) and mission (quantity and quality of good work). The same microeconomics of NFPs shows that in general all NFPs will face similar technology and input-market constraints as their FP counterparts, with the exception of financial inputs (equity markets in particular are absent) and workers (whose personal valuation of the NFP's mission leads them to a lower wage-benefit offer schedule; for example, volunteers in the extreme).

Business-as-mission firms will therefore have the same incentives as any firm to adopt a global-business-model approach to best-practice technologies, innovation, and cost saving in input markets (cost saving generates excess revenues that get plowed back into advancing good work). Indeed, business-as-mission firms have been quick to global-ize. Even small companies operate multinationally, joint venture with foreign partners, export, import, and outsource offshore.

So offshoring alone offers few new unexplored opportunities for business-as-mission firms. Cross-border worker exchange, however, is not merely a close substitute for offshoring, but a genuinely new frontier. Business-as-mission firms have not yet explored the growing potential to move workers across borders on temporary visas. Such worker movement need not be into a firm's home country necessarily, but rather could be between its affiliates and partners abroad. Nor is it merely a nascent pipe dream. Hundreds of bilateral agreements already exist that allow workers to move temporarily across borders, especially within a company. Many regional agreements facilitate it, even some to which the United States has been a party, for example, TN Visas in the North American Free Trade Area (Orrenius and Streitfeld 2006).

Christian business-as-mission firms, with their strong inter-personal style of meeting their purposes, ought to be as intrigued by this new frontier in globalization as they have been by offshoring.

Capsule

The global growth in offshoring and worker migration has created well-publicized new concerns in rich, developed countries about globalization, including loss of control over traditional workplace and local community as well as loss of jobs. Christian ethicists have of course contributed to shaping these concerns.

Less publicized are the large estimates of standard-of-living gains that these same trends create for globally engaged developing countries and their workers. Almost invisible in rich countries is the positive face of offshoring and worker migration. The same trends have created enormous, underappreciated economic opportunity for their own workers and communities. Higher-skill workers and others willing to move to build new skills are especially helped by offshoring from firms abroad, the growth of which is as intense as the offshoring by home firms. These same groups of workers increase personal productivity from both the growth and diversity of immigrant workers and entrepreneurs, who are best viewed as complementary inputs of human capital. Mid- and lower-skill workers are the beneficiaries of promising innovation in and expansion of adjustment-assistance policies.

And from the perspective of Christian business-as-mission firms, the opportunity to buttress both business *and* mission through strategic-worker movement around the world needs to be added to their well-established recourse to offshoring to do the same thing.

Questions for Review

1   In terms of the economic impacts, please discuss the similarities and differences between offshoring and worker migration. Then discuss the similarities and differences of each to conventional merchandise trade.

2.   If a rich nation could somehow eliminate both offshoring by its own firms and inward worker migration, what would be the

predicted domestic results? How do you think trading partners would respond? Who would gain and lose domestically and across countries?

3. In your opinion, what would the ideal trade adjustment-assistance program look like? What kind of assistance would it offer, and what would trigger that assistance? To shape your answer, use assessments of the new European Union program and U.S. reform proposals that began in the 2007–2008 congressional session (under the coordination of Senator Max Baucus).

4. According to the author, how can worker migration and offshoring contribute to the mission of a business-as-mission firm?

Notes

[1] Clear conceptions of these trends are important. In this chapter, offshoring describes outsourcing across national borders; outsourcing is a firm's reliance on a supplier or distributor outside the firm's own enterprise boundaries. Worker migration describes cross-border movement of workers themselves, usually time-limited (ranging from seasonal agricultural work to "worker circulation"—reverse migration back to one's country of origin after years of work experience in a host country)—and usually lacking in intentions to settle one's family, naturalize, or integrate with society beyond the workplace.

[2] See, for example, Herrera de la Casa and Meduna (2006) on the European Union's history of developing "EU citizen" rights for its member-country workers and families who move across EU borders for work. Multinational firms, though often deemed "juridicial persons" in home-country jurisprudence, are arguably temporary residents everywhere else. Occasionally they seem to have negotiated "rights" for themselves that exceed those of their host country's firms, as has been alleged in Dispute Settlement procedures negotiated under the North American Free Trade Agreement (NAFTA).

[3] Indeed, Grossman and Rossi-Hansberg (2006) begin their synthetic treatment of offshoring by recalling Adam Smith's famous pin factory, with its division of labor across observable *tasks* in which respective workers specialize.

[4] Farrell (2006) is a recent, representative book-length treatment of the global scope of offshoring, collected from studies by the McKinsey Global Institute. See also Collins and Brainard (2006) for a representative collection focused on global services offshoring.

[5] Tradability is gauged by high-information content, Internet transferability, and absence of any need for face-to-face content.

[6] Evolutionary growth of the "fittest" firms in global markets is a newly identified source of gains from globalization. Estimates of its importance for raising industry-level productivity and standards of living are extremely large compared to traditional gains from trade. See Bernard (et al. 2007) for a readable survey of the relevant research literature.

[7] Amiti and Konings (2007, Table 5), for example, find a strong negative correlation between Indonesian tariffs on imported inputs—reflecting barriers to Indonesian-firm offshoring—and labor productivity in manufacturing, which is presumably in turn correlated with Indonesian wages (as is the total factor productivity emphasized in the rest of their study). They include a comprehensive discussion of related literature on the effects of offshoring in poor countries. Moran (et al. 2005) is a useful collection in which many chapters show how poor countries and their workers gain by engaging integrated global-production networks among disintegrated firms.

[8] Likewise, at the turn of the twentieth century, many American firms lost their regional identification and became national in scope; and at the turn of the

twenty-first century, many European firms became genuinely European Union-wide in scope, rather than British, German, and others.

[9] Mattoo and Carzaniga (2003), Pritchett (2006), and Schiff and Ozden (2007) are recent, representative book-length treatments of worker migration as a services-sector trade frontier and as a poor-country strategy for development. See also the fourteen-member-country proposal to the WTO, WTO (2003).

[10] It is not wrong to think of such profit transfers as unwanted remittances of capital income *back* to rich countries. That conception helps highlight one development-*un*friendly aspect of traditional foreign investment.

[11] Lipsey (2006) shows that there is little trend in any of the various measures of world-services trade relative to world-goods trade—the ratios of one to the other oscillate between 20 and 30 percent over the past thirty-five (or more) years.

[12] Even the European Union has attenuated its implementation of treaty commitments to free cross-member worker mobility, and its newest members are hardly poor!

[13] See Freeman (2006, Table 2), based on his own database. The gap is measured as the ratio of earnings by occupation (or prices by good, or cost of capital) for the country at the eightieth percentile in cross-country rankings to the counterpart in the country at the twentieth percentile.

[14] Counting temporary-worker migrants as source-country residents implies that cross-border financial remittances are irrelevant. The entire earnings of the migrant are attributed to the poor-source country.

[15] Kirkegaard (2007) documents the large American gains that are possible by strategic worker-immigration concessions in the context of broader trade negotiations.

[16] See Gianmarco, Ottaviano, and Peri (2006) and Iranzo and Peri (2007) for empirical demonstrations of significant differentiated-task gains for the United States and the European Union.

[17] See Brooks (2008) for a recent book-length treatment of the broad movement. See also Johnson and Rundle (2006) and Eldred (2005) for its business-as-mission sub-family.

[18] The author is in the process of drafting a detailed demonstration of this continuum and this claim, building on the serious microeconomic literature on NFPs (for example, Glaeser 2003), especially that on NFPs-with-FP affiliates.

References

Amiti, Mary, and Jozef Konings. 2007. "Trade Liberalization, Intermediate Inputs, and Productivity: Evidence from Indonesia." *American Economic Review* 97 (December), 1611–38.

Bernard, Andrew B., J. Bradford Jensen, Stephen J. Redding, and Peter K. Schott. 2005. "Importers, Exporters, and Multinationals: A Portrait of Firms in the U.S. that Trade Goods." National Bureau of Economic

Research Working Paper 11404 (June). Cambridge, MA: National Bureau of Economic Research.

———. 2007. "Firms in International Trade." *Journal of Economic Perspectives* 21, no. 3 (Summer), 105–30.

Brooks, Arthur. 2008. *Social Entrepreneurship: A Modern Approach to Social Venture Creation.* Upper Saddle River, NJ: Prentice-Hall, 19–36.

Collins, Susan M., and Lael Brainard, eds. 2006. *Offshoring White-Collar Work—Issues and Implications. Brookings Trade Forum 2005.* Washington, D.C.: Brookings Institution.

Eldred, Ken. 2005. *God Is at Work: Transforming People and Nations through Business.* Ventura, CA: Regal Books.

Farrell, Diana, ed. 2006. *Offshoring: Understanding the Emerging Global Labor Market. McKinsey Global Institute Series in Critical Trends in Economics and Management.* Boston: Harvard Business School Press.

Freeman, Richard. 2006. "People Flows in Globalization." *Journal of Economic Perspectives* 20 (Spring), 145–70.

Gianmarco, I., P. Ottaviano, and Giovanni Peri. 2006. "Rethinking the Effects of Immigration on Wages." National Bureau of Economic Research Working Paper 12497. Cambridge, MA: National Bureau of Economic Research.

Glaeser, Edward L., ed. 2003. *The Governance of Not-for-Profit Organizations.* Chicago: University of Chicago Press.

Grossman, Gene M., and Esteban Rossi-Hansberg. 2006. "Trading Tasks: A Simple Theory of Offshoring." NBER Working Paper W12721. Cambridge, MA: National Bureau of Economic Research.

Herrera de la Casa, Ana, and Michal Meduna. 2006. "The EU Directive on Free Movement." *CESifo DICE Report* (April), 3–20.

Iranzo, Susana, and Giovanni Peri. 2007. "Migration and Trade in a World of Technological Differences: Theory with an Application to Eastern-Western European Integration." NBER Working Paper 13631 (November). Cambridge, MA: National Bureau of Economic Research.

Jensen, J. Bradford, and Lori G. Kletzer. 2008. "'Fear' and Offshoring—The Scope and Potential Impact of Imports and Exports of Services." Policy Brief 08-1. Washington, D.C.: Peterson Institute for International Economics.

———. 2007. "Measuring Tradable Services and the Task Content of Offshorable Services Jobs." Draft paper for the conference Labor in the New Economy (November 16–17). Washington, D.C.: Conference on Research in Income and Wealth (CRIW) and the National Bureau of Economic Research. Forthcoming in *Labor in the New Economy,* edited by Katharine Abraham, Michael Harper, and James Spletzer. Chicago: University of Chicago Press.

Johnson, C. Neal, and Steven Rundle. 2006. The Distinctives and Challenges of Business as Mission. In *Business as Mission: From Impoverished to*

Empowered, edited by Steffen and Barnett. Pasadena, CA: William Carey Library.

Kirkegaard, Jacob F. 2007. *The Accelerating Decline in America's High-Skilled Workforce: Implications for Immigration Policy*. Policy Analyses in International Economics 84. Washington, D.C.: Peterson Institute for International Economics.

Lipsey, Robert E. 2006. "Measuring International Trade in Services." NBER Working Paper 12271' (March). Cambridge, MA: National Bureau of Economic Research.

Mattoo, Aaditya, and Antonia Carzaniga, eds. 2003. *Moving People to Deliver Services*. Washington, D.C.: Oxford University Press and World Bank.

Moran, Theodore H., Edward M. Graham, and Magnus Blomstrom, eds. 2005. *Does Foreign Investment Promote Development?* Washington, D.C.: Institute for International Economics and Center for Global Development.

OECD. 2007. *International Migration Outlook*. Paris: Organization for Economic Cooperation and Development.

Orrenius, Pia, and Daniel Streitfeld. 2006. "TN Visas: A Stepping Stone Toward a NAFTA Labor Market." Federal Reserve Bank of Dallas. *Southwest Economy* (November–December), 10–13.

Pritchett, Lant. 2006. *Let Their People Come: Breaking the Gridlock on Global Labor Mobility*. Washington, D.C.: Center for Global Development.

Roberts, Adam. 2008. "Open Up: A Special Report on Migration." *The Economist* (January 5).

Schiff, Maurice, and Caglar Ozden, eds. 2007. *International Migration, International Development and Policy*. Washington, D.C.: World Bank.

van Welsum, Desiree, and Xavier Reif. 2006. Potential Offshoring: Evidence from Selected OECD Countries. In *Offshoring White-Collar Work. Brookings Trade Forum 2005,* edited by Susan M. Collins and Lael Brainard. Washington, D.C.: Brookings Institution.

———, and Graham Vickery. 2005a. "Potential Offshoring of ICT-Intensive Using Occupations." DSTI Information Economy Working Paper DSTI/ ICCP/IE (2004)19/FINAL. Paris: Organization for Economic Cooperation and Development.

———. 2005b. "New Perspectives on ICT Skills and Employment." DSTI Information Economy Working Paper DSTI/ICCP/IE (2004)10/FINAL. Paris: Organization for Economic Cooperation and Development.

Winters, L. Alan. 2003. The Economic Implications of Liberalizing Mode 4 Trade. In *Moving People to Deliver Services*, edited by Aaitya Mattoo and Antonia Carzanig. Washington, D.C.: Oxford University Press and World Bank.

World Bank. 2006. *Global Economic Prospects for Developing Countries 2006*. Washington, D.C.: World Bank.

WTO. 2003. "Proposed Liberalization of Mode 4 Under GATS Negotiations." World Trade Organization Document TN/S/W/14 3 (July). Geneva:

World Trade Organization. http://www.commerce.gov.in/trade/international_trade_trade_negotiating_committee_7.asp (accessed Jan. 1, 2008).

Yeoh, Brenda S. A. 2007. "Singapore: Hungry for Foreign Workers at All Skill Levels." Migration Information Source Article (January). Washington, D.C.: Migration Policy Institute. http://www.migrationinformation.org/Profiles/display.cfm?ID=570 (accessed April 12, 2008).

Zhou, Jianping. 2007. "Danish for All? Balancing Flexibility with Security: The Flexicurity Model." IMF Working Paper WP/07/36 (February). Washington, D.C.: International Monetary Fund.

PART III

International Aid, Development, and the Church

CHAPTER 7

FOREIGN AID, DEVELOPMENT STRATEGIES, AND POVERTY REDUCTION

Christopher B. Barrett

Globalization brings the suffering of the world's poor directly to the attention of those fortunate to have been born non-poor in high-income countries. And there is plenty of suffering. In 2004, an estimated 969 million people—more than 18 percent of the world's population—lived on less than $1 per day per person and were thus classified as "extremely poor" by global standards (Chen and Ravallion 2007). Indeed, outside of China, the developing world has not enjoyed any sustained progress over the past quarter century in reducing the number of extremely poor people. Meanwhile, in some regions the number of extremely poor people has increased significantly. In sub-Saharan Africa, even in the face of population growth, the extreme poor have consistently accounted for 41 to 48 percent of the sub-continent's residents since good estimates began around 1980.

For Christians especially, Jesus' injunction that "As you did it to one of the least of these my brethren, you did it to me" (Matthew 25:40 RSV) reminds us that to ignore the suffering of others is an offense against God. Hence the Christian's natural instinct to provide aid to the poor. However, good intentions and good deeds do not always translate into favorable results, as the checkered history of foreign aid makes clear.

Foreign aid—the transfer of government resources to poorer countries—has long been an essential part of any strategy to reduce poverty and hunger. It encompasses both short-term relief of suffering resulting from natural disasters and war as well as longer-term development to end chronic deprivation. The modern era of foreign aid began with post-World War II reconstruction, in particular the Marshall Plan, when the United States devoted 2 to 3 percent of its national income annually to restore war-ravaged Europe. Once European recovery was well underway by the second half of the 1950s, Europe's former colonies in Africa and Asia began achieving independence and became the new foci for foreign aid. Over the intervening half century, aid has become an industry, professionalized in United Nations agencies, multilateral-development banks, and a vast network of non-governmental organizations (NGOs) committed to humanitarian relief, long-term development, or both. Cassen (1987), Mosley (1987), and Tarp (2000) provide excellent histories of foreign aid.

Humanitarian Response to Disasters

One important impetus for aid is disaster response. The Gospels call Christians to emulate the Good Samaritan, to tend to those who suffer misfortune. Such suffering occurs on a large scale. Over the past quarter century, roughly two million people died and five billion were affected by some seven thousand natural disasters—geophysical or hydro-meteorological events such as droughts, earthquakes, floods, hurricanes, tsunamis, and volcanoes.[1] Extreme natural phenomena strike developing countries more often than developed ones. Moreover, the consequences, measured in terms of human mortality and displacement rates per disaster, are far greater in the poorest countries due to lower-quality construction, poor public health and emergency response systems, and meager private resources of the affected population to finance response and recovery (Stromberg 2007).

As a result, humanitarian response is typically most effective, per dollar spent, in poorer countries. Yet awareness of disasters that strike the poorest places tends to be lower for various reasons.[2] Lower awareness typically leads to markedly weaker humanitarian response to disasters in low-income countries by aid agencies and private donors. For example, flooding in 2001 in Angola, Brazil, Poland, and Thailand killed thirty to one hundred people in each country and affected tens of thousands (up to 450,000 in Thailand). Yet Poland received $15 million in international relief assistance, Brazil received $230,000, while Angola and Thailand each received less than $100,000 (Stromberg 2007). The same type of event, the same year, elicited markedly different responses for a range of reasons related to media coverage, geographical distance, sociocultural ties, and others. (Alesina and Dollar 2000). Although relief aid appears to respond to the severity of the emergency, many other factors come into play as well, often impeding the effectiveness of aid to provide relief to victims of disasters.

Aid for Development: Hypotheses and Successes

Although disaster relief draws the most attention, the overwhelming majority of foreign aid flows go not for emergency response, but for investment in longer-term development. The basic, original hypothesis motivating foreign aid for development was that capital access constrains investment in developing countries; thus foreign-aid flows can stimulate development by relaxing those financial constraints to foster faster economic growth, which allows the recipient country to reach its steady state growth rate faster than it would otherwise. This is crucial for long-term poverty reduction since economic growth appears necessary for sustained poverty reduction (Ravallion and Chen

1997). That original hypothesis has been supplemented in the past few decades by a corollary hypothesis: aid can change a country's steady state-growth rate by introducing improved technologies, markets, policies, or institutions. This refinement has led to some reconsideration of how and where to use aid to advance development objectives. In particular, this latter view encourages investment in global public goods that can potentially change the growth trajectories of nations and improve standards of living among the world's poorest peoples. Unlike conventional aid to developing-country governments or to nongovernmental organizations operating in such countries, aid for global public goods to benefit the poor is invested wherever important new technologies, policies, markets, or institutions are created. Somewhat ironically, sometimes development assistance therefore flows to entities (for example, research institutes) in developed countries.

Several of the best examples of highly successful foreign aid fall into this global public goods category. Aid has made possible historically unprecedented achievements in expanding food supply to reduce hunger and under-nutrition worldwide, in spite of rapid population growth and an essentially fixed cultivable land area on Earth. The Consultative Group on International Agricultural Research (CGIAR), formed in 1971, fosters research to find technical solutions to constraints impeding agricultural development in developing countries. More than $7 billion (1990 USD) invested in the CGIAR from 1971 to 2001 delivered an impressive estimated internal rate of return of roughly 34 percent per year (Raitzer and Kelley 2008). While many of the benefits of improved agricultural technologies have accrued to small-scale farmers in developing countries—and even to large-scale farmers in high-income countries—most benefits have accrued to poor consumers through real food-price reductions resulting from expanded food supplies and improved food quality, safety, and variety (Evenson and Gollin 2003).

Aid has likewise played a central role in eradicating diseases, such as smallpox and, soon, polio, and in reducing infant mortality through a suite of simple childhood interventions (growth monitoring, oral rehydration therapy to address diarrheal diseases, breastfeeding, and immunization) developed for delivery worldwide with minimal need for context-specific adaptation. The resulting improvements in life expectancy, child health, and school enrollment rates have been a boon to development in many low- and middle-income countries.

Focus has renewed, in recent years, on global public goods in part because of the cross-border spillover effects associated with phenomena such as terrorism, infectious diseases, and climate change. As threats to well-being have globalized, foreign aid has focused more on the production of global public goods to facilitate development and poverty reduction while simultaneously protecting higher-income nations.

This new trend is partly attributable as well to the rise of new actors on the global development stage. Private charitable giving, once relatively insignificant, has become influential. In its early years, the CGIAR was funded largely by the Rockefeller and Ford Foundations. This pattern has been especially pronounced in health-related aid, which is now financed roughly one-quarter by private philanthropic groups such as the Bill and Melinda Gates Foundation. Foundations and private philanthropists devote a much larger share of development aid to longer-term technology development projects for new cultivars, drugs, energy sources, vaccines, water treatment methods, and such.

Another area of growing attention concerns peacekeeping operations. Because of the adverse spillover effects commonly associated with violent internal and cross-border conflict—due to refugee movement, infrastructure damage, and political uncertainty, in addition to the obvious direct consequences of violence—the economic returns to expanding peacekeeping and security guarantees appear substantial. Indeed, Collier (2007) argues that nearly three-quarters of the world's poorest people have been caught at one time or another in war, and the typical civil war costs around $64 billion. Preventing or shortening conflicts thus yields returns that dwarf those of conventional aid flows. Collier (2007) claims that British military support for ending the civil war in Sierra Leone may be the most effective aid program in the United Kingdom's history.

Aid's Muted Effects on Growth

A vast amount of literature on the effects of aid on growth has yielded quite mixed results, however. Mosley (1987) long ago concluded that the overwhelmingly favorable evaluations of micro-level effects of aid could not be reconciled with macro studies that often struggle to find national-level evidence of aid's beneficial effects. Countering this, Dalgaard, Hansen, and Tarp (2004) concludes that most studies find a positive effect of aid on macroeconomic growth. Yet in perhaps the most persuasive recent study, Rajan and Subramanian (forthcoming) find little evidence of a robust positive relation between aid and growth. Needless to say, the relationship between aid and growth remains a hotly contested issue among researchers.

Why has the effectiveness of aid been so mixed, such that foreign aid seems to have underperformed relative to the expectations of the 1950s and 1960s? At least five distinct hypotheses exist.

Aid Insufficiency. One argument holds that aid has never lived up to its promise because donors have never given as promised. If the poor are caught in poverty traps, then small increments of capital are commonly insufficient to ignite rapid take-off; therefore large, discrete transfers may be necessary to spark development. Following this logic, Sachs (2005, 246) emphasizes, "foreign assistance is not a welfare handout, but is actually an investment that breaks the poverty trap once and for all." The problem of aid incrementalism gets further compounded because many aid commitments never get fully disbursed by donors, and a large share, estimated at roughly one-third, arrives late. For countries that depend on aid flows to finance basic government operations, the unpredictability of aid can impede investment in public goods and retard economic growth (Celasun and Walliser, 2008).

In 1970, the OECD countries committed to providing 0.7 percent of gross national income (GNI) as foreign aid. However, few donors have given at anything close to that level over the years. Only the Nordic countries (Denmark, Finland, Norway, and Sweden) and the Netherlands have done so consistently. Through the early years of the twenty-first century, average aid-flows from the high-income countries were consistently around 0.25 percent of GNI.[3] This share has increased to 0.30 to 0.33 percent in the past few years as global political leaders, persuaded by arguments such as Sachs' (2005), made high-profile commitments to increase aid flows, especially to sub-Saharan Africa in the 2002 Monterrey Consensus and the 2005 Gleneagles Declaration. The United States is the world's largest donor, consistently accounting for roughly one-quarter of total aid flows from the OECD countries, except for a period in the 1990s when U.S. foreign aid fell sharply, especially to Japan. Yet relative to the size of its economy, the United States has typically trailed the rest of the donor field, giving only about 0.1 percent of GNI throughout that past quarter century.

The weaknesses in the aid-insufficiency argument are several. First, the developing countries that have enjoyed the fastest growth over the past two or three decades—such as Botswana, China, India, Mauritius, Vietnam—have enjoyed rapid poverty reduction without any significant inflow of foreign aid. Rather, the real engine was a sharp, new commitment to homegrown reforms to get institutions, infrastructure, and incentives for private investment right. These countries made key, strategic investments in public goods and services to "crowd in" private investment, including foreign direct and portfolio investment that ultimately dwarfed aid flows.

Second, aid has always been and will always be tiny relative to overall income, to external trade, and, in recent years, to private commercial financial flows. Most developing countries receive aid amounting to only about 3 percent of their GNI (Tarp 2006). It would take more than $200 billion annually to bring every sub-Saharan African up just to a modest $2 per day per person standard of living, a sum more than ten times present aid flows to the continent (Barrett, Carter, and Little 2007). Plainly, aid cannot close the gap on its own; it must crowd in private investment in capital accumulation and job creation.

Net private financial flows to developing countries increased more than ten-fold from 1991 through 2006 to $195 billion, surpassing official aid flows in volume. Less than $15 billion of this was private giving; foreign direct investment accounted for nearly $130 billion, and portfolio investment another $60 billion. These flows are concentrated disproportionately in developing countries, such as China and India, enjoying the fastest economic growth and poverty reduction.

Separating cause from effect is exceedingly difficult, but the core point is that private financial flows are strongly associated with growth and, in successful cases, far more substantial than aid.

Self-Serving Aid. The second explanation for why aid has not generated greater growth in recipient-developing countries has to do with the self-serving nature of much foreign assistance. In some instances, this has been for international self-promotion, contrary to the Gospel directive "when you give to the poor, do not let your left hand know what your right hand is doing" (Matt. 6:3 NASB). Furthermore, a large share of aid is driven by donor-country commercial or geopolitical concerns, not an authentic and focused concern for the poor, as would be more consistent with Matthew 25:40. For example, Egypt and Israel—and more recently Iraq—have long been the primary recipients of United States government aid, not because of acute poverty or need, but for diplomatic reasons. Other donors behave similarly. France lavishes aid on its former colonies to the exclusion of other, needier nations, while most donors allocate funds in response to poor countries' voting patterns in the United Nations (Alesina and Dollar 2000).

Throughout the Cold War, aid was often given to rulers supportive of the donor in geopolitical contests, even when those leaders were known to be corrupt, ineffective, or both. Aid revenue squirreled away in private bank accounts overseas obviously had negligible growth or poverty reduction effects for the recipient country as a whole. But this consideration was often trumped by political concerns. The geopolitical drivers of aid flows also help explain why, when the Cold War ended, global aid flows—especially from the United States in the 1990s—fell precipitously.

Perhaps most disturbingly, much foreign aid is tied to the purchase of goods or services from the donor country; they are not unconditional gifts of cash. These restrictions reflect efforts by influential interest groups to siphon off foreign aid funds justified to the donor country taxpayers—and many legislators—on the basis of helping combat poverty and hunger abroad. The funds are still available for the ostensible purposes, but the fine print of the authorizing legislation obligates expenditures on particular activities or goods provided by a restricted set of providers. This generates profits for those who can manipulate the aid system, while rendering aid unnecessarily inefficient. For example, Barrett and Maxwell (2005) estimate that the United States food-aid budget could provide for roughly twice as many hungry people with a few simple reforms to end tying food delivery to the purchase of commodities in and shipment from the United States. Sachs (2005, 310) vividly explains that "in 2002, the United States gave $3 per sub-Saharan African. Taking out the parts for U.S. consultants, food and other emergency aid, administrative costs, and debt relief, the aid per African came to the grand total of six cents." The hijacking of aid flows by donor-country profiteers is one of the most shameful features of the current system, and addressing this should be a high priority of Christians.

Lack of Donor Coordination. Third, there has been an explosion of donor agencies and aid-supported development organizations in recent decades. In the 1950s, the United States was the only donor of any scale, and there were only a few large international development organizations (such as Catholic Relief Services, CARE, or OXFAM). Coordination among them was relatively easy. The proliferation of donors and implementers each pursuing their own agenda—and often in direct competition with one another—poses serious management challenges for poor countries with limited technocratic capacity to manage aid flows and large-scale development programs. Widespread lack of coordination among donors has become an increasing problem as recipient-country policymakers and their technical advisers have grown overwhelmed by a never-ending barrage of official missions and reporting requirements from donor agencies.

Even when funds flow to honest governments in needier countries, donors commonly earmark aid for their pet concerns, often disregarding both what recipients deem most essential to stimulating their own development and what other donors are funding. Donors overwhelmingly favor technical assistance and project funding over general budgetary support. The most recent example of mismatching relates to funding for HIV/AIDS, which is attracting the lion's share of health financing in development today, although the disease accounts for fewer deaths or illnesses than malaria, waterborne diseases, or hunger-related diseases.

This problem of poor donor coordination has been magnified by the emergence of new donors from fast-growing, middle-income countries such as China, Hungary, Korea, and Kuwait, as well as by the rapid rise of NGOs as key intermediaries in the aid business. As donors increasingly funnel resources through private NGOs, it constrains the recipient-country governments' ability to match flows to national priorities. Meanwhile, a decreasing share of foreign aid is being channeled through multilateral institutions such as United Nations agencies, the World Bank, and the various regional development banks that are designed to address the multiple interests of different donors. Despite growing awareness of the need for greater donor coordination among themselves, and with implementing agencies and recipient-country governments, little progress has been made in resolving this growing problem.

Ineffective Forms of Aid. The forms of aid most popular with donor-country governments for political reasons are not always the most effective uses of scarce aid dollars in terms of developmental effectiveness. Perhaps the most current example is debt relief. This is a topic of special interest to many Christians because debt forgiveness is rooted in the Pentateuchal concept of jubilee years and the Jubilee 2000 movement, which ignited much of the past decade's high-level attention to the issue of debt forgiveness, has explicitly Christian roots (Peters 1995; Smith et al. 2000).

Following twenty years' gradual emergence of a variety of debt rescheduling and forgiveness plans for developing countries, the leaders of the eight major industrial economies pledged in 2005 to completely forgive the debts owed by the heavily indebted poor countries (HIPCs) to a range of multilateral financial institutions and bilateral donors. In 2006, debt relief to low- and middle-income countries worldwide grew to just under $20 billion, accounting for almost 19 percent of the $104 billion in global aid flows. Of course, debt relief, like most other aid, is not targeted to the poorest countries. The largest beneficiary was Iraq, again underscoring the political roots of most foreign aid. Debt relief represents only 5 to 10 percent of net-aid flows to Africa. So in spite of the considerable attention it has received, debt relief plays a relatively modest role in foreign aid for the poorest countries.

Countries benefiting from debt forgiveness have indeed enjoyed a sharp increase in net aid transfers, from $8.8 billion in 1999 to $17.5 billion in 2004 (Gunter, Rahman, and Wodon 2008). Therefore, if well used, debt relief can free up significant funds for investment in education, health care, infrastructure improvement, and such. But in order to be eligible for HIPC debt forgiveness, countries have had to demonstrate favorable policies and institutions, conditions that have been independently associated with significant growth in net aid inflows over the past decade. So whether added flows are really due to debt relief or merely come in the form of debt relief remains an open question. This also raises a question of sustainability: will donor countries be able to sustain present aid flows once the stock of forgivable debt has been run down over the coming decade or two? No one really knows for sure.

Moreover, there are serious concerns whether debt relief benefits the right countries. It clearly does not benefit countries that sacrificed in order to service their debts on schedule so that they do not need debt relief. Nor does it help poor countries that do not meet HIPC criteria for other reasons, such as large fiscal deficits or political instability. The benefits from debt-forgiveness programs have been concentrated on countries that did not meet their contractual debt-repayment obligations but are now favored by donors, for whatever reasons, many of which reflect donor self-interest. HIPC-eligible countries are not uniformly the poorest countries. Indeed, Sanford (2004) argues that debt forgiveness is quite likely to divert scarce aid resources from the poorest countries to better-off beneficiary countries. If debt relief is ineffective in stimulating truly additional aid flows to poor countries, or if it merely diverts aid from better managed or needier countries to more politically-favored ones, its efficacy in stimulating growth and poverty reduction will likely prove limited.

Poor Aid Targeting. Just as Jesus reminds his disciples in the parable of the sower that seed must be sown in good soil to produce a good crop (Matt. 13:3–8; Luke 8:5–8), so is it widely believed that aid only works in hospitable institutional and policy environments. Burnside and Dollar (2000) present empirical evidence that aid only works in stimulating growth in countries that follow good macroeconomic policies. Their claim is that aid is ineffective in changing the policy regime in recipient countries and that inappropriate policies prevent aid from advancing growth and poverty reduction objectives; therefore aid is only effective in a favorable economic and institutional environment. As a result, *ex ante* evaluation of prospective-recipients' macroeconomic policies and institutional capacity has become central to aid-allocation criteria in recent years.

The problems with this argument are several. First, it is exceedingly difficult to establish what constitutes "good policy." Second, the Burnside and Dollar (2000) results appear fragile to the econometric specification and to the particular data series used; others have easily overturned their empirical findings with only modest tweaks to the data, the model or estimator used, or some combination of these (Easterly, Levine, and Roodman 2004; Hansen and Tarp 2001; Rajan and Subramanian forthcoming). While these critics agree that bad governance is indeed a constraint on growth, they disagree that growth has any added benefit in countries with favorable policies and institutions. Third, it is contestable whether it is quality of governance that drives economic development or vice versa. Sachs (2005) argues that corruption in Africa is more the product of that continent's poverty than its cause. Fourth, if policy and institutional criteria for aid eligibility orient recipient governments more toward donor concerns than toward those of their constituents, then state accountability and context-appropriate policymaking can suffer. Indeed, in its worst forms, aid may encourage outright corruption or have subtle but powerful effects that retard economic growth, as through distorted tax policies and real exchange rates (Adam and O'Connell 1999; Younger 1992).

Improving Aid Effectiveness

Given the mixed performance of foreign aid in stimulating economic growth and poverty reduction in the past, attention is increasingly turning to how to improve aid effectiveness rather than whether aid "works." There is a growing chorus of those who are in favor of returning to financing projects subject to rigorous project evaluation—often based on randomized controlled trials, much like drug testing—and reducing general budgetary support to developing country governments. Once potential projects have been thoroughly evaluated, scarce aid funding can then be allocated where the greatest benefits have been demonstrated (Easterly 2006; Banerjee 2007). These arguments in favor of evidence-based policymaking, including aid allocation, appear indisputable.

The arguments in favor of renewed focus on project aid with demonstrable results may, however, prove naive. Not all promising, prospective interventions are amenable to carefully controlled study using randomized-controlled trials, whether for political, logistical, or ethical reasons. For example, it is effectively impossible to randomize reforms or most macroeconomic interventions (for example, exchange rate policy). Large-scale infrastructure projects, such as airport or bridge construction, are not politically or practically amenable to randomization. And in the sphere of emergency response, randomization that requires withholding assistance from disaster-affected peoples would be simply unethical. Hence, the limited scope for using randomized-controlled trials to make aid work better by relying increasingly on rigorous research results.

Furthermore, project aid is largely fungible. Recipients can undermine donor intentions by shifting resources from areas supported, based on the criteria donors favor, into others that are more politically favored by the regime in power. Which brings us back to the Burnside and Dollar (2000) argument that growth and poverty reduction are driven primarily by the quality of policies and institutions in developing countries, which can be reinforced by aid but neither transformed nor superseded by development assistance.

Another, related development in recent years is greater emphasis on the role of aid in creating incentives for individuals to change behaviors in ways that foster long-term growth and poverty reduction (Easterly 2006). The most prominent current examples are conditional cash-transfer (CCT) schemes that pay cash to means-tested recipients if and only if they engage in pre-specified behaviors, such as keeping their children in school or vaccinating their family against infectious diseases. CCTs aim not only to provide immediate assistance to poor families but also to force long-term investment that improves the likelihood that children get a better chance to break free of their parents' poverty. Originally introduced and carefully evaluated in Mexico, CCT's have generated significant payoffs by multiple metrics—child health, school enrollment, family income, small business creation, and others—and as a result have rapidly spread to countries in Africa, Asia, Latin America and the United States to tackle chronic urban poverty.

Toward a Christian Approach to Foreign Aid for Economic Development

The moral imperative of the rich to help the poor compels a proactive approach to almsgiving and investment. The relevant question is not whether to give aid, but rather how, in what form, to whom, and when? Although aid has achieved much in specific projects, it is clearly not a major driver of macroeconomic growth and poverty reduction, although it can play an important role in financing key strategic investments, perhaps especially in high-return, global public goods, such as those related to agricultural or health-technology development or in peacekeeping. Aid can also be used to underwrite programs (such as CCTs) that improve poor people's incentives to invest in behaviors that foster long-term development. Indirectly, aid can therefore have a significant effect on development even if the complex and often lagged pathways of its influence may be difficult to tease out in macroeconomic time-series data.

It is equally clear that there are no one-size-fits-all approaches to stimulating development. Context matters, and the devil is often in the details of the design—monitoring and evaluating specific interventions and then scaling them up to larger populations. For Christians concerned about the well-being of those suffering material deprivation in low-income countries, it may be natural to have more faith in bottom-up approaches based on communities, firms, individuals, and widespread experimentation than on top-down approaches run by large aid agencies. While there are some beacons of hope amid the general chaos of the bilateral and multilateral aid agencies, most have become bureaucracies with low performance standards and minimal creativity, just as focused on international and internal politics as they are on the welfare of the poor they are chartered to serve. Creating incentives for people to come up with solutions to their own problems often proves more effective than trying to convince them to adopt approaches developed by outsiders.

Top-down approaches to growth and development, such as the financing-gap models that motivated foreign aid from the 1950s through the early 1980s, minimize the role of human agency and give primacy of place to capital accumulation as the engine of growth and poverty reduction. This is an outdated model of growth and development that seriously underemphasizes the role of technological and institutional change arising spontaneously and creatively from individuals and communities within poor economies through innovation and adaptation (Easterly 2006). To Christians, the top-down approach denies both the reality of individual and institutional sin, perhaps especially by those entrusted with power and resources, and the transformational power of human free will guided by God's grace. The more natural Christian approach is to favor bottom-up approaches founded on channeling scarce aid toward creating and reinforcing incentives for the poor to lift themselves and their communities from poverty through good governance, investment, and institutional and technological innovation.

Questions for Review

1. Does it matter how well aid performs in reducing poverty or stimulating economic growth? Isn't the giving enough? Explain

why or why not.

2. Why might it be difficult to find clear macroeconomic-growth effects of aid when so much of the literature finds strong project-level evidence of aid's positive effects?

3. Is disaster response assistance allocated fairly or effectively across countries? Why or why not? And what might be done to improve its allocation?

4. If the church has an obligation to help the poor and weak, does it follow that the church should advocate for development aid? If so, what forms of aid and for whom?

5. Give two examples of a bottom-up approach to development. Do you agreee that Christians should favor bottom-up approaches? Why or why not? Are there times when top-down approaches are appropriate?

Notes

[1] These figures come from the Emergency Events Database (http://www.emdat. be/), developed and maintained by the Centre for Research on the Epidemiology of Disasters (CRED) in Belgium.

[2] These reasons include the following: lighter media coverage of developing countries; high-income country residents' weaker personal identification with victims in low-income countries due to geographic patterns of migration and trade; and the generally lesser geopolitical importance of poor countries.

[3] Unless otherwise indicated, this and all other aid figures in this chapter come from the *Statistical Annex of the 2007 Development Co-operation Report* issued by the Development Co-operation Directorate of the Organization for Economic Co-operation and Development.

References

Adam, C. S., and S. O'Connell. 1999. "Aid, Taxation and Development in Sub-Saharan Africa." *Economics and Politics* 11, no. 2: 225–54.

Alesina, A., and D. Dollar. 2000. "Who Gives Aid to Whom and Why?" *Journal of Economic Growth* 5, no. 1, 33–63.

Banerjee, A. V. 2007. *Making Aid Work*. Cambridge, MA: MIT Press.

Barrett, C. B., M. R. Carter, and P. D. Little, eds. 2007. *Understanding and Reducing Persistent Poverty in Africa*. London: Routledge.

———, and D. G. Maxwell. 2005. *Food Aid after Fifty Years: Recasting Its Role*. London: Routledge.

Burnside, C., and D. Dollar. 2000. "Aid, Policies and Growth." *American Economic Review* 90, no. 4: 847–68.

Cassen, R. 1987. *Does Aid Work?* Oxford, U.K.: Clarendon Press.

Celasun, O. and J. Walliser (2008), "Predictability and Procyclicality of Aid: Do Fickle Donors Undermine Aid Effectiveness?" *Economic Policy* 23, 55:545–94.

Chen, S., and M. Ravallion. 2007. "Absolute Poverty Measures for the Developing World, 1981–2004." *Proceedings of the National Academy of Sciences* 104, no. 43, 16757–62.

Collier, P. 2007. *The Bottom Billion: Why the Poorest Countries Are Failing and What Can Be Done About It*. New York: Oxford University Press.

Dalgaard, C. J., H. Hansen, and F. Tarp. 2004. "On the Empirics of Foreign Aid and Growth." *Economic Journal* 114, no. 496, F191–216.

Easterly, W. 2006. *The White Man's Burden: Why the West's Efforts to Aid the Rest Have Done So Much Ill and So Little Good*. New York: Penguin Press.

———, R. Levine, and D. Roodman. 2004. "Aid, Policies, and Growth: Comment." *American Economic Review* 94, no. 3: 774–80.

Evenson, R. E., and D. Gollin. 2003. "Assessing the Impact of the Green Revolution, 1960 to 2000." *Science* 300: 758–62.

Gunter, B. G., J. Rahman, and Q. Wodon. 2008. "Robbing Peter to Pay Paul? Understanding Who Pays for Debt Relief." *World Development* 36, no. 1: 1–16.

Hansen, H. and F. Tarp. 2001. "Aid and Growth Regressions." *Journal of Development Economics* 64: 547–70.

Mosley, P. 1987. *Overseas Aid: Its Defense and Reform*. Brighton, U.K.: Wheatsheaf Books.

Peters, B. 1995. "An Introduction to the JUBILEE 2000 Campaign for International Debt Remission." *Bulletin of the Association of Christian Economists* 26: 14–20.

Raitzer, D. A., and T. G. Kelley. 2008. "Benefit-Cost Meta-Analysis of Investment in the International Agricultural Research Centers of the CGIAR." *Agricultural Systems* 96, no. 1, 108–23.

Rajan, R., and A. Subramanian. Forthcoming. "Aid and Growth: What Does the Cross-Country Evidence Really Show?" *Review of Economics and Statistics*.

Ravallion, M., and S. Chen. 1997. "What Can New Survey Data Tell Us about Recent Changes in Distribution and Poverty?" *World Bank Economic Review* 11, no. 2, 357–82.

Sachs, J. D. 2005. *The End of Poverty*. New York: Penguin Press.

Sanford, J. E. 2004. "IDA Grants and HIPC Debt Forgiveness: Their Effectiveness and Impact on IDA Resources." *World Development* 32, no. 9: 1579–607.

Smith, S. L. S., C. B. Barrett, D. R. Finn, and R. Hoksbergen. 2000. "Christian Ethics and the Forgiveness of Third World Debt: A Symposium." *Faith and Economics* 35: 8–19.

Stromberg, D. 2007. "Natural Disasters, Economic Development, and Humanitarian Aid." *Journal of Economic Perspectives* 21, no. 3, 199–222.

Tarp, F., ed. 2000. *Foreign Aid and Development: Lessons Learnt and Directions for the Future*. London: Routledge, 9–61.

———. 2006. "Aid and Development." *Swedish Economic Policy Review* 13, no. 2.

Younger, S. 1992. "Aid and the Dutch Disease: Macroeconomic Management When Everybody Loves You." *World Development* 20, no. 11: 1587–97.

CHAPTER 8

TRANSFORMATIONAL DEVELOPMENT:
THE ROLE OF CHRISTIAN NGOS IN SME DEVELOPMENT

Roland Hoksbergen[1]

Madame Lefèvre began a small popsicle business in Haiti about ten years ago. She began with one freezer and sold out of her house. Today, she operates a business with 22 freezers, 40 employees in the factory, and 500 merchants. Through this business, Mme. Lefèvre has affected her community by creating jobs that sustain hundreds of families in Port-au-Prince.

Empowering others through employment, Mme. Lefèvre has helped individuals rise from poverty through work. When poor people knock on her door and ask for money, Mme. Lefèvre gives them some popsicles and tells them to go out and sell. The next day they pay for a new load of popsicles from their sales the day before. Of her over 500 merchants, most arrive each morning and purchase the popsicles they will sell that day. Each merchant makes significantly more than the average Haitian who works in the informal sector.

Over the last ten years, Mme. Lefèvre has invested in machinery
and equipment, improved her worksite, and developed her staff.
The quality of her products has greatly improved, they are made
in more hygienic conditions, and she now competes well with
similar products on the market.[2]

Development, the Private Sector, and SMEs

Not long ago the world was divided along the bipolar lines of
the communist East and the capitalist West, and there was no global
consensus about the role of business in fighting poverty. Some thought
the private sector was the main culprit in creating poverty, and multinational corporations (MNCs) were viewed as especially evil (for
example, Barnet and Muller 1976). Nationalization of industries and
heavy government regulations were seen by many developing countries
as the best way to neutralize the threat. Even in the market-oriented
West, the development community was highly suspicious of private
business and believed that, particularly in "vulnerable" developing
countries, the private sector needed to be controlled and managed, not
celebrated and encouraged.

How times have changed since the collapse of communism!
Certainly there are people who harbor the same suspicions of business
as before, but there is no hiding the fact that there is a new appreciation
for the private sector, which is now seen as an essential partner in bringing about economic and social development across the world. This new
hopefulness is based partly on the success of the microenterprise movement, which has helped millions of people around the world generate
life-sustaining incomes through the small-scale production and sale of
goods and services. Building on this success, development theorists and
practitioners are now shifting their attention to the central role played
by small- and medium-sized enterprises (SMEs), like Mme. Lefèvre's,
that fall between micro enterprises and large, globally integrated,

multinational businesses. Widely recognized as a principle driver of job creation and growth, the SME sector is now being carefully studied to determine what and how it contributes to development and how it can be promoted and strengthened.

Among the wide variety of government ministries and multilateral institutions involved in promoting the SME sector are non-governmental organizations (NGOs), some of them Christian. One such NGO is Partners Worldwide:

> A faith-based international ministry dedicated to alleviating poverty and building God's Kingdom . . . by engaging businesspeople to use their business knowledge and resources for mentoring, equipping, and encouraging small and medium-sized businesses with the goal of creating and sustaining jobs (http://www.partnersworldwide.org/index.html).

Partners Worldwide (PW) began in 1997 and now works in over twenty developing countries with over sixty associations of business owners. These associations provide opportunities for partnership, mentoring, mutual support, finance, training, networking, and advocacy.

This chapter has two purposes. The first is to explain the vital role SMEs play in economic development and the conditions, resources, and qualities they need to thrive. The second purpose is to report on the findings of a recent empirical study led by this author. In addition to confirming what many others have found, namely that a healthy SME sector requires good governance, sufficient capital, technological and managerial know-how, and a skilled labor force, our study identified another critical factor for sustainable economic and social transformation—an encompassing social vision combined with a sense of calling to a life of service. It is in these areas where Christian business people and Christian NGOs have the greatest potential to make development interventions truly transformational.

The Role of SMEs in Economic Development

SMEs can be thought of as firms in the middle of a continuum. On one end are large, globally integrated firms that have operations in many countries and are often hugely influential in the economies of developing countries in both positive and negative ways. On the one hand, their investment brings capital, jobs, access to global markets, and world-class know-how; but on the other hand, there are possibilities of potential power imbalances and mismatches between the firm's goals and the local economy's needs (Schmitz 2004; Todaro and Smith 2009). At the other end of the continuum are micro enterprises, businesses that employ fewer than five people and have a reach no further than the neighborhood or village in which it is located (UNDP 1999). Micro businesses have become powerful vehicles for addressing employment and income needs of millions of the world's poorest people. Yet because of their limited resources and narrow market, they are typically not strong enough to generate sustainable and widespread economic growth.

SMEs fall between the two extremes, employing between five and two hundred people (UNDP 1999).[3] In rich countries they contribute an average of 51.5 percent of GDP (De Ferranti and Ody 2007). In developing countries, however, the sector is much smaller, producing only an average of 15.6 percent of GDP. This so-called "missing middle" in developing countries is a consequence of decades of development planning by national governments and international organizations like the World Bank that focused on large state-owned enterprises and infrastructure projects, rather than on small, privately owned businesses.

Development scholars have identified three major contributions SMEs make to economic development: job creation and income generation; the potential for integration into global markets; and local leadership that helps generate social justice and political stability through civic engagement.[4]

Job Creation. Perhaps the most obvious contributions made by SMEs are job creation and income generation. In economically developed countries, such as the United States, SMEs typically "generate two-thirds of private sector employment and are the principal creator of new jobs" (De Ferranti and Ody 2007, 2). Because SMEs are typically born and nurtured in the context of local market demands and conditions, they tend to use relatively more labor-intensive techniques than MNCs, which helps make them stable sources of jobs and income over time (OECD 2004; Berry 2002). SMEs also tend to be relatively flexible and can respond quickly to changing trends. Because they are homegrown, so to speak, their entrepreneurial spark is compatible with local conditions, yet they are outward- and forward-looking. Neither micro enterprises nor multinational corporations are as responsive. MNCs often have global perspectives that cause them to be less concerned with the local, and micro entrepreneurs are often content to meet the needs of their household and entertain no ambitions to expand.

Potential for Global Integration. Because of the complexity of operating successfully in a foreign country, MNCs often seek out and contract with local SMEs. These supply-chain relationships are known as "backward linkages," because they link global firms to local suppliers (OECD 2004). Filling such niches in global supply chains allows SMEs to add value to products sold in global markets, a possibility far beyond their individual capacities. Integrating into global supply chains also enables SMEs to learn new technologies and business processes and to create new nodes of comparative advantage.

The salmon-farming industry in Chile offers an insightful example. In 1986, seventeen national salmon producers formed an association with the intention of going global. In 1987 Chilean producers accounted for 1.5 percent of the global market in farmed salmon, but by 2001 that had increased to 32.4 percent. As companies progressed along the learning curve, their average costs fell, thus increasing their global competitiveness. The increase in sales of salmon also spawned the development of many additional supporting businesses in areas such as fish feed, packing materials, and production inputs. By 2001, 41,000 jobs had been generated by Chile's salmon-farming industry, most of them in SMEs (Maggi Campos 2006).

Civil Society Benefits. The third contribution SMEs make toward healthy development is to civic and social stability, and, generally, to good governance. As Pfeffermann points out, SMEs form "the seed-bed of the middle class," a constituency that demands and works for stable, well-governed communities (Pfeffermann 2001, 45). More than the distant leaders of multinational corporations, SME owners naturally care about the well-being and stability of the community and are thus willing to provide community and civic leadership. Korsching and Allen (2004) describe the contribution as "development *of* the community rather than development *in* the community" (emphasis added), meaning that a virtuous circle exists, such that SMEs promote good governance and social justice even as well-governed communities support productive, job-creating businesses.

The emphasis on SME development is not without its critics. Some believe the potential benefits of SMEs are overblown. Levine (2006), for example, is skeptical about the ability of SMEs either to create or adopt new technologies. He says that empirical evidence has not yet confirmed their job-creation potential either. Biggs and Shah (2006) point out that SMEs need relationships of trust and cooperation (with communities, suppliers, buyers, and others) to function efficiently. But they worry that this need for trusting relationships may foster the for-mation of exclusive "clusters," businesses that favor certain people (for example, ethnic groups) over others, thus contributing to community divisions. A third concern is that SMEs may get caught in a "race to the bottom." That is, in the interest of becoming suppliers for large multinationals, competition with other potential suppliers may push them toward lower wages and lower standards. For example, Mattel's recent recall of millions of toys was due to its local suppliers cutting corners, such as using lead-based paints that were slightly cheaper than safer paints (Barboza 2007). Some analysts refer to this as a choice between taking the "high road" (that is, legal compliance, good labor practices, and environmental stewardship) or the "low road" (that is, paying the lowest possible wages, disregarding environmental standards, or defying legal and community norms) (Loebis and Schmitz 2006). The challenge for Christian business associations and supporting NGOs is to encourage SME owners to take the high road.

Promoting the Growth and Expansion of SMEs

In light of the great, and largely untapped, potential offered by the "missing middle," development theorists and aid agencies have begun researching the challenges SMEs face and how to actively promote the SME sector. Evidence suggests two main areas that need to be addressed: the firms' internal capacities and the quality of the overall business climate (Brainard and LaFleur 2006). The novelty of the PW study is that for the first time it documents another key factor: an encompassing social vision combined with a sense of calling to a life of service.

Internal Capacities. It may not need to be said, but for SMEs to function well, their owners need an entrepreneurial spirit, a desire to grow a business, a willingness to accept risk, and the ability to organize a business enterprise. Such entrepreneurs also need financial capital, which allows them to plan ahead and to purchase the inputs needed to expand their business. But capital by itself is not enough, and many well-meaning development organizations have made the mistake of thinking that capital is the only input SMEs need. In order to use capital resources productively, SMEs need to have marketable products and the know-how to produce and market them efficiently. "Know-how" is a catchall term that includes not only technical knowledge but also management, financial, accounting, human resource, and marketing skills. None of this is simple or inborn. The truth is that the abilities to run a business well need to be nurtured.

Business Climate. The second basic need for SMEs to thrive is a healthy business climate. The quality of governance, including legal institutions and reasonable economic policies, is vital on this front and covers a broad range of topics. Among the main issues here is whether the government is stable, trustworthy, and responsive to people's needs. If the government favors one ethnic group over another and/or implements regulations that seem erratic or unfair, SME owners are less able to successfully grow their businesses. Sometimes business regulations directly hinder business development, such as when the steps to start a business are lengthy, arduous, and expensive, or when taxes are punitively high. Likewise, court systems that do not uphold property rights or legitimate contracts, regulatory bureaucracies that extract bribes, or monetary authorities that inflate the currency and repress financial markets all create conditions in which SMEs are unlikely to prosper. In general, if governmental and judicial institutions are weak and unresponsive to the needs of the nation's citizens, and if economic policies are erratic and unwise, then SMEs will not be able to thrive, and the country will not be able to take advantage of the SME sector's potential (OECD 2004; Brainard 2006).

Together, the SME's internal capabilities and the business climate reinforce each other. A good business climate fosters SMEs, but SMEs themselves can also serve as an empowered force to advocate for the type of governance, legal institutions, laws, and policies that the SME sector needs. Unfortunately, such empowered business leaders are often tempted to advocate for their own narrow self-interests at the expense of the broader community. To mitigate this temptation, it is important for SME owners to have a sense of purpose that includes responsibility to their communities, and this comes from being morally rooted (Korsching and Allen 2004).

How can such leadership be developed? Many development organizations are working to promote healthy businesses and a healthy business climate. Key players include multilateral organizations like the World Bank, developed-country governments (especially their foreign aid agencies like the USAID), and NGOs from the civil-society sector, including educational institutions like colleges and universities. Together, these organizations play distinct and sometimes overlapping roles in supporting both the internal capacities and the business climate that SMEs need. But their ability to nurture a sense of calling and responsibility to the community is more problematic. In contrast, calling and responsibility are central elements that Christian organizations like Partners Worldwide are able to make, vitally important contributions to SMEs that secular agencies have typically overlooked.

Partners Worldwide and the Promotion of SMEs

To fulfill its mission of strengthening SMEs in the developing world, PW has created an international group of affiliate business associations that seek to create "innovative solutions for economic growth and community transformation in regions of need."[5] When PW was founded, its members thought that finance was the most critical ingredient for SMEs in developing countries. Thus, early efforts focused on forming associations of business people that would become the source of financial capital. Over time, as affiliates matured and became more aware of the needs SMEs face, PW began to provide other resources such as organized training activities, mentoring opportunities, and conferences that allowed affiliate members to network and to hear and learn from like-minded business people.

Today, financial resources in the form of interest-bearing loans still play a role in PW's programming, but most of their efforts go into building business associations that will be sources of mentoring, training, networking, and advocacy activities. These relational activities, which many PW members see as their main contribution, occur both internationally and nationally.[6]

PW members are guided by a culture of service and a sense of calling inspired by the "business-as-calling" movement. Those within this movement recognize the unique and vital role of business in God's kingdom, and they take seriously their calling to steward their lives and resources for the benefit of the broader community.[7] PW members seek to affirm each other in their business calling, to encourage each other to live more faithfully in their business life, to mentor and counsel each other, to consult with and learn from each other, to grow in service together, and to organize into effective voices for advocacy. SMEs in the PW network are thus encouraged and supported in their efforts to take the "high road" in all that they do.

Helping businesses prosper is only the beginning. While celebrating these achievements, PW desires to see evidence of ethical business behavior, community leadership, philanthropy, and civic engagement, including advocacy to appropriate government bodies. PW believes that economic and social transformation is not sustainable without some level of what one might call spiritual transformation.

Partners Worldwide thus has a vision, a sense of purpose, and a set of strategies for achieving their purposes in promoting a strong, vibrant, ethically sound, community-enhancing SME sector. How effective these strategies have been in achieving lasting transformation was the subject of the 2007 study.

Findings from the 2007 Evaluation of Partners Worldwide

Supported by a grant from the U.S. Agency for International Development (USAID), PW requested an independent evaluation of their work,[8] which the author of this chapter led in the spring and summer of 2007. To gather relevant information, surveys were distributed randomly to 328 affiliate business owners and 209 of their employees in three countries: Kenya, Haiti, and Nicaragua. These surveys were followed by visits to each country to visit businesses and to interview business owners, business association leaders, PW staff, survey administrators, and selected others.[9]

There were two basic categories of questions. First, how and to what extent were the strategies actually implemented? And second, to what extent were the strategies effective?

Because PW does not dictate how affiliate associations should be set up or governed, there is a wide variety of associations, each reflecting the personalities of its membership, the business climate, and the particular needs of local businesses. For these same reasons, some associations have trouble getting organized, some fail and dissolve, and others grow and thrive. Some of these associations have over one hundred members, others just a dozen. Some focus on finance, others on mentoring and training.

In the midst of such diversity, itself a strength when local initiative and flexibility are desirable, the four main additional strategies of training, mentoring, lending, and networking were also implemented, though sometimes to varying degrees and in different ways. In Kenya, where business owners reported that capital on reasonable terms was not readily available, access to capital was the most highly valued aspect of the program. In Haiti and Nicaragua, on the other hand, though financial assistance was appreciated, training, generally done in specialist-led workshops, was ranked as most valuable. This may be partly because, in contrast to Kenya, business owners in Haiti and

Nicaragua reported that financial resources on reasonable terms were more available through other sources.

Mentoring is of special importance to PW because of its potential for building virtuous character and for transmitting values in addition to technical know-how. So central is mentoring to the PW vision that they called their USAID supported program "The Million Mentors Initiative," a title that captured their desire to see business mentoring spread around the globe. The plan is for successful businesspeople to develop relationships with new and promising entrepreneurs in the association so that "young" entrepreneurs can learn from more experienced mentors. Over time, those initially being mentored become mentors to others. Importantly, the evaluation showed that mentoring was a new concept for entrepreneurs in all three countries. To a significant degree, they had adopted the go-it-alone mentality of the world around them. Before joining the local PW affiliated-business association, entrepreneurs said they had understood business to be only about competition and profit maximization, and sharing one's ideas to assist or to generally encourage others did not fit in their picture. Association members reported in interviews that the idea of successful businesspeople giving honest advice and otherwise helping other businesses was a foreign one.[10]

Entrepreneurs in the associations thus took some time to understand and become comfortable with the idea of mentoring. But gradually, over a period of four years, they did, to the point where a strong majority of people interviewed wanted to continue the mentoring experience. More significantly, they wanted not only to continue to be mentored but also to mentor others. For many, this was a major transformation, what some called a spiritual transformation. In the surveyed group, over 60 percent of business owners had participated in mentoring relationships, some one-to-one and others in peer groups. In open-ended questions and in follow-up interviews, business people emphasized that their mentoring relationships helped them learn about particular skills and technical strategies and about vision, values, ethics, and character.

In terms of results, the achievement of both quantitative and qualitative goals was impressive, with most business owners reporting that PW strategies had contributed greatly to their success. Eighty-five percent of the entrepreneurs surveyed reported their business as successful or very successful, with 87 percent saying their participation in the association had been a major factor in their success. Over the last three years, 65 percent of surveyed businesses reported higher profits, 71 percent reported higher revenues, 76 percent reported that the value of their businesses had increased, and, more importantly, 72 percent said they were more successful than similar businesses that were not association members. Selected open-ended comments from the surveys, as shown in Box 1, give some indication of the benefits SME owners discovered through their involvement with PW affiliated associations.

Another major indicator of program success is the number and quality of jobs being created. From 2003 to 2007, about nine hundred new jobs were created in member businesses, and over four thousand were retained. Eighty-five percent of employees surveyed said they were "happy with their jobs," 90 percent said their job was "important or very important to their family's well-being," and 70 percent said their economic well-being had improved. All of which suggests that many employers were on the "high road" rather than the "low road" of trying to squeeze their workers for all they could.

The case of Kenya's John Matheri and Margaret Gichohu (see Box 2) is illustrative of what we found more generally to be true. The story is indicative of the advances being made in such qualitative goals as transmitting good values, encouraging ethical business practices, and improving general citizenship.

Strong majorities of those surveyed agreed or strongly agreed that their community involvement, charitable giving, ethical business practice, and their own mentoring of other business owners had

Box 1: Benefits of Membership in PW Affiliated Business Associations: Selected Comments from SME Owners

I attended business forums where I gained insights and skills, and I also met other members and exchanged ideas with them. *Kenyan restaurant owner with 18 employees*

I have developed as a leader and enjoy helping other people with ideas. *Nicaraguan businesswoman in the fabrication/sales of soda, popsicles and juices, with 12 employees*

I learned how to run my business in a Christian way and also got more clients buying my products. *Kenyan soft drink distributor with 18 employees*

It has been a blessing to receive a loan at a low interest rate and good conditions, which has allowed me to invest in my business. *Nicaraguan textile fabrication/sales businesswoman with 15 employees*

The association helps us in making our life better. *Haitian agriculture and breeding businessman with 20 employees*

I have made many friends, acquired leadership skills and have been able to assist many other people, which has been a source of joy and satisfaction. *Kenyan welding and metal fabrication businessman with 17 employees*

I made new friends who are business owners, learned many things about small scale business I did not know before and received spiritual nourishment. *Kenyan borehole drilling businessman with 13 employees*

I have become a better mentor and have increased my own competence in business management. I have been ethically transformed. *Kenyan bakery/confections/restaurant businesswoman with 8 employees*

I now know much more about business management and about the importance of improving product quality. *Nicaraguan producer of hammocks with 24 employees*

I like to see the solidarity among global associates in this association. *Nicaraguan coffee roaster with 24 employees*

Box 2: Meet John Matheri and Margaret Gichohu

"Now I'm a man of integrity. Before, I was not." That is why John Matheri is becoming more than just an employer; he is also a transformer of lives. Intent on both protecting and empowering young women, John and his wife Margaret Gichohu employ women—many from underprivileged communities of Nairobi—as seamstresses and salespeople of Alpha Embroidery, their growing business of interior design.

John and Margaret began their business in 1990 with a loan of $40, just enough to purchase a treadle-operated sewing machine. By 2001, they dedicated themselves fulltime to their growing business. It was their membership in a Kenyan business association called CHESS (Christian Entrepreneurs Savings and Credit Society) that made the growth of their business possible.

They also joined a 20-person cell group of other CHESS members and thus became the inspirational model of mutual mentorship that was built into the USAID-funded Million Mentors Initiative. In that cell group, and through a mentoring relationship with a North American businessman, John and Margaret found ongoing support as they shared mutual business concerns and increased their marketing contacts. Today, through Margaret's expertise in tapestry and John's entrepreneurial spirit, they produce a variety of high-quality products—cushions, curtains, and bedspreads—in a highly competitive field. Alpha Embroidery has found a niche in the city center market through unique interior designs and their ability to fill special orders. And, as Alpha Embroidery has grown, so has the opportunity to socially transform the lives of their employees.

John and Margaret now have 15 employees, most of whom are young women who dropped out of primary education. Some are former prostitutes who are now gainfully employed, able to support their children through honorable work. To provide such opportunities to these young women, John and Margaret assume the risk and extra expenses of hiring inexperienced workers; Margaret guides them through intensive training to acquire the skills needed to continue in the field of tapestry.

Over the years, John and Margaret's understanding of the importance of a locally-owned business has grown. Through their mentoring relationships, their outlook on their role as employers has been transformed. According to John, he learned from his cell group peers "that you can be a compassionate businessperson (and) succeed while still giving." As compassionate businesspeople of integrity, John and Margaret encourage their employees to be proud of who they are and what they do. Adapted from the story at www.partnersworldwide.org/aboutus/million.html.

increased and/or improved as a result of their involvement with PW. For those business owners who received mentoring, about 80 percent said mentoring had a major impact on their changes in these areas. Business owners interviewed on our follow-up visits readily told how their perspectives and behaviors had changed. On numerous occasions in Haiti and Nicaragua, the evaluation team heard from members how inspiring the overall vision of business-as-calling had been to them. Many owners saw this vision of business as a Christian calling to be the most significant contribution that PW was making.

Overall, the evaluation found that businesses and entrepreneurs in all three countries were growing in size and character. Growth in assets, profits, and employment were all evident in the production and marketing activities that were in full display on the site visits. Time after time, on visits to businesses chosen by the evaluators themselves, businesses were bustling and conversations revealed that the owners were optimistic and forward-looking. Business associations were active and for the most part highly appreciated by their members. Businesses were growing, and working people were finding productive and satisfying employment.

While the results of the evaluation were largely positive, some aspects of the program needed improvement. For example, PW had focused most of its attention on the SMEs themselves rather than on association structure and governance. Not surprisingly, some of the associations were having difficulty with self-governance issues, and PW offered little help. The evaluation thus led to a recommendation that PW pay more attention in the future to this important piece of association life. The evaluation also discovered that, as of yet, there was little evidence of involvement in advocacy activities, which had much to do with the relative youth of both the associations and the member SMEs. Whether advocacy becomes an important part of the activities of the associations as their member SMEs grow and as their organizations mature remains to be seen.[11]

Conclusions: Christian Mission and SME Development

A strong SME sector is a vital component of any economy and will be an essential part of any country's development prospects. The PW evaluation helps us understand how Christian NGOs can contribute to the growth and strengthening of this sector. Assisting SME development is fully consistent with the holistic, transformational vision of development articulated by Myers (1999) and others who seek to integrate the redemptive task in every area of life. Business leaders around the world have caught this vision and are beginning to steward the gifts of business capabilities that God has given them. Their stewardship includes using their gifts of entrepreneurship, financial resources, market connections, and management/marketing skills to create successful businesses that are one foundation of a thriving community. PW provides one experience that others can learn from.

It is common to think that the lack of finance is the major obstacle to the development of business. The PW evaluation shows that to be only partly true. While the provision of financial capital is clearly an important and highly valued contribution that Christian NGOs can make, potentially more important is the nurturing of spiritual and social capital. When business people see their work as a calling, it translates into virtues such as integrity, honesty, compassion, and others that are transmitted through mentoring and training, and by the vision of seeing business as a Christian calling to be used in kingdom service. It is striking that these same virtues are those that feed a thriving SME sector. Many secular organizations know that honesty, integrity, cooperation, citizenship, community involvement, environmental stewardship, and just treatment of workers are important. What they have much more difficulty articulating and promoting is the vision and the rationale that give life to these fine qualities. How fascinating, too, to expect that when such mission-inspired businesses engage in public advocacy, they will be driven by a vision that encompasses not only their own self-interested advantage but also justice for the whole community.

Questions for Review

1. Why are SMEs so important to a developing economy? What contributions do they make that microenteprises and multinational firms are less able to make?

2. What inputs, resources, and conditions do SMEs need to be successful?

3. If you were going to donate time and money to alleviate global poverty, would you donate to an organization that is promoting the development of private SMEs? Why or why not?

4. If you were to lead an NGO that promotes the development of SMEs, what would that NGO actually do? Does your answer accord with what Partners Worldwide does?

5. How important is it for SME owners to have "an encompassing social vision combined with a sense of calling to a life of service?" Is this asking too much of SME owners?

Notes

[1] I would like to acknowledge the special contribution of Jeremy Veenema, a Calvin College senior economics major who co-authored the Partners Worldwide evaluation report with me. He also contributed a great deal of the research for this chapter.

[2] Adapted from http://www.partnersworldwide.org/aboutus/million.html.

[3] There is no precise and accepted set of definitions for these different groupings of businesses. But the definitions are generally close. De Ferranti and Ody, for example, define SMEs as employing between 10 and 250 employees (De Ferranti and Ody 2007, 1).

[4] Some excellent sources on the potential benefits of SMEs are Berry (2002), Brainard (2006), OECD (2004), Pietrobelli (2006), and Schmitz and Nadvi (1999).

[5] http://www.partnersworldwide.org.

[6] As an NGO, PW is considered small, with an operating budget of only a few million dollars. Most of what it offers is related to the value of connecting business people with each other and then collaboratively using their skills, knowledge, and other resources in a way that fulfills their purpose in building God's kingdom.

[7] Some influential books in this movement are Baer (2006), Novak (1996), and Rundle and Steffen (2003).

[8] The evaluation study focused especially on one central PW program called the Million Mentors Initiative (MMI). This particular program was supported by a grant from USAID, which requires an independent evaluation. Because the MMI so captures the vision, purposes, and working plan of the whole of Partners Worldwide, this chapter will not distinguish between the MMI as an individual program and the work of PW in general. Indeed, PW saw this opportunity to evaluate the MMI as an opportunity to evaluate their work as a whole organization. The full report, as it was presented to PW and to USAID, may be accessed at http://www.partnersworldwide.org/aboutus/images/Million_Mentors_Final_Evaluation.pdf.

[9] As with any evaluation or empirical study of this sort, there are many issues related to the choice of methods, the possible biases that might exist, the reliability of the results, and others. Because these issues are not central to the purpose of this chapter, they are not discussed here. The results and findings presented here are among those in which the evaluators had the most confidence.

[10] On the other hand, there were also some entrepreneurs (not as many) who said that while the word "mentoring" might be new to them, they had some experience with developing relationships of trust and sharing and mutual assistance with other business people. They just had different ways of thinking about it and organizing it.

[11] Again, the full evaluation report is available on the PW web site at http://www.partnersworldwide.org/aboutus/images/Million_Mentors_Final_Evaluation.pdf.

References

Baer, Michael R. 2006. *Business as Mission: The Power of Business in the Kingdom of God*. Seattle: YWAM Publishing.

Barboza, David. 2007. "Why Lead in Toy Paint? It's Cheaper." *New York Times* (September 11). View at http://www.nytimes.com/2007/09/11/business/worldbusiness/11lead.html?scp=1&sq=why+did+mattel+suppliers+use+lead+paint%3F&st=nyt.

Barnet, Richard, and Ronald Muller. 1976. *Global Reach: The Power of Multinational Corporations*. New York: Touchstone Books.

Berry, Albert. 2002. "The Role of the Small and Medium Enterprise Sector in Latin America and Similar Developing Economies." *Seton Hall Journal of Diplomacy and International Relations* (Winter/Spring), 104–19.

Biggs, Tyler, and Manju Kedia Shah. 2006. "African SMEs, Networks, and Manufacturing Performance." *Journal of Banking and Finance* 30: 3043–66.

Brainard, Lael, ed. 2006. *Transforming the Development Landscape: The Role of the Private Sector*. Washington, D.C.: Brookings Institution Press.

———, and Vinca LaFleur. 2006. The Private Sector in the Fight Against Global Poverty. In *Transforming the Development Landscape: The Role of the Private Sector*, edited by Lael Brainard. Washington, D.C.: Brookings Institution Press, 1–28.

De Ferranti, David, and Anthony J. Ody. 2007. "Beyond Microfinance: Getting Capital to Small Medium Enterprises to Fuel Faster Development." Policy Brief 159 (March). Washington, D.C.: The Brookings Institution. View at http://www.brookings.edu/~/media/Files/rc/papers/2007/03development_ferranti/pb159.pdf, 2–3.

Hoksbergen, Roland, and Jeremy Veenema. 2007. Million Mentors Global Business Alliance: Final Evaluation Report (August 21). Partners Worldwide. View at http://www.partnersworldwide.org/aboutus/images/Million_Mentors_Final_Evaluation.pdf.

Korsching, Peter F., and John C. Allen. 2004. "Local Entrepreneurship: A Development Model Based on Community Interaction Field Theory." *Journal of the Community Development Society* 35, no. 1 (October), 25–43.

Levine, Ross. 2006. Should Governments and Aid Agencies Subsidize Small Firms? In *Transforming the Development Landscape: The Role of the Private Sector*, edited by Lael Brainard. Washington, D.C.: Brookings Institution Press, 66–73.

Loebis, Lienda, and Hubert Schmitz. 2006. Java Furniture Makers: Globalization Winners or Losers. In *Development and the Private Sector: Consuming Interests*, edited by Deborah Eade and John Sayer. Bloomfield, CT: Kumarian Press, 167–77.

Maggi Campos, Claudio. 2006. The Salmon Farming and Processing Cluster in Southern Chile. In *Upgrading to Compete: Global Value Chains, Clusters, and*

SMEs in Latin America, edited by Carlo Pietrobelli and Roberta Rabellotti. New York: Inter-American Development Bank, 109–40.

Myers, Bryant. 1999. *Walking With the Poor: Principles and Practices of Transformational Development*. New York: Orbis Books.

Novak, Michael. 1996. *Business as a Calling: Work and the Examined Life*. New York: The Free Press.

OECD. 2004. *Promoting Entrepreneurship and Innovative SMEs in a Global Economy: Promoting SMEs for Development*. Report from the 2d OECD Conference of Ministers Responsible for Small and Medium-Sized Enterprises (SMEs), June, held in Istanbul. Organization for Economic Co-operation and Development. View at http://www.oecd.org/datao-ecd/6/7/31919278.pdf, 10–12, 44.

Pfeffermann, Guy. 2001. "Poverty Reduction in Developing Countries." *Finance and Development* (June). View at http://www.imf.org/external/pubs/ft/fandd/2001/06/pfefferm.htm, 42–45.

Pietrobelli, Carlo, and Roberta Rabellotti, eds. 2006. *Upgrading to Compete: Global Value Chains, Clusters, and SMEs in Latin America*. New York: Inter-American Development Bank.

Rundle, Steve, and Tom Steffen. 2003. *Great Commission Companies: The Emerging Role of Business in Missions*. Downers Grove: InterVarsity Press.

Schmitz, Hubert, ed. 2004. *Local Enterprises in the Global Economy: Issues of Governance and Upgrading*. Northampton, MA: Edgar Elgar, 1.

———, and Khalid Nadvi. 1999. "Industrial Clusters in Developing Countries." *World Development* (Special Issue) 27, no. 1 (September), 1503–14.

Todaro, Michael P., and Stephen P. Smith. 2009. *Economic Development*. 10th ed. New York: Addison-Wesley, 719–25.

UNDP. 1999. "Small and Medium Enterprise Development." *Essentials: Synthesis of Lessons Learned* 1 (November). New York: United Nations Development Program, Evaluation Office. View at http://www.undp.org/eo/essentials/finalversionSMEprintver.doc, 1.

CHAPTER 9

THE ROLE OF THE CHURCH IN POVERTY ALLEVIATION IN AFRICA

Julius Oladipo

The issue of reducing mass poverty in Africa requires urgent worldwide attention. A wide range of institutions have roles to play: the southern and northern governments, international-development finance institutions, international and local NGOs, the private sector, and the church (the universal church and the churches in Africa). The focus of this chapter is on the distinctive position of the church in Africa in this task of alleviating poverty. The emphasis here is that the church deserves a prominent role in the process of economic and social development (and particularly in the social-service sectors).

Stabilization and structural-adjustment measures adopted in African countries have usually led to reduced government involvement in social services delivery. The expectation is that private enterprise and personal expenditures will make up the difference. This leads, typically, to the exclusion of the poor. This chapter presents the credentials of the church as a candidate that should be supported and enabled to fill the gap.

The definition of poverty given by the United Nations Development Program is adopted here. It states that poverty is a lack of productive resources, income, and capacities that contributes to individual and/

or group isolation, vulnerability, and powerlessness; to economic, political, and social discrimination; and to participation in unsustainable livelihoods (UNDP 1996). Poverty has various manifestations, including hunger and malnutrition, ill health, and limited or no access to education, health care, and safe residential and occupational environments. It has both *absolute* and *relative* dimensions. A distinction is also made between *structural* (or chronic) poverty and *transient* poverty. Officially defined poverty lines identify absolute levels of poverty, while relative poverty refers to an individual's or a group's position in relation to others. Structural poverty is rooted in socio-economic and political institutions, is experienced over the long term, and is often transferred across generations. In contrast, transient poverty is due to cyclical or temporary factors and is experienced over shorter periods of time.

We focus here on absolute, structural poverty. Alleviating the effects of disasters and emergencies is an important subject, but it is usually distinguished from the goals of socioeconomic development. By all official measures of absolute poverty, the people of the sub-Saharan African countries form the bulk of the world's poor.

An effective solution to a problem must be based on good diagnosis. Early theories of the causes of poverty took rather narrow perspectives. Now we recognize that the causes of poverty are complex and sometimes even contradictory. Political, economic, and social institutions and processes are implicated in producing and perpetuating poverty. Based on this view of the multidimensional causes of poverty, holistic approaches to poverty alleviation are being promoted. However, what is now known as holistic development has been the approach of the African church from its inception. Whenever we think of a mission station in any part of Africa, the following specific features come to mind: a church, a school, a health clinic, and a vegetable garden or farm. There is also the characteristic campaign of the church agents against the social ills of the time, which in earlier days centered on harmful traditional practices.

The Basis of the
Church's Service to the Poor

Defining the role of the church in development requires, first, defining the goal and content of development (see, for example, Samuel and Sugden 1987). Also required is an understanding of the mission of the church. There have been many efforts to define development; each of the various approaches to development work necessarily stems from the particular definition adopted. The *economic growth* perspective has dominated the public discourse, although over the last decade thinking has shifted from an economic-growth model to one that takes into account several factors, particularly the moral and equity dimensions. It can be argued that the shift in viewpoint has not yet brought about major changes in official approaches to development. However, it has been accepted in principle that development interventions ought to "wear a human face"; that is, at the policymaking stage, the possible effects of policies on the vulnerable groups in society ought to be considered. There is also global agreement that the yardstick for measuring development ought to be a society's ability to sustain a healthy and dignified standard of living without abuse of others or destruction of ecosystems.

The Christian *stewardship* view of development decries the unbridled quest for economic gain in which no one cares who or what is hurt in the process. This view hinges on the passage where God places humankind in "the Garden of Eden" to both work it and take care of it (Gen. 2:15). It emphasizes responsible and accountable use of God-given resources (see, for example, Bragg 1987).

True development improves the total person in a holistic manner, which is summed up in the meaning of *shalom*. That is the goal of development, from the Christian perspective.

A basic reason for the church's involvement in development is contained in Jesus' declaration concerning his mission (Luke 4:18–19): bringing "good news" to the poor. And his mission is our mission.

That humankind is created in the "image of God" also signifies that each person is entitled to a decent and dignified living. With this in mind, Kinoti (1994) has said, "The wretchedness of the African people dishonors their Creator . . . And we must overcome the disgrace of being the poorest people on earth." For the Christian, development work is not an option. The Christian is commanded to demonstrate her or his faith in good works. Hence, socioeconomic development is an imperative sphere of engagement for the church.

The Church's Track Record in Poverty Alleviation

The European voyages of world discovery were motivated by religion, commerce, and political expansionism. The effects of those three motives are indelible. The indisputably bright part of history is that Christian missionaries brought the message of spiritual redemption, and they ministered to the physical needs of the people. In many places, they introduced new staple crops and the use of animal power for farming. In most African countries, formal education, vocational-skills training, and modern health-care services were pioneered by the church. The management of these services subsequently passed from missionaries to nationals.

Many of the national leaders in African countries were educated in Christian schools. Nevertheless, in line with Western secular trends, these leaders decided that government can and should run these services on its own. In many African countries, the government took over church schools and hospitals. The result is well known. In many countries, when the government took over the schools, the church stepped up vocational training for youths, for instance, by introducing the concept of "village polytechnics." The church has also made a significant contribution in providing safe water to rural communities by means of boreholes, hand-dug wells, protection of springs, and rainwater-harvesting techniques.

The leaders of the church have taken their prophetic role very seriously. In almost every country in Africa, the voice of the church has been loud, clear, and consistent against the ills in society. The church played a major role in dismantling apartheid. When oppressed by a dictator—military or civilian—citizens have usually looked to the church to speak out on their behalf. And the church has been alert to the onerous responsibility, in some cases at the cost of its leaders' lives.

Civic education and election monitoring are recent additions to the work of the church in many countries, proving so effective that unpopular political leaders have realized they can no longer mislead and exploit the populace.

The voice of the church has been loud in the campaign to cancel the debt of the poorest indebted countries (for example, see Gitari 1999). In recent years, the debt crisis has worsened the already grievous conditions of poor countries. A large proportion of the limited foreign exchange goes into debt service. The reality is that in some cases the net flow of funds is now from developing to developed nations. The view that the creditor countries should be held responsible for their part in creating the problem underscores the moral dimension of the issue. "Cushioning" involves offering indebted countries additional but softer loans. An "improved" version being proposed is to let some proportion of debt-service payments be retained in the debtor country as grants for poverty alleviation. The plea of many churches is that what poor African countries need now is total debt cancellation, not halfway responses.

Much is known about the development work of the church in Africa, but only in a general way. Statistics are scarce. Various denominations and Christian NGOs produce separate reports for each country they work in. Collating information on all this work is overdue.

The Church's Core Competencies for Development Ministry

Obviously, alleviating mass poverty in Africa calls for radical but carefully thought out strategies. To be effective, approaches have to be multipronged. There are economic, sociocultural, and moral/advocacy dimensions. Also, every effort has to address the root causes of poverty rather than merely treating symptoms. In this section, we discuss those aspects of the development potential of the church in Africa that are not yet adequately explored.

In the economic dimension, there are both macroeconomic and microeconomic levels. Until recently, most thought that the church had nothing to contribute at the macro level. But now that bad governance is understood as a major factor in deepening poverty, all agents in a position to help secure positive changes in the polity are recognized as important.

Good governance is important for sound formulation and implementation of economic policy. Here, the church has recently taken up the role of "conscientizing" the citizenry to elect competent leaders, and it is monitoring elections to ensure that the people's choice is respected. Through its ongoing prophetic ministry, the church speaks out on any manifestation of poor policies or blatant misrule. Also, the church has often been called upon to serve as an informal arbitrator in trade disputes, particularly nationwide strikes.

However, there are other areas in which the church needs to be more purposively harnessed. In almost all African countries, the constitutions inherited at independence are inadequate to address contemporary challenges. The principles on which nationhood should be based are only vaguely stated. The role defined for government is all-pervasive and far outstrips its capacity, even if there is the will to deliver. The framework for making leaders consistently accountable to the citizenry is invariably lacking. Elections are based on the winner-takes-all principle rather than on power sharing. Provisions for smooth leadership succession are generally inadequate. Accordingly, the need for constitutional reform is widespread. The church is getting involved in the movement for reform, and it needs to be supported and strengthened in this role.

Guiding governance, in addition to the written constitution, should be the expressed will of the people. While the church needs to continue in civic education for the governed, there is also a need to raise consciousness of political leaders. The church should be enabled to convene, particularly at the district level, workshops on poverty. Leaders from across the political spectrum, local traditional leaders, and religious leaders could attend forums on principles and procedures of good governance.

Also, the civic education program should go beyond enlightening people about the electoral process. Communities must be able to demand accountability from their local elected leaders. Obviously, when these leaders blame their own poor performance on the national government, they are declaring themselves irrelevant and hence not qualified for reelection. However, people should not just keep quiet and wait for the next election. In this regard, to lead the way in assertiveness, the heads of church development departments, who in most countries are members of the government's district development committee, should insist on being de facto members contributing to the formulation and monitoring of the official district development budgets.

Most of the objectionable policies or practices of government could be corrected before they are officially adopted, if popular protests took place. Church leaders should have a proactive approach to their prophetic ministry. This would require, among other things, sources of information in the government policymaking offices that would allow the leaders and their professional advisers time to discuss the best way the church should react to any particular matter.

Certain regulatory features of world trade have worked unfairly against developing countries and have contributed to the current scale of poverty in Africa. The church in Africa needs actively to join the lobby that has been demanding redress in this sphere. It should work with its external supporters in the campaigns for a just world-trade order and for debt cancellation.

Microeconomics is a major area of the church's development ministry. However, there is much room for improvement. Although it is accepted that development efforts should address the systematic causes of poverty, the choice and design of interventions has often not focused on that goal. Most community-development programs offer relief to the poorest of the poor rather than changing livelihood opportunities for the whole mass of the poor. Lambs, kids, and heifers are given to poor and marginalized households. Self-help groups are assisted here and there. However, the whole mass of poor people in the village is not affected. Programs that relieve the tragic suffering of the poorest of the poor should not be neglected, and the church should recognize its capability to influence the whole village by introducing sustainable livelihoods that can be widely adopted.

Household cash-flow is a basic issue. The common practice is for small-scale farmers to sell their produce at giveaway prices during the harvest season to obtain cash for children's school fees and other family expenses, only to buy grain at much higher retail prices later in the year. Even where food production is not an issue, good output retention in the household is problematic. Traditional granaries to store grain are now used less. It is pointless, therefore, to promote adopting "appropriate technology" granaries in such a context. The church needs to design effective ways of addressing the household cash-liquidity problem.

Rural savings and credit schemes are relevant in this regard. The services of the few microfinance NGOs currently operating in Africa are generally not accessible to many would-be entrants. The goal of the rural savings and credit schemes of the church is to build up novices in microenterprise to a level where they can use the services of specialized microfinance NGOs. However, the church needs to adopt more effective activities in these schemes. Involving resource persons with relevant expertise would be very helpful.

As it has done in the past—for example, with coffee and cotton innovation in East Africa—the church in Africa can mobilize people to adopt sustainable innovations. Which innovations can the whole village embrace that will make a difference in the standard of living? For example, sericulture is one very promising possibility; and there are many other viable ideas to adopt.

Food security is a major theme in the church's development ministry. Increased production is frequently a great need. However, influencing people's dietary choices is probably a more basic requirement. Global dietary patterns are leading the African family to substitute imported foods for traditional staples, which wastes scarce foreign currency, among other things. Where drought-resistant crops are appropriate, the church could make a significant impact. In some semi-arid and arid areas where sorghum, millet, and cassava are the traditional staple crops, modern tastes have changed to rice and spaghetti, and the motivation for cultivating the former staples has waned. With new crop varieties and production techniques, the church may be in a position to revive interest in them. There is also the need to diversify the staple crops. There could be more sharing of crops across the tropics than has currently taken place. African soils can produce a much wider variety of foodstuffs than are cultivated at present. Irish potatoes were introduced by missionaries and widely embraced in many higher-altitude areas. The church can do this again with other products.

The church has been promoting appropriate small-scale irrigation technology on family farms, but only as a marginal activity and not in a vigorous manner. Small- and micro-scale irrigation and water-harvesting technologies are rarely used in sub-Saharan Africa, even though their viability has been dearly demonstrated in South Asia where they have been widely adopted. This is an area for urgent consideration in the anticipated poverty-focused discussions between the church and the World Bank.

The church has great strengths in promoting self-help groups and in enhancing their capacity for self-actualization. Church development-ministry organs should expand into forming and facilitating cooperatives and associations built around the objectives of marketing and input supply. They should also promote local processing facilities that add value to the primary products of each local economy. The church could spearhead preprocessing for export and promote linkages with already existing fair-trade organizations in the North that are promoting direct exports from small producers in the developing countries.

Small-scale African farmers need to recognize the competitive potential of high-value commodity trade, already demonstrated in, for example, tea, coffee, and cocoa production. The world is steadily supplied with tobacco (and other controversial crops) essentially by small-scale farmers. Rural cooperatives are an effective organ for pooling the limited output of individual small farms into large, exportable volumes. The basic requirements are to focus on a high-value crop and to establish linkage with non-exploitative buyers overseas—facilitated, possibly, by contacts within the universal church as well as by some Christian-owned commercial agencies.

The church can play a great part in promoting and diversifying export production. As Belshaw (1999) has noted: "The range of high-value products that have a growing world market has been tapped by only a few African countries to date. Product types include tropical fruits; flowers and vegetables of all types in the northern winter months; nuts; spices; livestock products; medicinal plants and aromatics."

The church has been working extensively on household income-generating activities, but its efforts need to be more imaginative. Village groups are assisted in poultry, pig, or bee-keeping enterprises. Everyone in the village adopts the idea. Soon, they discover that they have insufficient outlets to absorb the output. Then the church is blamed for having not done a thorough feasibility study. The same question of demand applies to vocational-skills training. Perhaps scores of youths in a village learn carpentry and masonry, but the village may not need more than two carpenters and three masons. Similarly, a church's vocational center for women annually graduates, say, five tailors, six embroiders, and seven craftswomen into the village. The sewing machine left up on a shelf testifies to the low returns from such training. It is evident that the church's development organs have the capacity to enhance skills. The question is, which types of skills do the villagers require for sustainable livelihoods? Increased attention should be given to that issue.

The observations above relate to some of the economic dimensions of the church's role. Next, we discuss competencies of the church in the sociocultural sphere. Creating awareness is a necessary activity, one area in which the church is roundly competent. Being rooted in the community, having a multidimensional knowledge of its people, and being regarded as a credible institution are significant assets of a church.

Social cohesion is a basic issue in Africa. It sets the atmosphere for productive engagement. It is an important component of development and an area in which the church has much proven capacity. Ethnic clashes, civil wars, and land disputes within and between communities continue to augment the miseries of the poor. The church needs to introduce, as a widespread program, regular intercommunity forums to discuss issues and take steps toward planning and implementing development and civic projects. Because it is known to be nonpartisan and because it already has credibility with the people, the church is usually in a better position than political leaders to initiate and facilitate these discussions. Similarly, youths of different ethnic groups could be brought closer through carefully designed, interethnic cultural and vocational activities.

Land is a common concern in almost all African countries. It is a thorny issue that politicians prefer to keep off the agenda. Here also, the church can play a key role. First, the church can convene local forums for redressing incessant communal land disputes. Second, the plight of peoples living in arid, famine-prone regions requires systematic discussion. Reclaiming the hard land, as Israel has done, is an option open to poor countries. Forcible resettlement is unacceptable, as is part of the population becoming perpetual receivers of relief handouts. The church could negotiate voluntary relocations of new farm households to underused areas, once these are provided with adequate production and social infrastructure.

The church's capacity to run institutional social services, particularly health care services and schools, is widely appreciated in Africa. The church can be counted on to effectively deliver sustainable health care and educational services. In health care, greater emphasis is being placed on preventive services, relative to curative medicine. Governments and the church have been active in this category because private health-care providers earn only limited profits in health care. Now that governments are reducing their involvement, the church is poised to be the main player in that arena. The possible advantages of church-state and church-private partnerships should also be examined in specific situations.

Cost-sharing has been promoted both as a requirement for the financial viability of the service institution and as a protection for those who receive services from the dependency syndrome. However, there is concern everywhere about how to help the poor afford even relatively low fees. Health insurance is being discussed but has not been widely explored; while it should receive increased attention, only social (subsidized) insurance would seem to be suitable for the poor. Such a conclusion emphasizes the importance of raising the productivity and incomes of the poor.

The church is campaigning against traditional harmful practices and restrictive beliefs. So far, however, this has merely been regarded as another activity of the development department rather than one that involves the whole mobilized potential of the church. It seems that church leaders will need to take extra time to study the particular and often local issues and start playing their full role as agents of change. The church has immense but only partially tapped potential in this area. Some African traditions, such as those involving high bride prices and expensive weddings and funerals, make the poverty situation worse. The church is in a position to influence communities to appropriately adjust with current realities.

Family planning or child spacing is a theme in the socioeconomic program of the church. Less rapid population growth is an important factor in poverty alleviation. Also, the scourge of HIV/AIDS is a matter of increasing concern to the church (see for example, Okaalet 2001).

The sociocultural dimension has several components, including the waning communal spirit, the increasing instability of marriage relations, the problem of street children, the widening generation gap, gender issues, and so forth. In all these areas the church, by its mission, has primary interest, is eminently competent, and can work effectively given the will and resources.

The moral guidance and advocacy dimensions are indisputably central to the mission of the church. The prophetic role of the church makes it not only the conscience of society but also a testimony and witness to the values and ethics of the kingdom of God. A concern with justice is at the center of poverty alleviation, and the church is characteristically equipped for advocacy. For example, the marginalization of women is a matter of importance in the poverty situation in Africa. The role that the church is playing and is further capable of playing is discussed by Abuom (2001).

Constraints Facing the Management of the Church's Development Ministry

In its development ministry, the church faces some basic challenges that need to be recognized and urgently addressed. Most of these are probably features of the general working culture of the church in

Africa. As the church wants to play a greater role, it needs to prioritize its use of resources. International partners need to note the top-priority areas for capacity-building support.

In the church's system, policymaking organs and reference committees are usually dominated by clergy, despite the availability of appropriate practicing professionals within and outside the churches' membership. Also, involving women in decision making has rarely moved beyond tokenism. Furthermore, while the church has been known to target its services to the whole community without discrimination, including nonmembers on project-management committees is not yet a common feature. The increasingly accepted concept of participatory management enjoins that these facets be considered.

While the church recognizes the importance of having appropriate professional expertise for the technical aspects of its sectoral services, such as health care, schools, and water-supply construction, church leaders generally appreciate less fully the place of professionalism in management aspects. Also, multisectoral approaches to community development require a level of expertise and intellectual capacity that is not yet fully appreciated.

Some church leaders have not made a distinction between a project that has been set up to serve the people and one intended to earn profit for running the church's internal administration. Requiring a hospital or a school to pay an annual "quota" into the church's administrative fund is no different from expecting dividends from shares in a commercial venture. The goals of poverty-focused development can hardly be attained when expecting such services to bring dividends.

In general, the church can be credited for integrity, but occasionally the temptation to dip into designated donor funds to meet other genuine unfunded needs is irresistible. Misapplication of funds needs to be detected and rooted out as a form of financial indiscipline. While financial management in the African church is progressively improving, there are still cases of weak financial systems and procedures where fraud goes undetected far too long. While excessive documentation is the bane of government service, the lack of paperwork is a pervasive weakness in the church's working environment in Africa. "Don't you trust me?" is the common reply when someone is asked to put things in writing or to back up financial transactions with documentary evidence.

There is a general tendency to be slow in implementing decisions. Although things move faster in the church's working environment than in government, there is much room for improvement in developing a sense of urgency about what needs to be done. Speed of response needs to be greatly improved.

Transport and communication are areas of widespread need. The church tends to target its services to underserved people in geographically remote locations, where communication is poor and the population is sparse and scattered over wide areas. Because of poor roads, maintaining a vehicle is a common problem. A maintenance culture is not yet widespread; ironically, physical assets obtained with scarce funds are left to deteriorate through poor or absent maintenance procedures.

The Church in Partnership Relationships

It is not unhealthy for the church in Africa to receive external funding support for its development ministry. What is not desirable is for the church to expect external funding for meeting its own internal "club needs." Church members should provide the funds for the internal administration of the church. They should fund the synod conferences and other administrative meetings. But in its ministry to the poor, the African church should not feel ashamed to solicit external funding support. It should see itself as providing a service to donors—by signposting them to worthy causes that deserve their funding support and by providing efficient and effective management of these funds to improve the lives and prospects of the poor. Sustainability should be promoted widely as a thematic priority, but we should all be clear about what is meant by "sustainability of social services." By their nature, long-term or welfare services to the poor can hardly be financially self-sufficient. Anywhere in the world, not-for-profit service and charity organizations typically depend on donor funds.

A significant feature of the church's development work in Africa is that it has been carried out in close partnership with international funding agencies and NGO support organizations. The two sides bring their distinctive strengths together to serve the poor—the African churches' contributions are identifying needs and managing projects, while the international churches' contributions are providing funds and technical support. The possibility of entering into a working relationship with official aid institutions, especially the World Bank, is currently being discussed; these funders could benefit from experience the church has acquired in its existing partnerships.

The World Bank has been perceived in different ways. For example, Mohammed Yunus, the founder of Grameen Bank, presents his perception of the World Bank's relation to a borrowing country as follows:

> They give you money. They give you all the ideas, expertise and everything else. Your job is to follow the yellow lines, the green lines, the red lines, read the instructions at each stop and follow them. The World Bank is eager to assume all the responsibilities. They don't want to leave any responsibility to the borrower, except the responsibility for the failure of the project (quoted in Hodson 1997).

The church is not familiar with such a relationship where its only role in forming agreements is to sign on the dotted line. The need to negotiate positions is obvious.

With reference to the early stage of a particular bank-funded project, Hodson (1997) states:

Through frequent supervision missions the Bank tried to ensure that the project design was closely followed. The level of micro-management of the project at times reached ridiculous levels with 15-member supervisory missions leaving hundreds of pages of notes and instructions, much of it based on an inadequate understanding of the situation.

Donors that provide aid grants to the church prefer, in the language of development, to be referred to as "partners." Although most of them are still grappling with the implications of that position, its importance is recognized in principle. The church cherishes partnership based on mutual understanding, mutual respect, and mutual accountability.

The business community—the commercial and manufacturing sectors—is virtually dormant in social development in Africa. But the theme of social responsibility is currently being promoted worldwide. The church leaders in a district could come together to approach profitable companies and factories in their locality to fund some specific community projects. The potential of involving local donors has not been adequately tapped. In addition to benefiting workers, suppliers, consumers, owners, and government (through taxes paid directly and indirectly), these businesses should be feeding back some returns to strengthen their local communities.

This chapter intentionally has not given any definition of "the church." For partner relationships to be effective, fruitful, and sustainable, the church needs to recognize and maintain its identity. There is ongoing debate about whether or not the church is an NGO. The church is an active and significant player in development; however, this is only a part of its mandate. Basic requirements for good partnership are to know and respect each other's distinctive qualities and peculiarities and to collaborate on the common ground.

This chapter originally appeared in Faith in Development: Partnership Between the World Bank and the Churches of Africa, edited by Belshaw, D., R. Calderisi, and C. Sugden. Oxford: U.K.: Regnum Books International (2001). Reprinted with permission.

Questions for Review

1. According to the author, what should be the goal of development, and how is that consistent with the mission of the church?

2. Identify some of the roles the church can play in development. Do you agree that these are appropriately the function of the church? Why or why not?

3. In regard to promoting holistic development, what has the church done well and what not so well?

4. Identify three areas in which the author says the development ministry of the church can be better managed.

5. Recent trends in development ministry have promoted activities, such as micro-lending, that can be financially self-sustaining. The author argues that "By their nature, long-term or welfare services to the poor can hardly be financially self sufficient." Do you agree? Why or why not?

References

Abuom, A. 2001. Women's Issues in Health and Education. In *Faith in Development: Partnership Between the World Bank and the Churches of Africa*, edited by D. Belshaw, R. Calderisi, and C. Sugden. Oxford, U.K.: Regnum Books International, 111–30.

Asante, R. K. O. 1998. "Sustainability of Church Hospitals in Developing Countries: A Search for Criteria for Success." Geneva: World Council of Churches.

Belshaw, D. 1999. "Poverty Reduction in Sub-Saharan Africa in the Context of the Decline of the Welfare State: The Strategic Role of the Church." *Transformation* 16, no. 4: 114–18.

———, R. Calderisi, and C. Sugden, eds. 2001. *Faith in Development: Partnership Between the World Bank and the Churches of Africa*. Oxford, U.K.: Regnum Books International.

Bragg, W. G. 1987. From Development to Transformation. In *The Church in Response to Human Need*, edited by V. Samuel and C. Sugden. Grand Rapids, MI: Eerdmans.

Gitari, D. M. 1999. "Development Opportunities and Challenges in Africa: Effects of International Debt Crisis on the Sub-Saharan Region." Processed.

van Hulten, M. H. M, ed. 1992. *Global Coalition for Africa: Documents on Development, Democracy and Debt*. The Hague: Netherlands Ministry of Foreign Affairs.

Goold, L., W. Ogara, and R. James. 1998. "Churches and Organisational Development: Churches and Organisational Development in Africa: Directions and Dilemmas for Northern NGOs." INTRAC Occasional Papers Series 20. Oxford, U.K.: International Training and Research Centre and CORAT-Africa.

Hodson, R. 1997. Elephant Loose in the Jungle: The World Bank and NGOs in Sri Lanka. In *NGOs, States and Donors: Too Close for Comfort?* edited by D. Hulme and M. Edwards. Basingstoke, U.K.: Save the Children Fund/ MacMillan Press.

Hulme, D., and M. Edwards, eds. 1997. *NGOs, States and Donors: Too Close for Comfort?* Basingstoke, U.K.: Save the Children Fund/MacMillan Press.

Kinoti, G. 1994. *Hope for Africa—and What the Christian Can Do*. Nairobi: African Institute for Scientific Research and Development.

Okaalet, P. 2001. Reducing Poverty by Combating AIDS. In *Faith in Development: Partnership Between the World Bank and the Churches of Africa*, edited by D. Belshaw, R. Calderisi, and C. Sugden. Oxford, U.K.: Regnum Books International, 131–41.

Samuel, V., and C. Sugden, eds. 1987. *The Church in Response to Human Need*. Grand Rapids, MI: Eerdmans.

TAABCO/CORAT. 1998. "The Role and Contribution of Development Projects (run by Churches and Christian NGOs) to the Development of

Civil Society: Report of a Study Done for the Swedish Mission Council and Swedish Pentecostal Churches." Nairobi: Interlife.

World Bank. 1989. *Sub-Saharan Africa: From Crisis to Sustainable Growth: A Long-Term Perspective Study.* Washington, D.C.: World Bank.

UNDP. 1996. "Progress Against Poverty: A Report on Activities since Copenhagen. UNDP Progress Report." New York: United Nations Development Program.

PART IV

Global Economic Stability, Growth, and the Environment

CHAPTER 10

THE INTERNATIONAL FINANCIAL SYSTEM:

THE GOOD, THE BAD, AND THE UGLY

Stephen L. S. Smith

In the United States, morning radio shows routinely update listeners on the day's trading on Asian and European stock markets. That the closing value of Hong Kong's Hang Seng Index is newsworthy is a telling sign of our era's deepening cross-national financial ties. The massive growth of international capital flows of all kinds in recent decades is a prominent feature of globalization, and the international financial system has drawn the spirited attention of globalization's critics and supporters alike.

At the time of this writing in late 2008, global attention is riveted on the U.S. financial crisis and recession. Has financial globalization deepened or ameliorated the crisis? This question is simply the most recent manifestation of a worldwide debate about the desirability of global financial liberalization, the pace of liberalization, and the means by which some poor nations have been induced to accept it. The behavior of key actors, especially the International Monetary Fund (IMF) and the World Bank, is particularly contentious.

This debate hits home both in rich countries fully integrated into global finance and in nations that have yet to fully integrate into the international financial system—poor and "emerging market" economies (such as China, India, Brazil, Mexico, and Thailand) whose weak financial systems make complete financial integration risky. Policy decisions must take many issues into account, and many of those issues are still unresolved. Is risk adequately regulated? Are floating exchange rates too volatile? How should debt default by national governments be handled? If these concerns are not addressed, the sixty-year global trend toward deeper financial liberalization may soon abate.

In what follows, I first analyze the policy environment within which international financial institutions and policy choices are shaped. There are fundamental economic constraints on what is possible. Financial integration brings real benefits but also real risks, and it is hard to design workable international institutions that mitigate that risk. This is the good and the bad. I then survey several prominent international financial issues, including regulatory and exchange rate questions, the role of international finance in the financial crisis of 2008, and sovereign default. The problem of the roles of the main international financial institutions (IFIs)—the IMF and the World Bank—is also considered.

I then consider Christian perspectives. Christian scholarship, to the extent that it discusses international finance at all, has focused on developing countries' problems. Christian views divide along ideological rather than theological lines. Those who find fault with market-based economies domestically tend also to object to global capital liberalization. In fact, in the turbulent globalization debate, Christians have been among the harshest critics of the IFIs and of global capital—painting them as "the ugly" in the global economy. I argue that much of this criticism, though not all of it, is misplaced. It ignores the extent of the gains of globalized finance, and it misdiagnoses its risks. In economics as in other aspects of life, ugliness is in the eyes of the beholder. The way forward in the international financial system is to move toward selective reforms in several areas, including sovereign bankruptcy mechanisms and more sophisticated, vigilant financial regulation, rather than repudiation of global capital markets.

Risks, Rewards, and Constraints in the International Financial System

There is in fact no international financial "system" in the sense of a unified set of institutions arising from comprehensive blueprints. Domestic (national) financial systems have central authorities that set financial and macroeconomic policies. The international financial system really is different: it has no central governance. The system today is best thought of as a motley collection of rules, practices, arrangements, and institutions that govern international financial transactions. Key actors are committed to capital openness and stability; the IMF and the World Bank handle certain pieces of governing the system. But outcomes are dictated by the willingness of sovereign states to collaborate—or not—on a case-by-case basis, inside and especially outside of the IFIs. Many important details are hammered out in crises rather than in cool contemplation.

Lack of institutionalized governance does not mean incoherence. Since the close of World War II, the international financial system has moved more or less continuously toward greater openness and liberalization. It now encompasses more types of financial flows, with fewer taxes and restrictions, than ever before.[1] Liberalization accelerated in the 1980s, driven by the shared vision of key nations (the United States, Japan, and the European Union) about the gains to be had from greater financial openness. The IMF also promoted capital mobility as a specific desirable aim, distinct from openness to foreign direct investment.

Front and center, international financial policy must navigate a severe tradeoff: the "trilemma" of global finance. There are three inherently desirable attributes of an international financial system: exchange rate stability, national autonomy/independence in monetary policy choices, and capital mobility. The trilemma is that it is impossible to achieve all three simultaneously. Only two out of three are feasible in any given period.

Theory and experience have borne out the trilemma at every turn. Countries that want exchange rate stability can achieve it by fiat if they are willing to impose tight controls on capital flows. To get capital mobility *and* exchange rate stability, they must dedicate monetary policy to stabilizing the exchange rate, giving up on using monetary policy for other aims (such as controlling interest rates). Countries that want full capital mobility along with a free hand to use monetary policy can achieve these aims—but they will need to live with fluctuations in their exchange rate. Countries can triangulate among these goals to a modest extent, achieving each in partial measure, but the tradeoffs are real.

Judgments about these tradeoffs often change over the course of development. The Bretton Woods system in the first decades after World War II emphasized exchange rate stability (members' currencies were fixed against the dollar) and limited capital mobility. But steady capital account liberalization and growth in international capital flows contributed to the abandonment of fixed exchange rates among industrial countries in the early 1970s. Present day poor countries tend to put a high value on exchange rate stability. The richer, emerging market economies have wanted to take advantage of capital mobility and have therefore faced hard choices about their exchange rate. In the past fifteen years they have moved toward flexible exchange rates, prompted at times by foreign exchange crises.

How important is capital mobility? Economic theory suggests that large gains can be had when residents in one nation buy or sell financial assets in other nations. Centuries of economic experience bear this out. Investment in capital abroad is an important way for individuals and nations to diversify their assets; this can yield substantially higher rates of return and reduce the variability of returns, compared to purely domestic investments. When capital can flow from regions where capital is abundant to regions where it is scarce, both regions are better off. Capital inflows can substantially mitigate shocks such as recessions or commodity price increases.[2]

Gains are not always obvious, so it helps to think about them as specifically as possible. Right now, for instance, most Chinese residents are allowed to invest only in Chinese bank accounts and stocks. That locks them out of the higher returns they could earn by investing globally, and it leaves them particularly vulnerable to domestic financial shocks. Being able to buy U.S. stocks would have protected Chinese savers from the 2008 collapse of Chinese stocks (which fell far more than U.S. stocks). U.S. retirees' pensions are paid from mutual funds, and these retirees benefit enormously from the fact that U.S. law lets *anyone*, worldwide, buy U.S. stocks. U.S. job growth is sustained by the fact that firms can borrow money from *any* bank, anywhere. When India experiences a recession because of a decline in global incomes, consumption there is not harmed as much as it would otherwise be, because currency depreciation makes foreign purchases of Indian goods and assets cheaper than before. Terms like "increased mean returns" and "lowered risk through diversification" sound like hopeless jargon to the nonspecialist, but they describe substantial benefits for real peoples' economic welfare.

But there are also risks. An economy that is integrated into the international financial system is potentially vulnerable to large, fast capital outflows.[3] Big sales of assets and big conversions of domestic funds into foreign currency, for quick removal from a country, can make asset prices and exchange rate values plummet. Large chunks of wealth can evaporate, and whole economies can be thrown into recession. The risk of big outflows is most associated with short-term or portfolio capital movements, though in a crisis all kinds of assets may be dumped.

This issue, typically triggered by a problem in a country's domestic financial system, can start with, say, a real estate bubble that bursts, causing stock prices to fall. Openness to international capital flows exacerbates this type of domestic financial system problem, as investors flee the economy. The problem can devastate a small country, which is what happened in Thailand in 1997 (the capital outflow also forced a currency devaluation, a problem discussed later).

Sometimes, problems originate in the international financial system. When a nation is open to international capital flows, a problem abroad may harm the domestic economy. In the Asian financial crisis of 1997–1998, this scenario took the form of "contagion." Crises in Thailand, Indonesia, and Malaysia made investors skittish about Hong Kong. Capital flowed out of Hong Kong. Speculators pressured monetary authorities to devalue the currency, even though Hong Kong's economy was sound.

One trend of the past sixty years is countries slowly learning to live with exchange rate instability as the price they must pay to reap the rewards of capital mobility and independent monetary policy. The substantial benefits of the latter outweigh the costs of the former—and those costs have turned out to be manageable.[4]

National policy choices are made in an environment remarkably free of formal institutional frameworks (with the notable exception of IMF conditionality cases, discussed later). No system of international rules governs investment flows, be they foreign direct investment or short-term portfolio capital. There is no formal system of exchange rate management, though G-8 treasury departments speak with one another regularly, and IMF members consent to various consultative and reporting requirements. No institution governs sovereign default or sovereign wealth funds. There is no international lender-of-last-resort, though in a pinch the IMF could pick up some of that role. This relatively open environment has allowed considerable experimentation with capital account policies and considerably different timetables for implementing financial liberalization. The downside is that solutions to pressing international financial problems emerge in an ad hoc and not-always-timely manner.

Even when binding international financial rules clearly would be helpful, they are difficult to attain. One reason is that rules-based systems constrain members' sovereignty and reduce policy flexibility. They would make it more difficult, for instance, to have competitive currency depreciation or to impose some kinds of temporary capital controls. Second, the costs of negotiating formal institutions are high. Free riders abound: everyone wants a stable global monetary system but would be delighted if other nations provided the resources to fund, say, a global lender-of-last-resort. A third sticking point is that it is particularly difficult to design forward-looking institutions flexible enough to deal with unanticipated future problems, especially when such design requires binding commitments of real resources. The experience of European Monetary Union (EMU) illustrates how difficult it can be to negotiate changes in international financial rules and institutions. EMU emerged from the European Monetary System initiated in 1979, but not until 2002 did it come to fruition with a real currency in citizen's hands, governed by a central bank. Given that a small number of states, with a high degree of shared interest in the project, took a quarter-century to negotiate and implement monetary union, in the next decades it is unlikely that large, powerful international financial institutions will be created. It is more realistic to expect progress in discrete steps on particular issues.

Prominent International Financial System Issues

There is a vast range of important financial system issues. What follows is a brief treatment of a few of these topics. In each of these cases, there is the potential for policy and institutional innovations.

Regulation, Regulatory Asymmetries, and the 2008 U.S. Financial Crisis

In September 2008, the United States experienced a dramatic credit crisis. Commercial lending and firms' access to working capital fell perilously. Hard on the heels of this crisis, stock values fell dramatically worldwide—quickly wiping out trillions of dollars of wealth. The United States and the EU entered a sharp recession. Is this unfortunate chain of events a symptom of weaknesses in the global financial system or of excessive global financial integration? Has the global financial system aggravated the problem or helped soften it?

The path toward an answer to these questions begins in the U.S. domestic financial system. A country's domestic financial sector is unlike any other sector of the economy: if it is not working well, nothing else works. A domestic financial sector provides essential short-term working capital and long-term credit for investments. Credit in an economy can be compared to oxygen for the body—without it, even otherwise healthy economies cannot long survive. Finance is an especially risky business. It is risky not simply because loans might go bad, leaving a firm strapped for funds, which is problematic enough. It is risky because depositors need short-term access to funds, while much lending must be long-term. Short-term demands for funds, rational or not, can therefore wipe out an otherwise sound firm.

For these reasons, national governments tightly regulate financial sectors to ensure the safety of deposits and the availability of credit. This regulation involves many standard features. Deposit insurance minimizes bank runs by calming depositors' anxieties about the safety of their funds. Strict loan standards and rigorous bank supervision guard against reckless lending, a moral hazard that emerges when banks can lend money that is protected by deposit insurance. Capital-adequacy rules and reserve requirements also help keep banks sound. And finally, a lender-of-last-resort, usually a country's central bank, is necessary to provide liquidity in credit crises. Western nations have a sorry history of bank failures and financial system crises stretching from the eighteenth to the twenty-first century, that proves how difficult financial regulation can be. Though regulation can never be perfect or complete, it must become more sophisticated as financial institutions evolve.

As global financial integration has increased, there has been enormous growth in non-bank financial institutions, in offshore banking (currency deposits held in other nations' banks), and in new financial instruments such as derivatives and securitized bonds. The latter are bonds constructed by bundling many small loans (such as mortgages) so that the interest paid on the bonds is derived from the individual interest payments on the component loans. It has been hard for national regulatory authorities to keep up with these innovations. And there are now several striking global regulatory asymmetries. Most of the standard regulations noted above are in place only domestically. Banks holding offshore deposits, for instance, are not required to hold reserves on those accounts. International bank branches and subsidiaries that operate abroad escape some home-country regulation and fit only uneasily under host-nation financial regulation.[5]

All these factors suggest a real risk: in a financial crisis, national central banks and treasury departments may not coordinate their actions sufficiently with counterparts in other nations. Disagreement about fundamentals, free rider problems when costly interventions might be needed, disputes about who should be the lender-of-last-resort, accidental breakdowns in communication—any or all of these might allow a regional financial crisis to become a global crisis.

The U.S. credit crisis of 2008 emerged from an unusual confluence of long-term and short-term factors. After technology stock prices crashed in 2001, the Federal Reserve lowered interest rates to ward off recession. This dovetailed with a substantial loosening of mortgage lending standards. Sub-prime lending ballooned, encouraged in part by government guarantees of mortgage-backed securities issued by Fannie Mae and Freddie Mac, and a housing price bubble emerged.

New products, such as credit default swaps (CDS), grew rapidly. CDSs gave financial firms a way to insure against mortgage defaults, but they were poorly understood, hard to model, and, because they were entirely new, unregulated. Once home prices started to decline, rising numbers of mortgage defaults caused the value of mortgage-backed securities to plummet. The balance sheets of many leading financial institutions toppled toward insolvency.

The Federal Reserve can be credited with following a wise course of slowly trying to unwind banks' bad debts, beginning with several high-profile bank bailouts in 2007. But the pace of failures accelerated in September 2008, resulting in a full-blown credit freeze. Once that crisis emerged, the Federal Reserve and Treasury were fully justified in seeking emergency powers and funding for supplying credit, though the details of their plans and subsequent changes to them are likely to be enduringly controversial.

The list of culprits is long and varied: executives at Fannie Mae and Freddy Mac; legislators who defended Fannie Mae and Freddy Mac; former Federal Reserve Chair Alan Greenspan, who resisted regulating new financial products; supporters of softened mortgage lending standards in the 1990s; ratings agencies that understated the risk of mortgage-backed securities; the Securities and Exchange Commission that, in 2007, removed the "uptick rule" so that short-selling stocks became easier; homeowners and sub-prime lenders who signed loans that were fraudulent on both sides. All these and many others share the blame.

The international financial system is strikingly absent from any realistic accounting of the sources of the U.S. financial crisis. The crisis is not intrinsically a global financial problem. Its consequences have been global, to be sure, in the European credit crisis that mirrors that in the United States and in the stock market losses and recession that are global in scope. But the crisis itself was triggered by a cluster of banal domestic regulatory deficiencies—and would have occurred even if the

United States were financially detached from the rest of the world.[6] History is full of examples of domestic financial system problems that generated financial crises entirely on their own, with no prompting from the international system. Domestic bubbles, manias, and regulatory mistakes are classic causes of credit crunches and recessions. So far, the U.S. experience very much fits this mold.

Furthermore, central banks and treasury departments around the world exhibited a high degree of cooperation and collaboration at the height of the crisis. The U.S. Treasury worked intensely with counterparts in Britain, France, and Germany. The Federal Reserve and the European Central Bank orchestrated their first jointly decided, simultaneous cut in discount rates—a genuinely historic event. There was some drama in Europe when Ireland increased its deposit insurance coverage ahead of similar moves by the rest of the region. This could have been destabilizing—risky even for sound banks elsewhere—if depositors had flocked to the perceived extra safety of Irish banks. However, other European nations raised their deposit insurance limits rapidly enough to avoid a problem. In sum, fears that a lack of global policy coordination could itself become a problem in a crisis were not borne out in this case.

Several policy implications for the international financial system are already apparent. First, it is essential that the regulatory fixes ultimately adopted do not fundamentally inhibit global capital flows.[7] There is no evidence that the international financial system contributed to the recession; in fact, access to funds from abroad has been helpful. Second, it is also clear that the United States has been helped by its large size, its continued economic strength relative to other nations, and by the fact that the Fed has not had to defend a fixed-dollar exchange rate. Thus the credit crunch and recession have not triggered massive capital outflows and crisis-exacerbating losses of foreign exchange reserves. Finally, the crisis underscored the importance of consultative arrangements between national central banks and treasury departments. Forums such as the new U.S.-China Strategic Economic Dialogue have renewed importance. Their regular meetings build trust, mutual knowledge, and important personal relationships among key ministers of state. However, the high level of cooperation achieved in 2008 cannot be taken for granted.

Exchange Rate Instability

The value of the U.S. dollar has been quite unstable in recent years. Against the Japanese yen, for instance, between 1999 and 2008 the dollar rose more than 30 percent, fell more than 30 percent, rose again by more than 20 percent, then fell by about 20 percent. Until the late twentieth century, most countries feared this degree of currency volatility and went to great lengths to stabilize currency values against gold, silver, or another currency. However, this too can be problematic.

Instability with Fixed Exchange Rates. Many poor countries fix their currencies against a major international currency. Their goal is to facilitate trade by stabilizing the price of foreign exchange. These countries also hope to fight inflation by "anchoring" their domestic price level with a fixed price link to the rest of the world.

The chronic shortcoming of a fixed exchange rate is that success hinges on having sufficient foreign currency reserves. Sustained capital outflows or trade deficits can drain a central bank's reserves and prompt a balance-of-payments crisis. At that point, the only options are to devalue, borrow additional foreign exchange reserves, severely contract domestic credit and raise interest rates, impose capital controls—or a little of all these. Soberingly, reserve losses can be triggered by almost anything, even mere rumors that the central bank is losing reserves. For this reason, virtually every country with a fixed exchange rate has a history of crises, many of them severe. When devaluations come, they tend to be big—say, 50 percent—and in the midst of economic contractions.

In recent years, balance-of-payments crises have taken place mostly in emerging market economies. The 1997 Asian financial crisis resulted from a series of classic foreign exchange crises. Thailand's real estate bubble burst, its stock market fell, its banks became less solvent, and suddenly Thai and foreign investors felt it prudent to take funds out of the country. Thus, in the presence of a fixed exchange rate, the domestic financial system problem became a foreign exchange crisis, and large devaluation and IMF-supervised borrowing ensued. Contagion quickly spread the problem as investors anticipated the same problems elsewhere and nervously withdrew funds from low-risk countries.

To some extent, then, the Asian crisis was related to unwise domestic financial sector regulation. But it is essential to recognize that the crisis was not inherently an emerging market phenomenon. This kind of crisis will occur in any fixed exchange rate context when a domestic financial system problem triggers large foreign exchange reserve losses. This is exactly what happened in Europe in 1991–1992 when the U.K. and Sweden were forced to exit the European Monetary System. In effect, they devalued against the deutsche mark.

Several important lessons stand out for countries that want to fix exchange rates. Short-term capital flows play a key role in precipitating balance-of-payments crises. Foreign portfolio investment, especially in mutual funds, is particularly mobile. Consequently, a strong case can be made for restrictions on short-term capital flows. Waiting periods or higher taxes on short-term funds repatriation may be wise. Many economists, including the notable proponent of globalization, Jagdish Bhagwati (2004), support such controls as a means of softening the effects of financial and exchange rate crises.

Looking at the Asian crisis in hindsight, the combination of fixed exchange rates and capital mobility appears unwise. Emerging market economies rightly judged capital mobility to be attractive. Had exchange rates been free to adjust to market values, there would have been less fallout from the initial domestic financial system problems. Currencies would have depreciated, to be sure, but events would have played out without severe regional contagion or heavy borrowing from the IMF. The floating exchange rates in place since the crisis have served countries well. It is telling that there have been no further crises. If emerging economies move more quickly from fixed to floating exchange rates in the future, a valuable lesson will have been learned.[8]

Instability with Flexible Exchange Rates. The developed economies have lived with floating exchange rates since the 1970s. It is now evident that trade and investment can prosper even in a situation of substantial daily and long-term exchange rate volatility, and there are macroeconomic advantages to letting exchange rates fluctuate. Foreign exchange risk in commercial transactions can be hedged (that is, insured against) using the forward market. Arbitrage in foreign exchange derivative products helps firms spread risk and craft portfolio holdings with optimal exposure to such risk relative to domestic assets. Successive rounds of hedging related to any single underlying "real" transaction help explain why the overall value of foreign exchange transactions is so high compared to the value of trade flows themselves.

At the same time, the changes in currency values allowed by floating rates help countries adjust to external shocks. They are automatic stabilizers. Basically, a currency appreciation or depreciation can offset an aggregate demand shock's effects on income. Currency changes also help correct macroeconomic imbalances, reining in large trade deficits or surpluses.

In principle, countries could use fiscal and monetary policies to engineer large exchange rate swings to benefit themselves at other nations' expense. Though countries have on occasion nudged their currencies toward depreciation, aggressive competitive depreciations have not materialized. In part, this is because foreign exchange markets are so large, and capital flows so liberalized, that it would be hard for a single central bank to push things in one direction. More important, however, the treasury departments and central banks of the G-8 countries have a long record of mutual consultation and cooperation. Their meetings are not window dressing. They have resulted in substantive, if informal, understandings about monetary policy. This kind of informal governance structure can result in coordinated action to address severe currency imbalances when they occur.

Systemic risks remain. There is no overarching agreement about how much flexibility will be allowed or when intervention should occur and by whom, so there will always be some chance that the system will dissolve into a morass of competitive depreciations. And exchange rates—which are financial assets whose value is set every moment on markets—are subject to overshooting in response to changes in the real economy and possibly to bubbles. Thus, the question of working out some kind of global, fixed exchange rate system, or system of allowable "bands" on exchange rate movements, will probably never go away. But so far, the large political capital necessary to work this out and the inherent loss in economic sovereignty have made such proposals unattractive.

Sovereign Defaults

Sovereign defaults—when a government is unable or unwilling to repay its debts to a foreign creditor—have occurred regularly for more than two centuries. In the early 1800s, for instance, several U.S. states were notorious for defaulting on loans from Europe. In the debt crisis of the 1980s, many Latin American countries defaulted on loans from private commercial banks. In the 1990s, many of the world's poorest nations (concentrated in sub-Saharan Africa) defaulted on loans from the IMF, the World Bank, and other official international sources.

There is no global mechanism to govern sovereign defaults. Corporate or household default in the domestic economy is tightly regulated in commercial law, with cases adjudicated by third-party judges. Sovereign defaults are handled in an ad hoc manner, because there is no easy way for a creditor to force a national government to pay up, nor is there collateral that the creditor can seize.

The debt crisis of the 1980s was resolved only when the threat to U.S. commercial banks, and thus to the stability of the U.S. financial system, proved dire enough to stir the U.S. Treasury to seek a solution. Treasury Secretary Nicholas Brady's 1989 plan offered a creative set of inducements (including U.S.-backed, debt-replacing Brady bonds) to persuade private commercial banks to write off a substantial portion of their outstanding loans *and* to convince nations to pay off their remaining debt. Treasury action was crucial in overcoming the free rider problem among commercial banks, each of which would have preferred that *other* banks write off loans.

The debt crisis of the 1990s played out differently. Poor country defaults on debt owed to the IMF and the World Bank threatened neither domestic nor global financial stability. The Jubilee 2000 Debt Forgiveness campaign of the late 1990s deserves credit for building public sentiment in favor of a solution and for pushing the IMF and the World Bank toward debt reduction sooner than would have otherwise been the case.

But forgiving these debts was costly to the rich country governments that fund the World Bank and the IMF. Forgiveness meant that World Bank and IMF funds would not be replenished, imperiling future lending and requiring hard cash to make up the difference. The World Bank and IMF's Multilateral Debt Reduction Initiative features slow implementation keyed to specific policy and poverty-reduction conditions. As of 2007, the plan had yielded approximately $100 billion in debt reduction. Annual debt payments per person have fallen from approximately $9 to $6 in the thirty-one countries that have received debt reduction so far.[9]

Ann Pettifor (2000), one of the architects of the Jubilee campaign, has written eloquently that it is fundamentally unjust for creditors such as the World Bank and the IMF to sit as bankruptcy judges over their debtors. I concur. However, in the absence of an international bankruptcy regime there is no immediate alternative. The Jubilee proposal advocates unconditional debt forgiveness, even for countries such as Sudan, where such forgiveness would buttress rogue regimes. This is unrealistic, given the size of the financial flows at stake. Unconditional debt relief that does not encourage steps to reduce the likelihood of future debt problems arguably falls short in Christian ethical terms as well.[10]

It is only a matter of time before sovereign default problems surface again in the global economy. In the interim, it would be wise to devise proper mechanisms to handle them. One plan, promoted by the IMF, would use the IMF as an international bankruptcy judge. Another plan, promoted by the U.S. Treasury, would require loan contracts to include covenants that spell out the framework for default negotiations.[11] Implementing some such mechanism should be a serious focus of global negotiation.

The Roles of the IMF and the World Bank

In principle the IMF and the World Bank play distinct roles. The IMF lends for short-term balance-of-payments problems. IMF programs, typically three years or shorter, emphasize regaining macroeconomic stability. The World Bank lends long-term, supporting specific development projects and a country's general development budget. In practice, poor country circumstances of the past thirty years have thrown the two institutions together. They are, bar none, the most controversial lightning rods for critics of the global financial system.

IMF lending has always carried stiff conditions. By definition, a country experiencing balance-of-payments difficulties needs some kind of policy adjustment. Typical policy conditions involve money growth targets, government spending and budget deficit targets, inflation targets, and specific financial sector practices relating to the balance-of-payments. A key change occurred at the World Bank in the early 1980s when it too started putting policy conditions on loans. Concerned that countries' policy choices were undoing the benefits of project and program lending, the Bank made development lending conditional on market-oriented policy reform. These structural adjustment programs (SAPs) aimed to rejuvenate economic growth. In a famous paper, John Williamson (1990) dubbed the combination of IMF and World Bank policy recommendations the "Washington Consensus."

During the 1980s, much of the developing world experienced slow growth at best and crisis at worst. The effects of the commodity price bust in the early 1980s rippled through the global economy. Most poor countries at the time had highly statist economic policy orientations, to an extent that casual Western observers had trouble comprehending. Thus, countries shared many common features that contributed to financial distress. The state owned many industries. Tariffs were layered on top of quotas on top of foreign exchange license requirements to protect domestic industries. State-dominated, domestic financial sectors used directed credit and interest rate controls to subsidize favored industries. The inflation tax was commonly used to cover the inevitable budget deficit that could not be financed in domestic financial markets. Countries often negotiated IMF and World Bank programs together, with the former typically a prerequisite for the latter.

Assessing the consequences of IMF and World Bank conditionality has spawned a huge literature, popular and academic, that often sheds more heat than light on matters. Did IMF and the World Bank conditions promote raw capitalism and "market fundamentalism"? Critics make this charge, but the reality is much more prosaic. In the context of statist economic systems, substantial liberalization will indeed seem liberal. However, the specific policy changes the IFIs mandated were such things as cutting average tariffs from 50 to 10 percent, or cutting a government budget deficit from 10 to 5 percent of GDP (to lower inflation), or cutting (non-means tested) urban food subsidies. These cannot fairly be called brutal free-market measures. Macroeconomic stability and a more liberalized economy are essential prerequisites for growth and sustained poverty reduction. Therefore, perhaps surprisingly, the IMF and the World Bank are on the ethical high ground regarding many specific policy conditions, which were and are pro-poor.[12]

This is not to say that conditionality worked well. In fact, it accomplished little. First and foremost, it ran straight into strong political forces within poor countries. Blanket statism has little going for it as an economic policy, but it is an effective way for regimes to secure power with patronage and rent. As Clapham (1996) argues, in asking sub-Saharan African states to reform economically, the IFIs were in effect asking regimes to undercut the basis of their own authority and legitimacy. Governments were able to resist conditions quite effectively, in part by making shows of partial compliance. It was and remains hard for the World Bank or the IMF to cut off countries' loans for non-compliance. "*Ex post*" policy conditionality that made aid contingent on actual policy reform or on specific welfare achievements might have worked better than the *ex ante* conditions the World Bank typically employed.[13]

But policy conditionality may have worked fairly well in the few countries that enthusiastically embraced structural reform. Mozambique, Uganda, and Tanzania are usually considered the World Bank's star pupils in Africa. Each of these nations experienced substantial economic growth between 1996 and 2006, after slow or negative growth over the reform years 1986 to 1996. In countries as poor as these, virtually any kind of growth helps the poor.[14]

The Bank continues to set conditions on the poorest countries. Compliance is necessary for participation in debt forgiveness programs. But thinking at the Bank has evolved considerably since the 1980s. It now favors slower reforms, with more attention to the complementary reforms necessary to make large reforms work.[15] It emphasizes the importance of institutional development, the state's capacity to regulate and govern economic policy coherently, honestly, and transparently.[16]

Looking ahead, to make aid more effective in the poorest countries the World Bank may need to apply further teeth on aid conditions and shift the focus of conditions toward governance criteria (even as it continues to emphasize sound policies).[17] Institutional changes will be necessary at the World Bank to empower it to direct aid toward well-governed countries with wise policies and away from countries that exhibit neither. This change may also be a key that unlocks sustained, higher aid flows from wealthy countries to the poorest.

IMF lending and conditionality present different issues. Critics charge that the IMF rigidly pursues complete capital account liberalization and rejects capital controls.[18] Critics also complain that the IMF tries to micromanage the financial systems of countries that are, in fact, reasonably competent in domestic financial regulation.[19] Both criticisms have hit home, so the IMF will likely be more flexible in future crises—at least with relatively wealthy emerging economies. Malaysia's robust economic growth in the decade after the Asian crisis suggests that capital controls and foregoing IMF funds can work well, at least in some cases.[20]

Academic studies of the future of the IMF reveal a consensus along several lines. First, there is general agreement that the IMF should act more quickly in crises. There have been no major developing-country financial crises since Argentina in 2001–2002, but there surely will be in the future. Shocks, policy mismanagement, and the difficulty of sequencing capital account and exchange rate reforms as poor economies grow guarantee future crises. Second, there is a consensus that the IMF should have stronger lender-of-last-resort capabilities. This would be especially helpful in large crises that spawn contagion.[21]

Finally, 2008 found the IMF on the verge of a major change in the distribution of Executive Board voting rights. These rights are linked to countries' GDP shares and are revised periodically to account for growth. China, India, and other developing countries are poised to make substantial gains. The U.S. share will stay roughly the same, while the European share falls. These welcome changes will improve the IMF's governance and raise its international legitimacy.[22]

Christian Perspectives

When Christian scholarship discusses international financial issues at all, it generally focuses on problems related to developing countries. The debt crisis of the 1990s, the Jubilee Debt Forgiveness movement, World Bank and IMF conditionality—these have attracted Christians' attention and comment. Surprisingly, not much of this has come from Christian economists.

Christian views divide along ideological rather than theological lines. Those who object to market-based economies domestically tend to be critical about global capital liberalization, too. In Christians' published writings on international economic issues, critics far outnumber supporters of economic globalization, and the critiques are generally from the left.[23]

Christian critics of economic liberalization have voiced some of the harshest complaints about the IFIs, conditionality, and the global economy in general. To take two straightforward examples among many, historically Anabaptist *Sojourners Magazine* regularly publishes critical takes on debt and the IFIs (including many articles written by Catholic authors).[24] Mainline Protestant denominations, such as the United Church of Christ, sharply denounce international finance and the Washington Consensus.[25] These critics argue that liberal trade and financial policies hurt the poor; that structural adjustment policies have hurt the poor for more than two decades; that unconditional debt relief is essential for poverty reduction in poor countries; and that poor countries are powerless to stop the IMF and the World Bank from opening their economies to transnational corporations.[26]

While there are indeed issues in the global economy that should be addressed, the generalizations made by economically leftist Christians miss the mark in many ways. They overstate the extent to which poor country poverty is influenced by external forces in the global economy. These critics rarely analyze the impact of developing countries' own policy choices or of "poverty traps" that are domestically rooted. Everything is blamed on the international system. For example, Herman (2007, 20) writes, "Repeated cycles of destructive indebtedness, are symptomatic of deeper injustices in the global economy," as if nothing within a poor country's sphere of policy autonomy can make a difference for good.

This literature also chronically ignores the welfare gains to the poor of economic growth and macroeconomic stabilization.[27] If those gains are off the table, it is no wonder global financial integration seems harmful. As Collier succinctly puts it, "Growth is not a cure-all, but the lack of growth is a kill-all." Collier's trenchant critique of leftist NGOs—"Many of them do not want to believe that for the majority of the developing world global capitalism is working"—is a fair critique of much Christian writing as well.[28]

From a Reformed Protestant view, Bob Goudzwaard's 1999 Kuyper Lectures (published in 2001) represent a substantive attempt to deal with international finance in both theological and economic terms. He too reaches for a radical framework to analyze global finance. The financial system today, he writes, is inverted. Speculative flows dominate real flows to the point where "the financial economy is overtaking and determining the development of the real economy . . . financial expectations do more to influence the real economy than the other way around" (24). He sketches a vision of human communities "hypnotized" by capitalism (27) and governments subject to the "whims of global capital, as if a new 'big brother' is watching them" (26). In this view, countries caught in financial crises are forced to be servants of speculators in the international capitalist system, and hunger for cheap capital and half-percentage point savings on mortgage rates encourages economic behavior so individualistic that it threatens communities.

Goudzwaard and other writers from the left are too eager to paint global finance as a villain and misdiagnose the nature and extent of its risks. Rather than viewing countries as "servants of capital," it is more accurate to understand countries as feeling their way toward optimal exchange rate and financial sector policies on a policy tightrope where mistakes are painful but not irremediable. Rather than viewing countries as selling their souls for the pottage of low interest rates, it is more accurate to think of properly regulated financial integration as strengthening communities by giving them access to more capital for all kinds of important investments while lowering overall risk.

As a fellow Christian economist, I affirm Goudzwaard's concern that nations and human communities not become "hypnotized" into serving an ideology rather than God. I affirm his conviction that the economy must first satisfy legitimate human needs, not speculators' whims. But when countries strive to attain the benefits of financial integration, while avoiding its costs, they are in effect striving to be faithful stewards of the national household. This is entirely reasonable in Christian ethical terms. As long as material well-being is a legitimate end and well-managed cooperative global finance can promote prosperity, it is hard to make a principial Christian ethical case against it.

Conclusion

International financial integration has real benefits and real risks. Christian economists would do well to study them as economists, of course, but also as Christians—that is, in a way that connects international financial issues with fundamental Christian normative concerns for justice, material well-being, and stewardship.

Scripture gives little specific guidance about international financial issues. Clearly, the Bible does not address questions about when or if a country should adopt a floating exchange rate or whether a global institution like the IMF should handle sovereign defaults. This does not mean that these issues should not matter to Christians. But it does mean that Christian scholars and citizens are free to think about financial system issues in prudential terms based on what the options might mean in terms of those important normative ends (justice, material well-being, and stewardship). What mix of institutions will yield the greatest gains and best mitigate risks? Christians and the church will be well served if Christian economists address these matters more extensively and forthrightly than they have up to this point.

When Christian economists consider these questions, I expect we will find that the best way forward in the international financial system is to not back off from fundamental capital mobility, but to complement it with selective reform in several areas. These might include sovereign bankruptcy mechanisms, strengthened international consultative mechanisms, more sophisticated and vigilant domestic financial regulations, plus related refinements in international capital regulations. Because international financial policies are of pressing relevance for economic progress in small, poor countries, Christian economists should be at the front of the line in thinking about domestic financial system development and the mixture of liberalization, global integration, wise regulation of capital flows, and aid that will best promote economic growth in these cases.

Questions for Review

1. What complaints are raised against financial globalization? How does the author respond to those complaints? Do you agree with the author? Why, or why not?

2. Explain the "trilemma" of global finance and the inherent problems this creates for developing economies.

3. To what does the author attribute the cause(s) of the U.S. financial crisis of 2008? Do you agree that it was ultimately

caused by internal (domestic) forces, not the United States' connection to the international financial system? Please explain.

4. In 2008 China, Japan, Korea, and several other regional states established an organization (dubbed the "Asian Monetary Fund") that would provide emergency loans to Asian countries experiencing financial crises. Is this a good idea? Why, or why not?

5. If Christians are concerned about the growth of individualistic behavior on markets and in Western society, what are the best means to promote a more biblical view of holistic, healthy behavior? What emphasis should the church place on financial institutions and issues, relative to other kinds of issues (spiritual, ethical, social, legal) it could address?

Notes

[1] The late nineteenth century was also a period of considerable international financial globalization, though the present period exceeds it in scope and depth.

[2] Evidence on these points is provided in Obstfeld (1998) and Henry (2007).

[3] Fast capital inflows are also problematic, but beyond the scope of this paper.

[4] The actual pattern of capital flows sometimes surprises. In the past decade, capital has flowed into the United States, though as the world's most capital-abundant country, capital outflows might have been expected. The inflow pays for the U.S. trade deficit, and it reflects both low U.S. savings (Summers 2004) and that the U.S. is a safe, profitable haven for capital owned elsewhere (Poole 2001).

[5] One exception to the generalization in this paragraph is the Bank for International Settlements, an international organization that sets bank reporting and capital adequacy standards for members. The points in this paragraph are covered in many textbooks. See, for example, Krugman and Obstfeld (2006).

[6] The recession that began in 2008 is different from other recent recessions in that it was triggered by an asset price bubble and credit crunch; but it is not unprecedented. Because it involves a general loss of wealth, it is likely to have greater widespread effects and be deeper than is typical. But it is a garden-variety financial crisis, historically speaking. It can be fought by expanding credit, by the Federal Reserve continuing to act as lender-of-last-resort, and by fiscal stimulus. The essential issue is to avoid large policy mistakes going forward.

[7] These fixes almost certainly will consist of some mix of improved reporting requirements on holdings and risks of new financial products; tighter lending standards; and refinements in mortgage default rules.

[8] The other option is to move to some kind of "super fix" that pegs the currency irrevocably so that balance-of-payments crises cannot recur. Dollarization (using the U.S. dollar as a national currency) is one way to achieve this and may be attractive to small countries.

[9] IDA/IMF (2007).

[10] See Smith (2000).

[11] See Fisher (2003) and Adams (2005) for brief discussions.

[12] Economic liberalization does not prevent countries from implementing means-tested social welfare and poverty-reduction programs. It also does not preclude carefully crafted state assistance to selected industries. These should be easier to implement in stable, growing economies.

[13] Collier (2007) reviews the difficult politics of SAPs and the pros and cons of *ex post* vs. *ex ante* conditionality.

[14] Studies that attempt to estimate the net effect of actual policy reforms and compare them with relevant counterfactuals are rare. Sahn, Dorosh, and Younger (1997) found that structural adjustment brought modest gains to the poor, on net. See also Mosley, Harrigan, and Toye (1991, 1995).

[15] For instance, construction of market infrastructure along with trade liberalization so that trade literally can grow.

[16] Much of this is detailed in a remarkably candid World Bank volume (Zagha 2005), reviewed by Rodrik (2006).

[17] Collier (2007), for instance, champions *ex ante* governance conditionality.

[18] As in Bhagwati (2004), noted above.

[19] This is the gist of Feldstein (1998). See also Feldstein (2003).

[20] Other criticisms of the IMF are less compelling. Stiglitz (2002) argues that sharp economic contractions could have been avoided if the IMF and domestic monetary authorities had expanded bank credit during the crises. Rogoff (2003) offers a riposte. When financial system crises occur (originating domestically or internationally), some kinds of painful adjustments usually must be made, and the sooner the better.

[21] Examples of this literature are Caballero (2003, 31–38), Fisher (2003), Meltzer (2000), and Truman (2006).

[22] The United States is officially on record as supporting these changes. See Adams (2005).

[23] For a Catholic perspective generally supportive of global finance, see Cleveland (2001 et al.).

[24] See, for example, Herman (2007).

[25] United Church of Christ (2003).

[26] Each of these assertions is drawn from Herman (2007).

[27] See Levin and Smith (2005) for one Christian ethical perspective on macroeconomic stability issues.

[28] Quotes are from Collier (2007, 190).

References

Adams, Timothy D. 2005. "The U.S. View on IMF Reform." Speech presented at the Conference on IMF Reform. Washington, D.C.: Institute for International Economics (September 23).

Bhagwati, Jagdish. 2004. *In Defense of Globalization.* New York, NY: Oxford University Press.

Caballero, Ricardo J. 2003. "The Future of the IMF." *American Economic Review* 93, no. 2 (May).

Clapham, Christopher. 1996. *Africa and the International System: The Politics of State Survival.* Cambridge, NY: Cambridge University Press.

Cleveland, Paul, Gregory M. A. Gronbacher, Gary Quinlivan, and Michel Therrien. 2001. *A Catholic Response to Globalization: Applications of Catholic Social Teaching.* Grand Rapids, MI: Center for Economic Personalism.

Collier, Paul. 2007. *The Bottom Billion.* New York, NY: Oxford University Press.

Feldstein, Martin. 1998. "Refocusing the IMF." *Foreign Affairs* (March/April).

————, ed. 2003. *Economic and Financial Crises in Emerging Market Economies.* Chicago: University of Chicago Press for the National Bureau of Economic Research.

Fisher, Stanley. 2003. "Globalization and Its Challenges." Richard T. Ely Lecture. *American Economic Review* 93, no. 2 (May).

Goudzwaard, Bob. 2001. *Globalization and the Kingdom of God.* Grand Rapids, MI: Baker and Washington, D.C.: Center for Public Justice.

Henry, Peter Blair. 2007. "Capital Account Liberalization: Theory, Evidence and Speculation." *Journal of Economic Literature* XLV (December), 887–935.

Herman, Christina Cobourn. 2007. "Jubilee: A Sabbath from Suffering." *Sojourners Magazine* 36, no. 8 (August).

International Development Association and International Monetary Fund. 2007. "Heavily Indebted Poor Countries (HIPC) Initiative and Multilateral Debt Relief Initiative (MDRI)—Status of Implementation" (September). View at http://siteresources.worldbank.org/INTDEBTDEPT/ProgressReports/21656521/HIPCProgressReport20070927.pdf.

Krugman, Paul R., and Maurice Obstfeld. 2006. *International Economics: Theory and Policy,* 7th ed. Boston, MA: Addison-Wesley.

Levin, Andrew, and Stephen L. S. Smith. 2005. Macroeconomic Stability and Poverty Reduction. In *Attacking Poverty in the Developing World,* edited by Judith M. Dean, Julie A. Schaffner, and Stephen L. S. Smith. Waynesboro, GA: Authentic.

Meltzer, Allan H. 2000. "Report of the International Financial Institution Advisory Commission." Washington, D. C.: U.S. Government Printing Office.

Mosley, Paul, Jane Harrigan, and John Toye. 1991. *Aid and Power: The World Bank and Policy-Based Lending in the 1980s,* 1st ed., 2 vols. London: Routledge (2nd ed. 1995).

Obstfeld, Maurice. 1998. "The Global Capital Market: Benefactor or Menace?" *Journal of Economic Perspectives* 12, no. 4: 9–30.

Pettifor, Ann. 2000. "Debt Cancellation, Lender Responsibility and Poor Country Empowerment." *Review of African Political Economy* 27, no. 83 (March), 138–44.

Poole, William. 2001. "Does the United States Have a Current Account Deficit Disorder?" Remarks before the Business and Community Leaders Luncheon, The Lannom Center, Dyersburg, TN (April 10).

Rodrik, Dani. 2006. "Goodbye Washington Consensus, Hello Washington Confusion? A Review of the World Bank's *Economic Growth in the 1990s: Learning from a Decade of Reform.*" *Journal of Economic Literature* XLIV, no. 4 (December), 973–87.

Rogoff, Kenneth. 2003. "The IMF Strikes Back." *Foreign Policy,* no. 134 (January/February).

Sahn, David E., Paul A. Dorosh, and Stephen D. Younger. 1997. *Structural Adjustment Reconsidered: Economic Policy and Poverty in Africa*. Cambridge, U.K.: Cambridge University Press.

Smith, Stephen L. S. 2000. "Christian Ethics and the Forgiveness of Third World Debt." *Faith and Economics*, no. 35 (Spring), 8–12.

Stiglitz, Joseph E. 2002. *Globalization and Its Discontents*. New York: W. W. Norton.

Summers, Lawrence. 2004. "America Overdrawn." *Foreign Policy* (March/April).

Truman, Edwin M., ed. 2006. *Reforming the IMF for the Twenty-First Century*. Washington, D.C.: Institute for International Economics.

United Church of Christ. 2003. "A Faithful Response: Calling for a More Just, Humane Direction for Economic Globalization." Statement adopted by the 24th General Synod of the United Church of Christ. Minneapolis, MN (July). Submitted by Justice and Witness Ministries, a Covenanted Ministry of the United Church of Christ.

Williamson, John. 1990. What Washington Means by Policy Reform. In *Latin American Adjustment: How Much Has Happened?* edited by John Williamson. Washington, D.C.: Institute for International Economics.

Zagha, Roberto, ed. 2005. *Economic Growth in the 1990s: Learning From a Decade of Reform*. Washington, D.C.: World Bank.

CHAPTER 11

CHRISTIAN VALUES AND THE CASE AGAINST FINANCIAL GLOBALIZATION

John P. Tiemstra

The objections that many Christians voice about globalization have their basis in a number of social-ethical norms that are held by many both inside and outside the Christian faith. (See for example, the statements of the World Alliance of Reformed Churches 2004; the Reformed Church in America 2005; and the United Church of Christ 2003. See also Bob Goudzwaard's 2001 Kuyper lectures.) There is great concern that globalization does not benefit all populations worldwide, but that it particularly favors economic elites, especially within the richer countries. The special concerns Christians have for the welfare of the poor—and for the prominence that the Bible gives to this issue—make globalization a very important issue for many Christians and justify engaging the resources of the church in the struggle against it.

Other values are also at stake. There is a great concern that the pattern of economic development that results from globalization will turn out to be ecologically unsustainable. The Christian meaning given to the natural world as God's good creation makes ecological integrity a religious issue. Economic development calls for specialization in the production process and for the markets for particular goods to be as broad as possible. This leads to production technologies that concentrate particular organisms and particular waste materials at particular locations, undercutting healthy ecological diversity and hence sustainability. It also leads to large expenditures of energy to bring products and services to remote markets, which contributes to dependence on unsustainable use of fossil fuels.

As a missionary religion with universal aspirations, Christianity depends on its ability to appeal to the consciences of people from all nations. Therefore, it is bound to respect cultural diversity and value freedom of conscience. Globalization is problematical when countries that are historically Christian and have a colonizing past demand conformity to their own cultural practices as a condition of full participation in the international community. This happens when the United States and Europe demand acceptance of particularly Western business practices and regulations as a condition of admission to global economic institutions.

In this chapter I argue that globalization can be made to serve the values of prosperity, sustainability, and diversity if (relatively) free trade in goods markets is coupled with restrictions on the freedom of movement of financial capital. In so doing, the danger of global financial crises is greatly reduced.

Analysis of Globalization

In the view of the critics, what is it about globalization that causes these problems? In a word, competition. The globalization of markets means that there are more participants on both the buying and the selling side. This means that competition is more intense, and there is competitive pressure on businesses to focus all their energy on increasing economic efficiency and reducing costs, so they can make enough profit to survive. Competition in both product and factor markets means that businesses must keep prices low and so must seek the lowest cost inputs worldwide. Labor-intensive activities migrate to low-wage countries, and wages elsewhere fall. Businesses and their home-country government pressure host countries that compete for investment and jobs to relax labor and environmental regulations, keeping private costs low. Harmonizing regulations worldwide levels the playing field for businesses and enhances the mobility of capital. Thus, intensified competition in product markets leads to all the problems identified with globalization: losses in standard of living realized by ordinary working folk, a race to the bottom in environmental standards, and declining national independence in setting regulatory policies and establishing culturally appropriate business practices.

The defenders of globalization among mainstream economists and Christians in the global north do not accept this analysis. The mainstream analysis suggests that wider geographic scope and greater competition in product markets have beneficial effects in all these areas. As economic development reaches new areas, "ladders of comparative advantage" (Bhagwati 2004) assure that there will be wage gains for even unskilled workers. Growing incomes often lead to growing resources devoted to environmental protection, especially as the very poor are lifted out of destitution and no longer have to resort to short-term exploitation of the environment to keep body and soul together. Cultural products compete in a global marketplace where people can choose movies from Hollywood or Mumbai, music from Nashville or Rio or Cape Town, and news from CNN, BBC, or Al Jazeera, even as best business practices spread worldwide.

But even some of the defenders of product-market globalization raise questions about the desirability of globalizing financial markets. While defenders of free international mobility of financial capital have often claimed that open markets will direct these resources to their highest and best use, presumably in helping poor countries to develop, experience has shown that resources have mostly flowed away from less-developed countries to the safe havens of the developed North. Proponents of financial globalization are left to claim that the main benefits come in the form of institutional reforms necessitated by membership in the global financial institutions, but these claims are speculative (Kose et al. 2006).

The problems caused by financial globalization are all too real, as was discovered in the 1994 Mexican peso crisis, the worldwide financial crisis of 1997–1998, the Argentinean collapse in 2000, and other incidents before and since. So mainstream economists like Bhagwati (2000; 2004) and Stiglitz (2006), while defending globalized-goods markets, question globalization of financial markets, because they limit macroeconomic flexibility in the face of differing conditions in different countries, because they lead to demands for worldwide conformity to Western policies and practices, and because of the potential damage from global financial crises.

In my view, the degree of competition in global-goods markets is overstated (Tiemstra 2007). Even in markets where the number of serious competitors has grown significantly with globalization, entry barriers are still significant (indeed, maybe more significant than in a world of protected national markets), and global branding of goods confers significant market power on preferred vendors. Thus, multinational enterprises have power in goods markets that gives them discretion to behave in a socially conscious manner if they choose. The major constraint on social responsibility is the fickleness of the "electronic herd" of global investors (Friedman 2000), those ready to stampede out of the stock of any company that does not manage its affairs exclusively for the benefit of the shareholders and out of the bonds of any state that does not favor business above all other constituencies.

The Case Against Global Financial Markets

As mentioned above, many economists who support free trade in goods and services nevertheless believe that the global integration of financial markets is not such a good idea.

There are two reasons that are commonly cited: (1) the inherent instability of financial markets and the lack of institutions capable of handling global financial crises, and (2) the need for countries to manage their own domestic macroeconomic policies (the "optimal currency area" argument). Three additional reasons are less commonly cited: (3) the desirability of accommodating differing cultural practices concerning the treatment of asymmetric information, (4) the desirability of maintaining differing national regulations concerning financial accounting and reporting, and (5) the advisability of reducing the competitive pressure on global corporations to maximize shareholder value at the expense of other constituencies. These five prongs to the case against financial globalization are discussed in turn.

Inherent Instability of Financial Markets

Financial markets, unlike most markets for goods and services, are subject to periodic crises in which a public event or a generalized loss of confidence leads to a collapse in asset prices. This instability results from the uniquely important role of asymmetric information in these markets and from their vulnerability to "rational bubbles." Asymmetric information leads lenders to require margin equity, collateral, and other forms of protection. When these break down (for example, the value of collateral declines), asset values are in jeopardy. In a rational bubble, financial investors bid up the price of assets, not because they believe that the assets are really worth that much, but because they perceive that other people are overestimating the value. This can lead to assets selling for far more than anyone truly believes they are worth, which is not a sustainable situation. When the crash comes, it could lead to a seizing up of the financial system, so that payments cannot be made and economic activity collapses. Uncertainty about the value of assets leads to unwillingness to buy them from people who need to raise money to fund new projects. This is the story of the real estate bubble in the United States that collapsed beginning in the fall of 2007. The fallout from this collapse rapidly spread internationally, because investors across the globe owned compromised, U.S. mortgage-backed securities and because weakened American financial institutions were counterparties to financial contracts in many different countries.

Two features of global financial markets make this worse. International or cross-cultural information flows are even more subject to asymmetric information problems than is the case within a single country. Also, no intergovernmental institution is capable or obliged to serve as the lender of last resort in the event of an international crisis. Though various national, central banks can play this role and have done so in the past, there is no institution that everyone can look to with confidence as the backstop. The current concern with "moral hazard" in emergency lending leads many observers to believe that national central banks may choose not to play this role in the future, especially if their domestic financial markets are not immediately threatened. This was apparently the case when the Asian crisis spread to Russia in 1998. In the current (2007–2008) crisis, the international coordination of rescue operations by the leading central banks has been impressive, and the international institutions (the International Monetary Fund, the World Bank, and Bank of International Settlements) have played a limited role. But mistakes have been made, too, and the central bankers' best efforts did not prevent financial markets from seizing up worldwide in the fall of 2008. As I write, the consequences for the real economy have yet to be seen.

Independent Macroeconomic Policies

The second commonly cited argument is that financial globalization makes it impossible for countries to pursue macroeconomic stabilization policies that are appropriate for their domestic economic situations. Many developing countries have chosen to fix their exchange rates against the currency of the United States or of another major developed-world trading partner. By taking this approach, they sacrifice the possibility of adjusting their macroeconomic policies to their own domestic circumstances in exchange for diminished currency risks leading to expanded trade volumes and for the inflation discipline of the developed-country partner. The overvaluation relative to the yen of dollar-linked Asian currencies set off a financial crisis ten years ago that finally spread to Russia and Brazil. More recently, Argentina had to break its dollar link when tight U.S. monetary policies led to unbalanced conditions in that country.

Thirty years of experience have taught us that even countries with flexible exchange rates lose some of their macro-policy independence when international capital flows are unrestrained. Monetary policy actions in any major country ripple through the rest of the world as capital flows and exchange rates respond to changing interest rate differentials and changing prospects for profit growth (Epstein 1996). The Fed cannot ignore the actions of the European Central Bank any more than Argentina can ignore the Fed.

These first two objections are the ones customarily offered by mainstream economists (Bhagwati 2000; Stiglitz 2006). Further objections are based on a broader view of social values than the mainstream analysis typically entertains. These values include cultural autonomy and diversity, and social responsibility of business for fairness to its stakeholders and for ecological sustainability.

Cultural Diversity, Business Practices, and Asymmetric Information

Different cultures have different traditions for handling the problem of asymmetric information in financial markets. Countries in the Western tradition tend to follow what I call the "litigious-society" approach. According to this approach, lenders write elaborate contracts with requirements for specific performance and extensive monitoring. Deals are structured so that borrowers have incentives to avoid risk. Litigation is available to enforce these provisions. In contrast, countries in the Eastern tradition follow the "crony-capitalism" approach. In these systems, personal, ongoing relationships and repeated deals among the same parties lead to a high level of personal knowledge and opportunities for retaliation when deals go bad. Litigation is rarely necessary.

We are all quite familiar with the costs of the Western approach. Contracts are long and complex and often have to be litigated. This requires the services of expensive lawyers, and an elaborate judicial system has to be maintained by government. In the worst cases, businesses devote many resources to "loophole-mining" or even to outright dishonesty. The wave of business scandals that began with Enron and continues with the sub-prime mortgages mess gives us a textbook on how this approach can fail.

The main cost of the Eastern approach is that there is very little opportunity for outsiders to create an economic space for themselves, because it is extremely difficult for them to find financing if they don't have social connections. In the worst cases, money goes to politically connected borrowers who divert funds to personal use or pay back loans with government funds and who bribe the lenders with kickbacks.

Western countries tend to think that everyone should handle asymmetric information problems the same way—the Western way. Westerners are comfortable with the tradeoffs made in the litigious-society approach. But this is certainly not the only way to handle the issue, and whether it is the best way depends on the analyst's values and cultural point of view. In a world of capital mobility, there are advantages to a uniform approach. However, we can preserve a diversity of approaches by sacrificing capital mobility. In this way, people of differing cultural and religious backgrounds can live their lives in a way that is consistent with their own worldviews. (I have written extensively about this in Tiemstra 2006.)

Accounting and Reporting Standards

When investors from different countries are evaluating securities from all over the world for their portfolios, it is much easier if the same accounting and reporting standards are in place worldwide. Differences in these standards amount to a barrier to capital movement, since different standards raise the cost of analyzing foreign securities. So the demand is made for uniformity, meaning conformance with Western (in practice, U.S.) standards.

What we give up in the process of achieving this uniformity is diversity in cultural understanding of how to handle the questions that arise in evaluating income, assets, and liabilities. The debate among the cognoscenti on rules versus principles in accounting standards is one area where lay readers of the business press can eavesdrop on these issues. No set of rules can cover every conceivable case. So how broad do we make the "principles" of the generally accepted accounting principles? Why should every society have to accept the judgments and tradeoffs made in the U.S. business context? The frequency and scope of reporting is a similar issue. Many people believe that the quarterly reports required by the Securities and Exchange Commission are much too frequent and that this requirement foreshortens the time horizons of American corporate management to the detriment of long-run competitiveness. Financial analysts and journalists might disagree, but why must this questionable choice be imposed on the rest of the world?

Interestingly, the United States now seems to be experiencing the other side of this issue, with increasing political pressure to relax the Sarbanes-Oxley regulations in order to attract more capital and more investment banking business to New York. Mostly Wall Street and the corporate community have exerted this pressure, so it has a self-serving flavor. All regulations have their purposes and their historical roots, and Sarbox was passed to restore confidence in U.S. markets in the wake of the business scandals of the 1990's. Its effect on attracting financial services business to New York has been disputed (Doidge, Karolyi, and Stultz 2007).

The Tyranny of Profit Expectations

Quarterly financial reporting feeds the tendency of investors and analysts to focus primarily if not exclusively on financial results in their investment decisions. The same tendency is reinforced by the difficulty of understanding the social and environmental context in which foreign businesses operate. Where a potential investor does not understand social and environmental dimensions of business performance in the context of a distant country, the easy thing to do is to look for financial profit. Conservative U.S.-market ideology, mainstream normative economics, and Wall Street institutions that evaluate and reward exclusively financial criteria add to the problem. If a corporation does not meet profit expectations, there are plenty of other stocks to consider.

Focusing on profits and short-run profitability growth distorts the way businesses are managed everywhere in the world. Failure to deliver profits to distant investors risks the firm's ability to raise capital or even the stability of corporate control. Investment in the long-run sustainability of the organization is neglected. The neglected areas are the ones with the longest payoff horizons: research and development; new technology; and investments in the labor force, such as education, health, career ladders, and retirement. Environmental and social investments in the local community are neglected, since there is no prospect of payoff to the distant investors and no easy way to evaluate performance.

The increased focus on short-term profit growth in global business is often blamed on hypercompetitive global-product markets or even on global-labor markets. But even in a competitive-market setting, businesses could perform well on all aspects of the triple bottom line if the owners permitted it. A consensus on the value of social and ecological objectives is part of the business culture of many nations, notably in Europe, and could easily be cultivated even in the United States. Certainly there is a lot of talk in management circles about the triple bottom line. Tyranny of profit expectations in the hypercompetitive, single-minded, global-capital market has created many of the problems we associate with globalization, now made a byword among progressives in every part of the world.

Conclusion

Liberalized global markets for goods and services require a functioning international-payments system, but they do not require absolutely free global mobility of capital. Liberalized global-capital markets bring with them special problems that cannot be solved with specially tailored regulation, and the benefits such markets bring are easy to overstate. Many commentators have called for measures that would impede the global mobility of capital (Kennedy 2003).

Restricting global-capital mobility will not by itself realize all of the important values that Christians rightly demand that globalization should serve. There will still be much work to be done, by governments and by non-governmental organizations, to ensure that the living standards of ordinary workers are universally improved, that cultural diversity and national autonomy are respected, and that economic development is sustainable. But removing the extra complications that result from the misguided attempt to establish a global market for financial capital will make the rest of the job of reforming global economics that much easier.

Questions for Review

1. Is it important for different societies to preserve their distinctive business practices? Or is there one best way to do things? Please explain.

2. Would restricting global-capital movements be a good way to prevent global financial crises? Or would it be better to create a global central bank to intervene in such cases, as the Federal Reserve intervenes in U.S. markets when crises arise?

3. Do businesses have obligations besides "maximizing shareholder wealth"? Can management keep shareholders happy while still serving other goals, such as providing security for workers or protecting the environment?

4. When the Federal Reserve was established in 1914, the idea was that there could be a different monetary policy in each of the twelve districts. Why has that turned out to be impossible? Would it be a good thing if it could happen? Should countries also be able to have their own monetary policies?

References

Bhagwati, Jagdish. 2000. *The Wind of the Hundred Days*. Cambridge, MA: MIT Press, 123–27, Chap. 1–3.

———. 2004. *In Defense of Globalization*. New York: Oxford, Chap. 13.

Doidge, Craig, George Andrew Karolyi, and René M. Stultz. 2007. "Has New York Become Less Competitive in Global Markets?" Charles A. Dice Center Working Paper 9. Ohio State University.

Epstein, Gerald. 1996. International Capital Mobility and the Scope for National Economic Management. In *States against Markets*, edited by Robert Boyer and Daniel Drache. London: Routledge, 211–24.

Friedman, Thomas L. 2000. *The Lexus and the Olive Tree*. New York: Anchor, Chap. 7.

Goudzwaard, Bob. 2001. *Globalization and the Kingdom of God* (containing his Kuyper lectures at Calvin College). Grand Rapids: Baker.

Kennedy, Joy. 2003. Currency Transaction Tax. In *Civilizing Globalization*, edited by Richard Sandbrook. Albany: SUNY Press, 111–19.

Kose, M. Ayhan, Eswar Prasad, Kenneth Rogoff, and Shang-Jin Wei. 2006. "Financial Globalization: A Reappraisal." IMF Working Paper WP/06/189. Washington, D.C.: International Monetary Fund.

The Commission on Theology. 2005. Globalization, Ethics, and the Earth. In *Acts and Proceedings of the 199th Regular Session of the General Synod* (June). New York, NY: Reformed Church in America, 344–64.

Stiglitz, Joseph E. 2006. *Making Globalization Work*. New York: Norton, Chap. 9.

Tiemstra, John P. 2006. "Financial Globalization and Crony Capitalism." *CrossCurrents* 56, no. 1 (Spring), 143–59, 26–33.

———. 2007. "The Social Economics of Globalization." *Forum for Social Economics* 36, no. 2 (Fall).

United Church of Christ. 2003. "A Faithful Response: Calling for a More Just, Humane Direction for Economic Globalization." View at http://www.ucc.org/justice/issues/globalization/.

World Alliance of Reformed Churches. 2004. "Covenanting for Justice in the Economy and the Earth." Excerpt from *Perspectives: A Journal of Reformed Thought* 21, no. 5 (May 2006). View full version at http://www.ucc.org/justice/issues/globalization, 6–10.

CHAPTER 12

TRADE GROWTH, ENVIRONMENT, AND POVERTY:

MUST THERE BE A TRADEOFF?

Judith M. Dean[1]

By all accounts, China appears to be a great illustration of the success of globalization. If by globalization (a very murky term) we mean increased participation in global markets via trade and foreign direct investment (FDI), then China has benefited greatly from globalization in recent years. From its significant trade liberalization in 1992 to its WTO accession in 2001 and beyond, China has continued to open its economy to world markets. The results have been dramatic. As shown in Figure 1, in just the first five years of the 1990s, China's GDP more than doubled, and its trade (exports plus imports) grew by 140 percent. FDI inflows increased more than ten-fold, making China the largest recipient of FDI in the developing world in 1995.[2] Over the next ten years, China's GDP continued to grow dramatically, while its trade grew an additional 400 percent, and its FDI inflows more than doubled.[3]

There is considerable evidence that this recent growth, which is integrally connected with the global market, has benefited the poor in China. As Table 1 shows, average real income per capita more than doubled from 1995 to 2005. Infant mortality fell by about 38 percent,

Figure 1. China's GDP, Trade, and FDI, 1990-2005

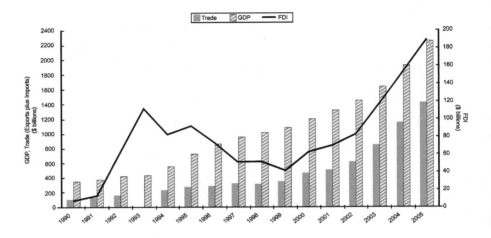

Sources: GDP: World Bank, *World Development Indicators, 2008;* trade and FDI data: *China Statistical Yearbook 2007.*

and the mortality rate for children under five-years old fell by about 40 percent. The share of China's population over the age of six classified as illiterate fell by nearly 50 percent between 1995 and 2000 and has been roughly stable since. China is still clearly a low-income developing country. The U.S. data in Table 1 remind us that the gap between China and wealthy industrialized countries is still startlingly large. Nevertheless, these data do suggest that China has made significant progress in raising the well-being of poor people.[4]

While these data present a positive picture, the popular press has been quick to link China's growth with its pollution problems. For example, a recent *New York Times* article stated:

But just as the speed and scale of China's rise as an economic power have no clear parallel in history, so its pollution problem

Table 1. Selected Poverty Indicators

	China			US
	1995	2000	2005	2005
Real GDP per capita (constant 2000 dollars)	658	949	1,449	37,267
Mortality Rate, infant (per 000 live births)	37	33	23	6
Mortality Rate, <5 years old (per 000)	46	41	27	7
Illiteracy Rate (% of people >6 years old)	16	9.5	9.2	na

Notes: All data except illiteracy rates are from World Bank, *World Development Indicators, 2008*. China's illiteracy rate for 2000 and 2005 are from the *China Statistical Yearbook* (various issues), and for 1995 is from Cao (2000). The US does not publish comparable data on illiteracy.

has shattered all precedents. Environmental degradation is now so severe, with such stark domestic and international repercussions, that pollution poses not only a major long-term burden on the Chinese public but also an acute political challenge to the ruling Communist Party.[5]

While major improvements have been made in pollution regulation since the mid-1990s (OECD 2005) and some progress has been made in achieving cleaner water and air, China's own State Environmental Protection Agency (SEPA) recently stated that "[t]he conflict between environment and development is becoming ever more prominent. Relative shortage of resources, a fragile ecological environment and insufficient environmental capacity are becoming critical problems hindering China's development" (SEPA 2006).

SEPA's annual *State of the Environment* report shows evidence of improvement in both water and air quality. From 2001 to 2005, the percentage of monitored sections of China's rivers classified as extremely polluted fell from 53 percent to 34 percent, while the percentage classified as relatively clean rose from 20 percent to 24 percent.[6] But this means that the majority of China's rivers were still moderately to highly polluted in 2005. In 2006, 48 percent of major lakes and reservoirs were still listed as heavily polluted (SEPA 2007). Urban air quality also improved between 2000 and 2005. The percentage of cities with extremely polluted air fell from 33 percent to about 11 percent, while the percentage of cities with relatively clean air rose from 37 percent to 51 percent during this time. Still, the air quality in nearly half of China's monitored cities ranked moderately to highly polluted in 2005.

Christians are called to be good stewards of the earth God has given us. Since that responsibility does not stop at national borders, Christians may be tempted to advocate restraints on trade or FDI in hopes of improving the environment in poor countries such as China. If we follow this line of reasoning, however, a serious conflict arises. Christians are also called to care for the poor. Economists from both ends of the political spectrum have long hailed the benefits of trade for raising living standards. Interventions in trade to correct environmental problems will likely reduce incomes in poor countries. Since traded goods account for a large share of national income in many poor countries, these effects would be significant.

Are Christians facing an irreconcilable conflict? Must we choose between our responsibility to help the poor and our responsibility to be good stewards of the environment? My answer is no. Both *sound* environmental policy and *compassionate* policies toward the poor call for freer, not restricted, trade. Supporting policies that open world markets will help the poor and encourage development of effective environmental policy. In fact, new evidence suggests that trade growth may contribute indirectly to a cleaner environment.

Why Is Trade Seen as Detrimental to the Environment?

Some of the large literature on trade and environment suggests that trade growth and environmental degradation in poor countries may be causally related. The basis of these arguments is the supposition that low-income countries have relatively lenient environmental standards compared to industrial countries, hence a comparative advantage in pollution-intensive goods. Here we will focus on two arguments of particular importance to developing countries. The first is the argument that trade growth will shift production within poor countries toward pollution-intensive (or "dirty") goods. The second is that foreign investors will shift production of dirty goods to poor countries, turning these countries into "pollution havens."

Trade Growth May Shift Production in Developing Countries toward Dirty Goods

As a low-income country grows, three forces are thought to affect its environment. Higher incomes tend to increase demand for all goods and services. This increases the *scale* of production and thereby the use of all inputs, including environmental resources. The *composition* of the country's output shifts toward its area of comparative advantage, which is assumed to be relatively "dirty goods." Both of these effects aggravate environmental damage. Higher incomes also generate pressure for more stringent environmental regulations, giving producers incentives to find cleaner production *techniques.* This effect tends to reduce environmental damage. For low-income countries, the scale and composition effects are thought to outweigh the technique effect, implying that the net effect of growth is detrimental to the environment. Only at higher income levels is the net effect assumed to be beneficial. This view suggests an "inverted-U" shaped relationship between income growth and environmental damage.[7] To the extent that trade growth raises incomes, it too will contribute to these scale, composition, and technique effects.

Increased Foreign Investment May Create "Pollution Havens" in Poor Countries

Some studies argue that stringent environmental standards in industrial countries have induced firms to relocate to poorer countries, where these standards are relatively weak. In any country, emissions taxes or other types of environmental regulations raise the cost of polluting and thus raise the cost of production. Firms have an incentive to abate pollution, either by "end-of-pipe" methods (for example, installing equipment that reduces emissions) or by changes in the production process itself (for example, adopting greener technology). But that too is costly. To reduce the costs of environmental compliance, firms may shift some or all of their operations to countries with less stringent standards. Thus, increased FDI from industrial countries into poor countries may be motivated by firms looking for a location where standards are relatively weak. Since the incentives to relocate will be strongest for relatively dirty industries, this will lead to a clustering of relatively dirty industries in developing countries. This argument is often referred to as the pollution-haven (PH) hypothesis.[8]

Why Is Trade Seen as Beneficial to the Poor?

A thorough examination of the relationships of trade, economic growth, and poverty is beyond the scope of this chapter.[9] Here we will simply summarize three important arguments that suggest freer trade is likely to help reduce poverty. Freer trade is expected to raise national income, to potentially accelerate income growth, and to generate direct benefits to poor households.

Increased National Income

While economists may disagree about many issues, nearly all of them agree that, in general, international trade raises the overall income of a country. There are two fundamental reasons underlying this conclusion. First, trade allows a country to have access to many goods at relatively cheaper prices than their domestic counterparts, while simultaneously finding more profitable markets in which to sell many other goods. Second, trade shifts production toward the goods in which the country has a comparative advantage. Since this reallocates productive factors from less-efficient sectors to more-efficient sectors, overall national output increases. Together, these two effects raise real national income.

Why does this matter? As Table 1 shows, the gap is vast between the per capita income levels of industrial countries such as the United States and developing countries like China. Since the majority of the world's poor live in low-income, developing countries—China, India, and large parts of sub-Saharan Africa—expanding national income is critical to reducing poverty (Dollar and Kraay 2002; Ravallion 2001; Berg and Krueger 2003).

Accelerated Growth Rate

More recently, economists have posited that freer trade may also increase a country's *rate* of growth by raising the productivity of a country's labor and capital. The channels through which this can occur include exposure to increased competition in the global market; access to new technology via trade in information or imitation of new products; increased FDI that may bring new technology; economies of scale in production as firms now sell in a global market; and access to cheaper imported inputs. While many studies have indeed found evidence that more open economies grow faster, these studies are not without limitations. Trade liberalization is difficult to quantify, and other factors interrelated with trade policy often affect growth simultaneously, making it hard to discern the effects attributable to trade alone (Rodriguez and Rodrik 2001). Opening up to trade does not guarantee that a country will grow faster. But as Berg and Krueger (2003) note, "[O]ne striking conclusion from the last 20 years of evidence is that there are no examples of recent take-off countries that have not opened to an important extent as part of the reform process."

Direct Benefits for the Poor

While freer trade is widely known to generate gainers and losers *within* a country, there are reasons to believe that poor people within developing countries would be among the gainers. Two of those reasons are that developing-country trade restrictions have historically been biased against the sectors in which the poor work and against the goods the poor consume. From the 1960s until the 1990s, many countries followed import-substitution development strategies, which entailed high trade barriers to promote the growth of capital-intensive, import-competing manufacturing industries. These barriers inevitably depressed the relative price of agricultural products, reducing returns to farmers. They also shifted resources away from low-skilled, labor-intensive manufacturing (such as textiles, electronics, clothing, and shoes), the type of manufacturing in which many developing countries have a comparative advantage and many poor workers are employed. Many of the goods produced in these sectors are basic consumer goods, such as clothing or household products. Since these goods make up a disproportionately large part of the expenses of poor households, these trade barriers raised the cost of living particularly for the poor.

Clearly, freer trade alone cannot solve global poverty. Other policies are required to fully address the root causes of poverty. In addition, the benefits of freer trade can be magnified or impeded by a country's other domestic policy choices. And certainly war, disease, famine, financial crisis, lack of rule of law, and natural disaster can reduce or negate the benefits of freer trade. But to echo both the WTO Doha Ministerial

Declaration (WTO 2001) and Watkins (2002), increased isolation from global markets would deprive the poor of the tremendous opportunities offered by international trade.

Investigating the Case That Trade Growth Is Detrimental to the Environment

Most economists agree that trade restraints make bad environmental policy. Environmental damage is generated by the production or consumption of goods, *regardless* of the market in which they are sold. Trade restrictions affect exports and imports of goods and only indirectly affect production and consumption. Thus, they do not address the root causes of environmental problems. As a result, while trade restrictions definitely generate additional costs in the economy, they may or may not achieve environmental objectives.

To illustrate this point, consider Indonesia's 1986 ban on exporting raw logs.[10] Though not implemented for an environmental reason, the policy was hailed by many environmental groups in the industrial world as a good way to reduce deforestation of tropical forests. But the export ban immediately shifted the sale of Indonesia's logs to its domestic market, dramatically depressing the domestic price of raw logs. As a result, local wood-processing industries expanded production and relied more heavily on the use of this cheaper wood. It only took a year or so before Indonesia's production of raw logs exceeded its previous level (Repetto and Gillis 1988). The export ban not only failed to reduce deforestation, it actually increased it. The ban was also extremely costly, since revenues fell with the inability to sell globally, and resources were shifted toward industries in which Indonesia did not have a comparative advantage.

A much more effective and less-costly approach to environmental stewardship is to design well-formulated environmental regulations that directly target the source of the environmental damage. In this case, a better approach would have been to raise the stumpage fees (the cost of felling a tree), and to lengthen harvesting contracts. The first policy would have helped to incorporate the environmental costs of deforestation directly into the price of felling a tree. The second would have helped encourage wise harvesting and replanting. Finally, policies to raise the incomes of poor subsistence farmers would have reduced their incentive to clear forested land (the main cause of the deforestation problem at the time). Together, these policies would directly target the sources of the environmental problem, therefore correcting the problem in a more efficient way.

In addition to the previous important argument, there is new evidence that the connection between trade growth and the environment may be a more favorable one than previously thought. Trade growth may actually foster cleaner rather than dirtier production. FDI may introduce cleaner technology to developing countries rather than create pollution havens.

Trade Growth May Foster Cleaner, Not Dirtier, Production

While it may be reasonable to assume that low-income countries have less stringent environmental standards than richer countries, it is not necessarily true that this gives the poorer country a comparative advantage in dirty goods. The use of the environment is only one of many "inputs" into production. Comparative advantage is affected by the costs of other inputs as well, such as capital equipment, skilled labor, unskilled labor, and others (Copeland and Taylor 2003). Since industries themselves differ in the intensity with which they use these inputs, so will the relative importance of environmental costs differ across industries.

Dean and Lovely (2008) were able to collect China's data on emissions of four pollutants for about thirty Chinese industries and three Chinese utilities. One of the interesting things they found was that China's major exports are not produced by the most polluting

Table 2. Export Shares and Pollution Intensity by Chinese Industrial Sector 2004

		2004 Share of Total Mfg Exports	2004			
			COD	SO2	Smoke	Dust
			(kilos per thousand yuan output, 1995 yuan)			
Top 5 Mfg Industries by Export Shares	Communications Equipment	**15.7**	0.03	0.03	0.03	0.01
	Office and Computing Machinery	**15.1**	0.03	0.03	0.03	0.01
	Wearing Apparel	**8.6**	0.44	0.35	0.17	0.02
	Textiles	**8.2**	0.73	0.70	0.27	0.03
	Machinery	**7.2**	0.05	0.18	0.12	0.08
Top 5 Mfg Industries by Pollution Intensities	Basic Metals	4.1	0.12	1.26	0.50	**0.90**
	Food Products and Beverages	2.6	**1.59**	0.59	0.66	0.04
	Non-metallic minerals	1.7	0.14	**4.26**	**3.24**	**14.07**
	Wood	1.0	0.92	1.15	**1.38**	**0.58**
	Paper	0.4	**6.95**	**1.86**	1.08	0.07

Notes: Extracted from Dean and Lovely (2008).

industries. Table 2 shows the five manufacturing industries with the highest shares of China's manufacturing exports, and the five manufacturing industries with the highest pollution intensities in terms of water pollution (measured by chemical oxygen demand, or COD) or air pollution (measured by SO_2, smoke, or dust) in 2004.[11] Communications equipment and office and computing machinery are by far the largest in terms of export share, and they are the fastest growing industries since 1995. They are also the cleanest of the sectors. The most polluting sectors, such as paper and non-metallic minerals (for example, cement) have, in fact, very low shares in China's manufacturing exports.

There also seems to be mounting evidence that trade growth might actually foster cleaner production in poor countries. A study by Dean (2002) examined the impact of freer trade on China's water pollution emissions over time. Dean found some evidence that freer trade might have shifted the composition of output toward more water polluting industries, but it also raised incomes, which tended to reduce emissions growth. The evidence suggested that the net effect of trade liberalization was beneficial for China. Antweiler, Copeland, and Taylor (2001) studied the impact of trade growth on SO_2 emissions across a large group of countries. Although they did find some evidence of a detrimental composition effect from trade growth, they also found evidence that the technique effect was stronger than anticipated, yielding a small net beneficial effect on emissions.

In their 2008 study, Dean and Lovely find that as China's trade has grown, the pollution intensity of almost all manufacturing industries has fallen (for all four pollutants). This finding suggests that China has benefited from a positive "technique effect," as emissions per real dollar of output have fallen across a wide range of industries. Their analysis also reveals that China's trade has been shifting toward relatively cleaner sectors over time. For example, the share of exports accounted for by textiles and leather products has fallen, while the share accounted for by office and computing and communications equipment has grown dramatically. These growth sectors are characterized by low air and water pollution intensities (see Table 2). Linking the industrial pollution intensities to detailed trade statistics, Dean and Lovely find that, contrary to popular expectations, Chinese exports are less water-pollution intensive, and generally less air-pollution intensive, than Chinese imports.[12] They also find evidence that both Chinese exports and imports are becoming cleaner over time. Interestingly, recent work by Levinson (2007) shows cleaner trends in U.S. exports and imports as well. Levinson also attributes this largely to cleaner production techniques.

Finally, there is some evidence that international production fragmentation may lead to a shift in the composition of trade toward cleaner goods and cleaner techniques. Production fragmentation involves splitting production processes into discrete, sequential activities (fragments) that take place in different countries.[13] This "processing trade" alone accounts for about 56 percent of the growth in China's exports and 41 percent of the growth in China's imports between 1995 and 2005. If highly fragmented industries (such as computers and other high-tech products) are relatively clean, then the composition of China's output and trade would shift toward cleaner goods as these activities expand. If FDI expands the range of cleaner fragments produced in China, this will also tend to make China's production and trade cleaner. Lastly, if the foreign-invested enterprises responsible for most of this trade bring greener technologies than those used by domestic producers in China, this will tend to make trade even cleaner.

Dean and Lovely (2008) find evidence that both the changing composition of Chinese exports and the changing industrial production techniques have worked to make Chinese trade cleaner. They also find strong evidence that Chinese processing exports are cleaner than Chinese ordinary exports. Finally, their statistical testing suggests that processing trade has played a key role in explaining the drop in the pollution intensity of Chinese exports over time, and FDI inflows have contributed to this cleaner trend.

FDI May Bring Cleaner Technology Rather Than Pollution Havens

The underlying argument for the PH hypothesis is a microeconomic one, related to a firm's production costs. To the degree that a firm's costs are heavily determined by *non-environmental* costs (for example, labor costs, capital costs, communications, transportation, and others), it is likely that environmental stringency may have little impact on a firm's decision making. For example, it is easy to understand why IBM might not locate in Nepal, even if the country had no environmental regulations, due to Nepal's lack of high-skilled workers and inadequate electricity, transport, and other infrastructure. In fact the extensive literature on the determinants of FDI suggests that most foreign investors are attracted by locations with large and/or growing markets, relatively large pools of high-skilled workers, other foreign investment (agglomeration), and good infrastructure. Head and Ries (1996), Cheng and Kwan (2000), Amiti and Javorcik (2008), and Dean, Lovely, and Wang (2007) all find that these determinants matter for the location of FDI in China.

Early empirical studies suggested that environmental stringency had no discernible effect on international investment flows.[14] Though FDI in pollution-intensive industries did occur, there was little evidence that it had been influenced by pollution-abatement costs or had flowed faster into developing countries relative to industrial countries. More recently, a study by Eskeland and Harrison (2003) examined data on the pattern of industrial-country FDI across industries within Mexico, Venezuela, Morocco, and Cote d'Ivoire. The authors found little evidence that foreign investment was relatively higher in "dirtier" industries. Javorcik and Wei (2004) examined the foreign investment choices of multinational firms locating across Eastern Europe and the former Soviet Union. Although they found some evidence that FDI was deterred by tighter environmental standards, their results were not robust to alternative proxies for environmental stringency.

In contrast, some studies examining FDI location choice in the United States find evidence consistent with the PH hypothesis. Keller and Levinson (2002), List and Co (2000), and List, Millimet, and McHone (2004) all find that regulatory costs deter investment in U.S. states with relatively stringent standards. But we do not know whether behavior observed in the United States also characterizes FDI flows into developing countries—the focus of concern in the pollution haven debate. While a U.S. focus makes it easier to obtain firm-level data and environmental stringency measures, the United States is a high-standard, industrial country, and it receives the vast majority of its capital inflows from other industrial countries. Blonigen and Wang (2005) argue that the factors determining FDI location are systematically different for developed and developing countries.

Recent work by Dean, Lovely, and Wang (2007) takes a close look at the location choices of foreign investors choosing to produce in China. Though only a single-host developing economy, Chinese provinces vary dramatically in terms of income and environmental stringency. Unlike many other developing countries with severe water pollution problems, China has a national price-based, water pollution-control system.[15] Data collected by China's National Statistical Bureau and by the World Bank allowed Dean, Lovely, and Wang to measure Chinese provincial-regulatory stringency and Chinese industrial-pollution intensity. Using data on 2,886 manufacturing-equity, joint-venture (EJV) projects in China during 1993–1996, the authors test the impact of water pollution regulations on FDI location choice, using data on the average levies charged in different Chinese provinces. They also test for differences in firm response by pollution intensity and by source country.

This study finds no evidence of the PH hypothesis for the sample of EJVs from *OECD-source* countries, regardless of the pollution intensity of the industry. However, projects in highly polluting industries from *ethnically Chinese sources* (Hong Kong, Macao, and Taiwan) are significantly deterred by pollution taxes. Although these findings are consistent with the behavior at the heart of the PH hypothesis, they put the focus on developing-country investors rather than those from industrial countries and on highly polluting industries only.

How do we explain this finding? One answer may be that FDI from industrial countries brings with it green technologies. Rich countries' higher environmental standards have induced innovation and production of environment-friendly technology (Bhagwati 2004). FDI from these source countries often employs newer, cleaner technology, even in low-standard locations. In contrast, entrepreneurs from poorer countries with lower standards typically hold on to the older, less-friendly technologies and may import them in second-hand machinery. Thus, we might expect environmental regulations to affect decisions of investors from poorer rather than richer countries. While Dean, Lovely, and Wang have no direct evidence on the role of technology, their results are consistent with this view. If foreign investment from industrial countries is not deterred from locations with stringent standards because it embodies cleaner technology, investment by high-income countries in the developing world has the potential to improve environmental outcomes in host countries.

Our Response as Christians

On the surface, the experience of developing countries like China might suggest that while trade growth is likely to benefit the poor, it may cause serious environmental damage. This presents a potential conflict for Christians who want to both help impoverished people and be good stewards of the environment. Fortunately, a closer look suggests that there is no necessary tradeoff between these two worthy goals. Environmental economics teaches us that the most effective policies to reduce pollution are those policies that address the problem directly. Trade restrictions do not do this. At best they are unnecessarily costly, and at worst they are ineffective or damaging to the environment. Rather than trying to solve environmental problems through trade restrictions, Christians should approach the problem directly by encouraging sound environmental policies in developing countries. In China's case, this might include technical assistance to improve the design and implementation of environmental regulations, as well as environmental monitoring and enforcement mechanisms (OECD 2005).

Arguments made in this chapter suggest that trade liberalization is not only likely to benefit the poor, it may also help improve environmental quality. Because trade growth raises incomes, it can strengthen a country's ability to develop environmental regulations and to pay for a cleaner environment. New evidence from China and other countries suggests that these effects are stronger than previously thought. In addition, the rise of global production chains means that developing countries may find opportunities to specialize in stages of the production process of skilled-labor, intensive goods. New evidence suggests that these industries use relatively clean production processes compared to many traditional manufactured exports. Finally, new evidence suggests that foreign investment may be an important vehicle for transferring cleaner technologies to the developing world. Thus, Christians might do well to support more open markets at home and abroad.

Questions for Review

You are sent to the World Trade Organization to participate in the upcoming round of world trade talks, a round in which many developing countries are active participants. While there, you hear the following views expressed. How might you respond to these views?

1. The Christian faith is irrelevant when it comes to improving the environment or reducing poverty.

2. Trade restrictions can be beneficial because they slow growth, reducing the pressure on a country's environment.

3. Reductions in *rich* countries' trade barriers could help reduce poverty in poor countries.

4. Participation in global markets should help poor countries develop better environmental policy.

5. China's experience clearly shows that freer trade means dirtier growth.

6. China's experience clearly shows that foreign investors merely exploit poor countries' environments.

Notes

[1] The views in this chapter are those of the author alone. They do not necessarily represent the views of the U.S. International Trade Commission nor any of the individual Commissioners.

[2] See Broadman and Sun (1997); Henley, Kirkpatrick, and Wilde (1999).

[3] Comparable data for GDP, trade flows, and FDI inflows in constant dollars were unavailable.

[4] The World Bank recently reported that it had overstated China's economic growth and its success in poverty reduction, due to the World Bank's underestimation of China's inflation in its purchasing power parity calculations. Since some of the World Bank's GDP measures and some poverty measures (such as headcount) are based on these erroneous data, they are not reported in the table above.

[5] *New York Times*, "Choking on Growth." View at http://www.nytimes.com/2007/08/26/world/asia/26china.html.

[6] Quality is designated by grade levels, with grades I and II reflecting the highest qualities, and grades V or "worse than grade V" reflecting the lowest qualities. See http://english.sepa.gov.cn/standards_reports/.

[7] Evidence on the existence of an inverted-U relationship between income and environmental damage is mixed and highly dependent upon time period, countries evaluated, and pollutants examined. For a recent survey of this evidence, see Copeland and Taylor (2004). For surveys covering the broader literature on trade and environment, see Dean (2001) and Copeland and Taylor (2004).

[8] A corollary is that developing countries may purposely undervalue environmental damage in order to attract more foreign direct investment (FDI). This, in turn, could generate a "race to the bottom," with all countries lowering environmental standards to attract and retain investment.

[9] This section draws heavily on material from Dean (2005). For an in-depth exploration of this topic, see that paper and the studies it references. A thorough survey of the entire literature can be found in Winters, McCulloch, and McKay (2004).

[10] This discussion draws on material from Dean (1997).

[11] COD measures the mass concentration of oxygen consumed by chemical breakdown of organic and inorganic matter in water. Industrial SO_2 emissions include the sulfur dioxide emitted from fuel burning and from the production processes on the premises of an enterprise. Industrial smoke (or soot) emissions include smoke emitted from fuel burning on the premises of an enterprise. Industrial dust emissions refer to the volume of dust suspended in the air and emitted by an enterprise's production processes.

[12] That is, the pollution intensity of China's imports, had they been produced in China.

[13] See Arndt and Kierzkowski (2001) for discussion of the causes of fragmentation.

[14] Reviews of the literature can be found in Dean (2001) and Copeland and Taylor (2004).

[15] Though China's environmental regulation system is far from perfect, it is remarkable for a low-income, developing country. For thorough discussions of its strengths and weaknesses, see Wang and Wheeler (2005) and OECD (2005).

References

Amiti, Mary, and Beata Smarzynska Javorcik. 2008. "Trade Costs and the Location of Foreign Firms in China." *Journal of Development Economics* 85: 129–49.

Antweiler, Werner, Brian Copeland, and Scott Taylor. 2001. "Is Free Trade Good for the Environment?" *American Economic Review* 91: 877–908.

Arndt, Sven, and Henryk Kierzkowski. 2001. *Fragmentation*. New York, NY: Oxford University Press.

Berg, Alan, and Anne O. Krueger. 2003. "Trade, Growth, and Poverty: A Selective Survey." *IMF Working Paper* WP/03/30. Washington, D.C.: International Monetary Fund.

Bhagwati, Jagdish. 2004. *In Defense of Globalization*. New York, NY: Oxford University Press.

Blonigen, Bruce A., and Miao Grace Wang. 2005. Inappropriate Pooling of Wealthy and Poor Countries in Empirical FDI Studies. In *Does Foreign Direct Investment Promote Development?* edited by T. Moran, E. Graham, and M. Blomstrom. Washington, D.C.: Institute for International Economics, 221–43.

Broadman, Harry, and Xiaolun Sun. 1997. "The Distribution of Foreign Investment in China." *World Economy* 20: 339–61.

Cao, Gui-Ying. 2000. "The Future Population of China: Prospects to 2045 by Place of Residence and by Level of Education." IIASA Interim Report IR-00-026. Austria: International Institute for Applied Systems Analysis. View at http://www.iiasa.ac.at/Admin/PUB/Documents/IR-00-026.pdf.

Cheng, Leonard K., and Yum K. Kwan. 2000. "What Are the Determinants of the Location of Foreign Direct Investment? The Chinese Experience." *Journal of International Economics* 51: 370–400.

China Customs. 2007. *China Statistical Yearbook*. View at http://www.stats.gov.cn/tjsj/ndsj/2007/indexeh.htm.

Copeland, Brian R., and M. Scott Taylor. 2003. *Trade and the Environment*. Princeton, NJ: Princeton University Press, 7–71.

———. 2004. "Trade, Growth and the Environment." *Journal of Economic Literature* 42.

Dean, Judith. 2005. Why Trade Matters for the Poor. In *Attacking Poverty in the Developing World*, edited by J. Dean, J. Schaffner, and S. Smith. Federal Way, WA: World Vision and Authentic Media.

————. 2002. "Does Trade Liberalization Harm the Environment? A New Test." *Canadian Journal of Economics* 35: 819–42.

————, ed. 2001. *International Trade and the Environment.* The International Library of Environmental Economics and Policy Series (November 2001). U.K.: Ashgate Publishing.

————. 1997. "Are We Turning Poor Countries into Pollution Havens? Understanding the Trade/Environment Debate." *ACE Bulletin* 30. View at http://www.gordon.edu/ace/pdf/Dean=Bulletin30.pdf, 7–14.

————, and Mary E. Lovely. 2008. "Trade Growth, Production Fragmentation, and China's Environment." NBER Working Paper 13860. Cambridge, MA: National Bureau of Economic Research.

————, Mary E. Lovely, and Hua Wang. 2007. "Are Foreign Investors Attracted to Weak Environmental Regulations." World Bank Working Paper 3505 (Revision). Washington, D.C.: World Bank.

Dollar, David, and Aart Kraay. 2002. "Growth Is Good for the Poor." *Journal of Economic Growth* 7, no. 3: 195–225.

Eskeland, Gunnar S., and Ann E. Harrison. 2003. "Moving to Greener Pastures? Multinationals and the Pollution Haven Hypothesis." *Journal of Development Economics* 70: 1–23.

Head, Keith, and John Ries. 1996. "Inter-City Competition for Foreign Investment: Static and \Dynamic Effects of China's Incentive Areas." *Journal of Urban Economics* 40: 38–60.

Henley, John, Colin Kirkpatrick, and Georgina Wilde. 1999. "Foreign Direct Investment in China: Recent Trends and Current Policy Issues." *World Economy* 22: 223–43.

Javorcik, Beata S., and Shang-Jin Wei. 2004. "Pollution Havens and Foreign Direct Investment: Dirty Secret or Popular Myth?" *Berkeley Electronic Journal of Economic Analysis and Policy* 3, no. 2 (Article 8).

Keller, Wolfgang, and Arik Levinson. 2002. "Pollution Abatement Costs and Foreign Direct Investment Inflows to the U.S. States." *Review of Economics and Statistic* 84: 691–703.

Levinson, Arik. 2007. "Technology, International Trade, and Pollution from U.S. Manufacturing." Resources for the Future Discussion Paper RFF DP 07-40. Washington, D.C.: Resources for the Future.

List, John A., and Catherine Y. Co. 2000. "The Effects of Environmental Regulations on FDI." *Journal of Environmental Economics and Management* 40: 1–20.

————, Daniel L. Millimet, and W. Warren McHone. 2004. "The Unintended Disincentive of the Clean Air Act." *Berkeley Electronic Journal of Economic Analysis and Policy* 4, no. 2 (Article 2).

OECD. 2005. *Governance in China.* Paris: Organization for Economic Cooperation and Development, Chap. 17.

Ravallion, Martin. 2001. "Growth, Inequality, and Poverty: Looking Beyond the Averages." *World Development* 29: 1803–15.

Repetto, Robert, and Malcolm Gillis, eds. 1988. *Public Policy and the Misuse of Forest Resources.* New York, NY: Cambridge University Press.

Rodriguez, F., and Dani Rodrik. 2001. Trade Policy and Economic Growth: A Skeptic's Guide to the Cross-National Evidence. In *NBER Macroeconomics Annual* 2000, edited by Ben S. Bernanke and Kenneth Rogoff. Vol. 15. Cambridge, MA: MIT Press, 261–325.

SEPA. 2006. *Environmental Protection in China 1996–2005.* Beijing: Information Office of the State Council of the People's Republic of China. www.sepa.gov.cn/english (accessed July 2006).

———. 2007. *Report on the State of the Environment in China 2006.* Beijing: Information Office of the State Council of the People's Republic of China. www.english.sepa.gov.cn/standards_report/soe/SOE2006 (accessed February 2008).

Wang, Hua, and David Wheeler. 2005. "Financial Incentives and Endogenous Enforcement in China's Pollution Levy System." *Journal of Environmental Economics and Management* 49, no. 1: 174–96.

Watkins, Kevin, and Penny Fowler. 2002. *Rigged Rules and Double Standards.* U.K.: Oxfam Publishing.

Winters, L. Alan., Neil McCulloch, and Andrew McKay. 2004. "Trade Liberalization and Poverty: The Evidence Thus Far." *Journal of Economic Literature* 42, no. 1 (March), 72–115.

Development Data Group. 2008. *World Development Indicators.* Washington, D.C.: World Bank.

WTO. 2001. Ministerial Declaration. WTO Document WT/MIN(01)/DEC/1. Geneva: World Trade Organization.

CHAPTER 13

GLOBAL CLIMATE CHANGE AND THE CHURCHES

Donald Hay

Climate change is *the* global environmental issue. It is *global* because the emission of greenhouse gases at any point on the globe adds to the stock of such gases in the atmosphere as a whole and can thereby have an impact at any other point on the globe. It is *environmental* because there is now a scientific consensus that greenhouse gas concentrations in the atmosphere are major contributors to global warming, with potentially catastrophic effects on the environment over the next hundred years. In this chapter, we review current orthodoxies on the science of global warming, outline the adverse consequences for the global environment and for human flourishing, consider critically the economic analyses and policies that have been presented to combat global warming, and then ask whether and how the churches might respond.

Global Warming: The Science and the Predicted Impacts

The growing realization that the atmosphere is warming is the result of a remarkable effort by the scientific community in the last twenty years. Specifically, the Intergovernmental Panel on Climate Change (IPCC) was formed by the United Nations Environment Program in 1988 and presented its first Report in 1990.[1] Further Reports followed, and the most recent, the Fourth Report, was published by the Panel in 2007. The pattern of these Reports is that scientific findings first advanced in 1990 as significant possibilities are now more firmly established.[2] The Fourth Report summarizes the latest findings of the scientific panel. First, concentrations of greenhouse gases (carbon dioxide, methane, and nitrous oxide) in the atmosphere have increased markedly in the last ten years. Second, there is now considerable evidence of global warming, from observations of increases in global average air and ocean temperatures, widespread melting of snow and ice, and rising average sea level. There is also detailed evidence of the variance of climate change across the continents of the world. As examples, Arctic temperatures have increased at almost twice the global rate in the past one hundred years, and more intense and longer droughts have been observed in tropical and subtropical regions since 1970. Third, the Report is unequivocal in attributing observed climate change to human activities: "Most of the observed increase in globally averaged temperatures since the mid-20th century is *very likely* due to the observed increase in anthropogenic greenhouse gas concentrations."[3] The Report effectively rules out "natural variations" in the earth's climate due to solar or volcanic activity as an explanation, since the changes are far outside the observed range of such variations. Finally, the Report essays some predictions of the likely path of climate change over the twenty-first century. For the next two decades, a warming of about 0.2 degrees Celsius is expected in each decade. Thereafter, the prediction depends on assumptions about the level of emissions of greenhouse gases and on the feedbacks from the carbon cycle. In a range of models, the lowest expected rise in temperature by the end of the century is between 1.8 and 4 degrees Celsius.

Writer's of the Stern Review (Stern 2007)[4] analyzed the sources of greenhouse gas concentrations in the atmosphere, which determine the rate of global warming. The level in 2000 was about 430 parts per million (ppm) CO_2e,[5] an increase of more than 50 percent since before the Industrial Revolution. This increase has been driven by emissions from the burning of fossil fuels for power, transport, buildings, and industry and by agriculture and deforestation. Currently, the former accounts for about 57 percent of emissions and the latter for about 41 percent. The pattern of emissions shows that they are driven by economic development. The level of emissions in 2000, if continued into the future, would generate increased concentrations, year on year, of 2.7 ppm per year. The projection on a "business-as-usual" scenario (that is, no action taken on the growth of emissions) is that concentrations will reach 550 ppm CO_2e by 2035. About three-fourths of additional emissions during 2004 to 2030 are expected to come from developing economies; China alone will be responsible for about one-fourth. By contrast, emissions have been falling in the developed economies in the last twenty-five years; however, about 70 percent of the existing concentration in the atmosphere is the result of emissions by these economies in the last hundred years.

Consistent with the IPCC Report, the Stern Review predicts a rise in global mean temperature of 2 to 3 degrees Celsius, and possibly much more, by the end of the century. Under these assumptions, there is a deeply concerning catalogue of predicted effects. These include the following:[6]

- A change in the pattern of average rainfall, with some regions becoming drier and others receiving more rainfall. But, more seriously, climate scientists predict greater variability of rainfall, with increased incidence of both droughts and floods. The melting of glaciers will affect water supply to economically important river systems in Asia and Latin America.

- A serious effect on food supplies. In tropical and subtropical regions, an increase of 3 degrees Celsius will add between 250 and 550 million people to those already at risk of starvation. Most of those added will be in regions where the risk is already high, such as Africa and South Asia.

- Increased incidence of malaria and other tropical diseases, malnutrition, and diarrhea in tropical and subtropical regions.

- A rise in sea level brought about by melting ice caps. A conservative estimate is that 150 to 200 million people will be displaced from coastal areas in countries such as Vietnam, Bangladesh, China, and India.

- An increase in the number and intensity of extreme weather events such as hurricanes and tornadoes. Peak winds in tropical storms increase exponentially with the increase in temperature, and, as a rule of thumb, storm damage to infrastructure and buildings increases with the cube of wind speeds.

- Increased extinction of species. A conservative estimate is that a rise of 2 degrees Celsius will result in the extinction of between 15 and 40 percent of species worldwide. Particular concerns are that the Amazon basin will dry out and the rainforest die off.[7]

Economic impacts will likely differ across different regions of the world. Developing countries are believed to face the greatest economic risks for three reasons. First, the experience of natural disasters in recent years has underlined the negative impact of extreme events on economic activity, health, poverty, and the budgets of national governments. The second reason relates to the sensitivity of developing economies and populations: their economies are dependent on agriculture and natural ecosystems, they are experiencing rapid population growth concentrated in the largest cities where living conditions are poor, and the general level of health is low. Third, developing countries lack adaptive capacity in knowledge, resources, and public infrastructure. For example, greater variability of rainfall will call for constructing additional water storage systems, which may be beyond the resources available to governments. The predictions are that the effects of global warming will be particularly severe in Africa and South Asia. The fear is that these effects will lead to mass displacement of populations (due to coastal flooding or crop failures) and to regional conflicts, as displaced people migrate in search of better conditions and scarce resources such as water.

By contrast, developed countries will not suffer significantly from modest climate change of 2 to 3 degrees Celsius. The effect of modest change on agriculture should be beneficial, since crops are not close to their limits of cultivation and yields should increase with greater warmth and the carbon fertilization effect. Moreover, the farming sector is sophisticated technologically and well placed to adapt. A major concern, however, is greater frequency of severe weather events: storms, floods, droughts, and heat waves. The costs in human terms of hurricane Katrina in 2005 and of the European heat wave in 2003 are indicators of the possible adverse effects of global warming in developed economies. Even so, these economies probably have the technological capacity, the financial resources, and the ability to deliver large infrastructural projects that enable them to adapt. This relatively sanguine evaluation does not apply should global temperatures rise by 4 to 5 degrees Celsius, in which case global changes in sea level would probably make it impossible to secure major cities, such as London, New York, and Tokyo, against frequent incursions by the sea.

The Predicted Economic Costs
of Global Warming

What do all these impacts add up to in terms of economic costs? The Stern Review (Stern 2007, Chap. 6) presents some estimates: for 2 to 3 degrees Celsius warming, the costs are equivalent to 0 to 3 percent of world GDP in perpetuity; for 4 to 6 degrees Celsius warming, the costs are 5 to 10 percent of world GDP in perpetuity. In every scenario, economic costs are much higher in poor countries than in rich countries. These estimates are much contested in part because the evidence base is thin, particularly in poor countries, and because there are three unresolved technical issues of economic analysis.

- The impacts of climate change develop over time, as greenhouse gas concentrations in the atmosphere build up. The challenge is estimating the present value of the costs of damage that may not arise until the second half of the twenty-first century, and possibly later. Much hinges on the choice of a discount rate. A high rate, reflecting current market rates (the return on a broadly constructed portfolio of U.S. stocks currently yields about 7 percent), would generate low values for costs incurred many years hence. This is equivalent to saying that we do not give much weight to the environment our great-grandchildren will inherit. Others argue that the discount rate should be low, reflecting our genuine concern for our descendants. For this reason, writers of the Stern Review advocate the use of a discount rate as low as 1.4 percent per annum. The difference between 7 and 1.4 percent can be seen by noting that the present value of a cost to be incurred one hundred years hence is 100 times greater if the discount rate is 1.4 percent rather than 7 percent.[8] This difference explains why some economists call for immediate action on climate change on the basis of a 1.4 percent discount rate, while others suggest a more gradual approach on the basis of a 7 percent discount rate, taking action later in the century when the economic costs are nearer at hand.

- The evaluation needs to be specific to those people on whom the impact of climate change will fall. The intuitive point is that a dollar loss means a great deal more to a person living on an annual income of less than $100 in sub-Saharan Africa than to a wealthy person in North America or Europe. An ethical judgment has to be made to determine the relative weights applied in these two cases.[9] A higher weight on costs accruing to people in poorer countries increases the global cost estimates substantially.

- The climate change models typically give a range of outcomes about a mean prediction. Some of those outcomes may have extreme impacts but a relatively low probability of occurring. For example, the fourth IPCC Report (2007) notes a 3 percent probability of the increase in temperature exceeding 6 degrees Celsius over the next one hundred years. Such an increase would indeed take the Earth into "uncharted territory" as far as environmental and economic impacts are concerned. An analysis that simply weights the costs by a low probability of occurrence will probably fail to account adequately for their seriousness. Weitzman (2007) suggested that it may be worth taking immediate measures to reduce CO2e emissions as an "insurance" against extreme, but low probability, impacts.

There is one other issue concerning the estimation of costs. The starting point is a "business-as-usual" scenario. In this scenario, no action is taken, and the growth of greenhouse gas emissions and hence atmospheric concentrations are predicted solely on the basis of the predicted growth of population and world GDP, allowing for technical change to improve the efficiency of the use of fossil fuels. This scenario omits taking action, within nations and multilaterally, as evidence accumulates on the adverse effects of global warming. Ignoring these actions altogether fails to take into account the known capacity of the human race to rise to new challenges. But there may be considerable variation in responses regionally, since in developing economies, technical information and organizational capacity may be lacking.

Policies to Address Climate Change

In standard economic analysis, global warming is an excellent example of an externality; that is, an effect of an economic activity that impinges on others but for which there is no market. Emissions of carbon dioxide from heating or cooling my home, from driving my automobile, or from traveling by plane add to the concentration of greenhouse gases in the atmosphere, hence imposing a cost on others for which they are not compensated. But neither I nor the companies that supply goods and services to me are held to account for the costs arising from these activities—no market for these "external effects" exists. If a market did exist, then we would have to pay more for heating our homes, driving our automobiles, and traveling by plane; and that, in principle, would induce us to reduce our emissions. In the absence of a market, the solution is to impose environmental taxes proportional to the CO2e generated so that we face up to the full costs of our activities. This requires us to identify the costs accurately so the tax can be set at the appropriate level. Unfortunately the analysis is far from straightforward, for the reasons advanced in Section 2—uncertainty about the appropriate discount rate for future costs, and the need to assign different weights for costs falling on the rich and the poor. It is not entirely surprising that when Tol (2005) reviewed estimates from twenty-eight independent studies, he found values ranging from zero to hundreds of dollars per additional ton of carbon released into the atmosphere.

Economists of the Stern Review (Stern 2007) take a different tack, proposing an agreed target range of stabilized greenhouse gas concentration between 450 to 550 ppm CO2e in 2050. The rationale is that to achieve less than 450 ppm would involve draconian policy measures. The upper limit of 550 ppm is based on predictions that once concentrations exceed that level we are into uncharted territory; in particular, catastrophic environmental changes cannot be ruled out. To stay within this upper limit will still require vigorous action: emissions would need to peak within ten to twenty years, and emission levels in 2050 would have to be no more than 75 percent of current levels.[10] That would not be the end of the matter. To stabilize CO2e in the long run will require emissions no greater than the capacity of the environment to absorb carbon dioxide: the best estimate is that emissions will need to be cut by 80 percent from their 2000 levels.

The trajectories for emissions are critical for devising actual policies. Specifically, any delay in implementing a reduction strategy implies a higher "starting point" in terms of concentration, requiring thereafter more aggressive reductions in emissions. There is considerable debate among economists about these trajectories, largely due to different assumptions about the appropriate discount rates. With a higher discount rate than that proposed in the Stern Review, a case can be made for a more gradual approach. Nordhaus (1994) is most persuasive among those advocating a gradual approach. With a higher discount rate, the present value of costs of global warming is much lower currently but will become more pressing later in the twenty-first century. In the meantime, the resources that might have been devoted to reductions in greenhouse gas emissions could be channeled into projects where the returns are currently higher, such as investment in human resources in developing countries.

How will these CO2e concentration targets be achieved, and what will be the costs? Measures might include stopping deforestation around the world, reducing consumer demand for carbon-intensive goods and services, investing in technologies to improve energy efficiency in the use of fossil fuels, and introducing low-carbon, alternative technologies for energy. In the Review, estimates that the costs of achieving the target of 550 ppm CO2e are in the range of -1 to +3.5 percent of world GDP in each year up to 2050, with a mean of about +1 percent. These estimates rely on very optimistic assumptions about improvements in energy efficiency and on reductions in the cost of low-carbon technologies. The lower estimates reflect additions to GDP resulting from the growth of new industries and services related to climate-change policies. In the context of continuing growth in the world economy, the costs (if such they turn out to be) represent a very slight reduction in the expected growth rate.[11]

Policy options can be broadly classified under the headings mitigation and adaptation. The former seeks to reduce emissions, while the latter seeks to reduce predicted damage.

Mitigation

There is a well-developed literature on the merits of tackling emissions by either taxes or quotas.[12] A target for stabilizing greenhouse gas concentration at a particular level by a given future date implies a specific trajectory of emissions, and hence quotas, over time. To achieve those quotas by setting taxes requires knowledge of the responses of households and firms to those taxes: the less responsive, the higher the tax rate required to achieve a particular quota in a particular period. The level of tax in each period should be preannounced so households and firms can chose an adjustment path for their own emissions. For example, household responses to higher costs of energy based on fossil fuels might include action to reduce consumption (turning off unnecessary lights, decreasing use of central heating or air conditioning, traveling less by automobile and plane), though the responses may not be immediate, since households may need time to adjust their lifestyle.

Firms will have similar incentives to adopt energy-efficiency measures, to keep their costs down.[13]

In practice, it is typically easier for quotas to be imposed on producers than on households, but with the additional feature that allocated quotas or "permits" should be tradable. Tradable permits are the most efficient way to reduce emissions, since those firms and regions that can reduce emissions at relatively low costs can profit by selling some of their quota to firms or regions for which reducing emissions is more difficult. The initial allocation of quotas has no effect on the outcomes, but it does create revenues for firms that can sell quota. These revenues accrue to the owners of those firms rather than to the public sector, as in the case of a directly imposed environmental tax. Not surprisingly, businesses are keenly interested in the procedure by which initial quotas are allocated. The typical scheme involves "grandfathering," allocations based on recent emissions history of the firms involved. An alternative mechanism would involve the authorities auctioning permits to firms: a market price would then emerge, and firms would purchase permits according to their need to generate emissions and their capacity to reduce them.[14]

Adaptation

Adaptation will typically require both private and public action. In the private sector, households and businesses will adjust their activities in a variety of ways, such as insulating homes and offices against extreme temperatures, strengthening buildings to withstand severe weather, and relocating to avoid flooding. A similar adjustment will unfold in agriculture. If climate changes increase the risk of crop failure with current varieties of plants, there will be incentives to develop a greater number of resistant plants, either by selective breeding or by genetic modification. Some kinds of adaptation will require investing in what are essentially public goods, such as flood defenses, drainage systems in large cities, and water conservation and storage. These have to be provided by the public sector and financed by taxing all who will benefit from them.

The Stern Review economists are optimistic about the prospects for adaptation in the developed market economies. Assuming an increase in temperature of 2 to 3 degrees Celsius, their cost of adaptation is estimated at 0.05 to 0.5 percent of GDP annually. This estimate depends on households having access to both the information and the finance to carry out alterations to homes, such as better insulation and storm proofing.[15] There is much less optimism about developing economies. First, as noted above, the economic consequences of global warming are likely to be more severe, particularly in agriculture and extreme weather events. Second, much less is expected in terms of private adaptation activities. Markets are poorly developed, and the private sector lacks the financial resources and innovative capacity to respond to market signals. Much will therefore depend on incorporating responses to global warming in the long-term development process, involving partnerships among local communities, governments, and international aid and development agencies.

This global problem requires that policy for mitigation should also be global, if it is to be effective; so international, collective action is essential. But such action is fraught with difficulties. The main problem is that it is in the interest of any one economy to stay outside an agreement, since it can then "free ride" on the commitment of the others to reduce carbon emissions without incurring any of the costs. It will therefore be difficult to get nations to sign up in the first place; and even if an agreement is reached, it may collapse because of incentives to cheat. But self interest and cheating can be overridden by commitments to behave responsibly to "save the planet." Scott Barrett (2005), in analyzing collective action in a review of 190 arrangements for environmental protection, shows that reaching agreements and sustaining them is far from a hopeless project.[16]

The Responsibility of the Churches

According to Bookless (2007), the non-Christian world takes one of two contrasting stances on environmental matters. The first is anthropocentric, which claims that the created order is here simply for our use and enjoyment. Our only ethical imperative is not to deprive other human beings of their share or future generations of their opportunity to use and enjoy. The second stance sees the human race as no more than a part of an integrated biological system, with no special rights to the resources on offer, or at least no greater rights than any other participant in the system. The problem with these two positions, as noted by Stott (2000), is that the former position regards human beings as gods, and the created order is the loser; while the latter treats nature as god, and the human race is demoted.

The economic analysis described above assumes a largely anthropocentric stance:[17] the natural order is solely for our use and enjoyment, and the analysis is largely directed toward ensuring that the environment will be preserved for future generations to use and enjoy.[18] That is, the anthropocentric stance focuses almost exclusively on human beings as producers and consumers, rather than beings in the image of God with the capacity to enter into relationships with God and other people and with a mandate to care for the earth. That does not mean we have to discard the economic analysis, but we should be careful in the use we make of it.

Two biblical strands are especially relevant to the issue of global warming. One is the biblical mandate to care for the earth and to utilize its resources to support human flourishing.[19] There is widespread theological agreement that God is revealed in the Bible as the creator and sustainer of the natural order—the earth is his. The human race is entrusted with the role of covenantal stewardship, as spelled out in Genesis 1 and 2. In Genesis 1:26–28, we are given responsibility for the resources of the earth to sustain human flourishing: but in Genesis

2:15, that responsibility is defined in terms of "tilling" and "keeping," where the latter implies a requirement to preserve and sustain the earth as it has been entrusted to us.

A second biblical strand is concern for the poor and disadvantaged, since the evidence suggests that climate change will have its greatest negative effects on poor people in developing countries. This theme has been explored by Wright (2004, Chap. 5) and Van Til (2007), among many others, tracing the concern for the poor expressed in the Old Testament. The texts include themes relating to the settlement of Israel in the Promised Land, ensuring that every family would have a share in the allocation of land, and providing support for those who had fallen on hard times until their land could be restored to them or for those who, for other reasons, had no family land. In Matthew 25:31–46, the parable of the sheep and the goats, Jesus identifies feeding the hungry, clothing the naked, and receiving the stranger as indicators of righteousness.

How might these theological insights affect Christian support for policies to address climate change? First, a Christian might argue for a low discount rate to be used in assessing the costs of climate change and the benefits of taking action to combat it. As stewards of the created order, we have a responsibility to generations of our descendants to ensure that we do not undermine their capacity to serve in the same way. Second, we might wish to give a greater weight to the preservation of the natural order for its own sake: within the framework of economics, it would matter little if the human race lived in a totally despoiled environment so long as it was able in perpetuity to produce and consume even more than it does now. Third, the assignment of higher "weights" to benefits and costs that affect the poor than to those that affect the rich is fine as shorthand for designing policies that will benefit the poor: but it is a thin representation of a commitment to the poor as entitled to live productive lives without encountering problems arising from global warming. To put it another way, the poor have rights to a world that has not been despoiled (and so have the rich, of course). We need to ensure that their livelihood and development opportunities are protected, even at the cost of the standard of living of the rich. While at times there can be a tension between the mandates to care for creation and to care for the poor, these are not irreconcilable as Dean shows in Chapter 12 of this book.

Clearly few Christians are in a position to influence the choice of discount rate and the weights for costs and benefits to rich and poor people. For the majority of Christians, there are three areas where action is more appropriate.

The first is personal and local.[20] Christian households in developed countries should be aware of their carbon footprint and take action to reduce it. The actions might include reducing the use of energy generated from fossil fuels (turning down the central-heating thermostat, using less air conditioning, insulating the house better), using public transport instead of private automobiles (and lobbying for improvements in public transport where it is inadequate), flying less, and generally consuming less of everything. Churches should do the same. Churches should also give their support to Christian-based environmental projects both at home and abroad; these are an educational tool for Christians. Such support gives credence to Christian advocacy concerning environmental change, since what is said to governments can be based in practical understanding of the issues involved.

The second area is that of Christian, development NGOs. Most are already acutely aware of the impact of climate change, both current and prospective, on the lives and livelihood of the poorest people with whom they work, especially in Africa and South Asia.[21] Indeed the issue of sustainability is already a key element in many of their projects. But there is of course a limit to what can be achieved locally if the problem is global climate change.

The third area is persuasion in the public arena. If we believe that mankind has a responsibility to sustain the environment, then it is incumbent upon us to make our voices heard. This persuasion can be through denominational bodies or through the establishment of lobby groups that bring together informed Christians from a variety of churches.[22] Such advocacy will carry greater weight if it is backed by evidence that the churches are also taking action to reduce their collective carbon footprint.

Conclusions

The concept of "double listening" was proposed by John Stott to describe the challenge facing Christians living in the secular world:

> We are called to double listening, listening to both the Word and the world. […] I am not suggesting that we should listen to God and to our fellow human beings in the same way or with the same degree of deference. We listen to the Word with humble reverence anxious to understand it, and resolved to believe and obey what we have come to understand. We listen to the world with critical alertness, anxious to understand it too, and resolved not necessarily to believe and obey it, but to sympathize with it and to seek grace to discover how the gospel relates to it (Stott 1992, 27–28).

This concept needs to underlie any Christian commentary on a complex global issue like climate change. Listening to the Word, we note the requirements to exercise covenantal stewardship and to have a particular concern for the poor. Listening to the world, publications such as the Fourth Report of the IPCC and the Stern Review are key documents for understanding the science and economics of global warming; and the Christian community should not hesitate to read them constructively, but not uncritically.

So what should be done? A first objective is to arrive at an international understanding of the problem, including agreement on a target range for the stabilization of CO_2e concentrations and on a trajectory for emissions over the next few decades. Ideally, a global price for carbon emissions needs to be established to enable "efficient abatement" of carbon emissions around the world.[23] However, it will probably be easier to get international agreement on a global quota for emissions reduction, which is then divided among the economies. A market in emissions quotas should be encouraged to identify the global price for emissions given the targets. The remaining issue is the basis for allocating the quotas. International grandfathering of emissions is not equitable, since it would implicitly permit greater emissions by the developed economies. These economies have been responsible historically for about 70 percent of the existing concentrations of CO_2e; they stand to lose least from global warming; and they are well placed to respond to global warming by mitigation and adaptation. It would therefore be equitable for the allocations of emissions-reduction targets to be more stringent for the developed countries, even allowing developing countries some room to increase their emissions as their per capita incomes grow. Evidently, the aggregate quota would have to decrease over time to follow the agreed trajectory for reduction in emissions.

A Christian should have reservations about our ability to resolve major world problems supposing we can analyze them sufficiently and present the nations with rational and equitable solutions. He or she might well be pessimistic about the capacity of fallen humanity to act sensibly in this way and want to know who has the power to decide what is going to be done. For example, we should be alert to the power of rich nations to set the international allocation of quotas in their own interests. The churches therefore need to act as the consciences of their national political authorities in the development of policies; but if their voice is to be heeded, they must be seen reducing their own carbon footprints.

Questions for Review

1. Climate science can at best predict a range of possible global warming outcomes over the next one hundred years. How should this uncertainty affect our evaluation of the recommendations for urgent action in, for example, the Stern Review?

2. Why is the choice of discount rate so critical to the framing of climate-change policy? Assess the arguments for choosing high or low rates.

3. Moderate climate change could be quite beneficial for the developed economies of North America and Europe, but generate high costs in Africa and Southeast Asia. What then are the arguments for requiring the governments of developed economies to implement policies to reduce their CO2e emissions?

4. What are the main difficulties in implementing policies to combat climate change at the national and international levels?

5. What, if anything, can and should the churches do to combat climate change?

Notes

[1] A prime mover was the distinguished U.K. climate scientist and Christian, Professor (later Sir) John Houghton. He was one of the first scientists to alert the international community to the dangers inherent in global warming, and he served as chair of the Panel that produced the first scientific report in 1990. In his book, *Global Warming: The Complete Briefing* (2004, 3d ed.), he gives one of the best "popular" accounts of the science and makes clear his own Christian position on the issues.

[2] This is not to say that everyone in the scientific community agrees. See, for example, Carter (et al. 2006) for a strongly worded critique of IPCC methods and findings as summarized in the Stern Review. This disagreement generates a problem for writing this chapter, since the author lacks the expertise to evaluate the competing claims. The IPCC Report is assumed to represent the majority scientific opinion.

[3] IPCC (2007, 10).

[4] The Stern Review (2007) was commissioned by the U.K. Treasury in July 2005 and involved a large team of economists under the direction of Lord Nicholas Stern, a distinguished economist who had previously served as chief economist to the World Bank. The Review presents a comprehensive and up-to-date survey of the literature on the economics of climate change and is a useful and accessible source text for those who want to know about the issues. Whether its analysis and policy prescriptions are correct is a (sometimes hotly) disputed issue in the economics literature.

[5] CO_2e is carbon dioxide equivalent for all greenhouse gas effects produced by carbon dioxide and other gases such as methane and nitrous oxide.

[6] This list is drawn from the Stern Review (2007, Chap. 3). The scientific bases are robustly criticized in Carter (et al. 2006). The criticisms are that the scenarios chosen for analysis are generally "worst case," that caveats and weaknesses in the underlying studies are not acknowledged, and that no allowance is made for countermeasures, including improved technologies, to mitigate the effects. The Stern Review does in fact address mitigation and adaptation in detail in later chapters.

[7] This list of damages does not include possible sudden and major impacts of climate change on the natural environment, the so-called "tipping points" (see Lenton 2008). The assumption that the environmental effects of global warming will be linear extrapolations from current conditions could be quite wrong. Climate scientists are seriously considering a possibility that the North Atlantic Thermohaline Circulation might slow down or stop altogether, resulting in a severe cooling of the winter climate in Western Europe.

[8] There is much more that could be said on this topic, but that would take us deep into technical issues of economic analysis. See Weitzman (2007) and Nordhaus (2007) for a discussion.

[9] In economic analysis, these are referred to as utility weights.

[10] The cuts in emissions required would be even greater if global warming is accompanied by a weakening in the natural capacity of the global environment to reabsorb carbon dioxide.

[11] The Stern Review (2007, 278) suggests that over the period to 2100 the costs of mitigation would be equivalent to reducing world growth in GDP from an assumed 2.5 percent pa under "business-as-usual" to 2.49 percent pa.

[12] See Hepburn (2006) for an accessible and comprehensive discussion of the issues in the context of regulatory policies in general.

[13] The hope sometimes expressed that carbon-saving measures will develop autonomously and that behavior will change voluntarily, without a change in prices, shows a curious misunderstanding of how markets actually work. Moreover, the experience of the market economies is that changes in relative prices generate changes in behavior and technologies in a relatively short time.

[14] In practice the experience of emissions trading schemes is quite limited. The most ambitious example is the European Union's Emissions Trading Scheme (EU ETS), which was launched in January 2005. There is general agreement that the Scheme had a defect in that too many grandfathered quotas were issued by national governments, so the trading price tended to be low. In the next phase of the Scheme, the quotas are likely to be tighter, reflecting greater European commitment to tackling climate change and a higher price is likely to emerge in the market. EU ETS was the subject of a special issue of *Climate Policy* (Grubb 2006).

[15] The analysis is based on global warming of no more than 2 to 3 degrees Celsius: if the actual outcome is twice that temperature range, then the scale of the effects may be such as to rule out adaptation (for example, many major coastal cities will just have to be abandoned).

[16] Agreements on carbon emissions will be more difficult because the scale and corresponding costs are so much greater. The experience of the Kyoto Protocol is illuminating in this respect.

[17] Though not entirely, there is the occasional nod in the direction of a requirement to maintain biodiversity and ecosystems, and not only for the use that future generations might make of them.

[18] The analysis, in common with modern economic analysis generally, works within a utilitarian framework to identify what makes for human flourishing. The objections to this framework from the standpoint of a Christian understanding of humanity are analyzed in Hay (1989, Chaps. 2 and 3).

[19] There is extensive literature on this point, and all we can do is to indicate the main lines of thought. Wright (2004, Chap. 4) gives a full exposition and summary of the Old Testament texts to derive their ethical implications. DeWitt (1994, 1997) and Sider (2000) provide a succinct summary of the relevant biblical materials.

[20] The websites www.creationcare.org and www.coolingcreation.org have many useful suggestions on practical actions that churches and Christian households can take.

[21] The U.K. evangelical development and relief organization, TEARFUND, has been particularly aware of climate change issues in the developing world. See www.tearfund.org for more details, particularly their 2005 report, "Dried Up, Drowned Out."

[22] The website www.christiansandclimate.org gives information about the Evangelical Climate Initiative.

[23] Industries and regions with low marginal costs of emissions reduction will do more than those with high costs, and the global cost of emissions reduction will thereby be minimized.

References

Barrett, Scott. 2005. *Environment and Statecraft: The Strategy of Environmental Treaty Making*. New York, NY: Oxford University Press.

Bookless, David. 2007. Towards a Theology of Sustainability. In Chap. 2 of *When Enough Is Enough*, edited by R. J. Berry. Leicester, U.K.: Inter-Varsity Press.

Carter, R. M., C. R. de Freitas, I. M. Goklany, D. Holland, and R. S. Lindzen. 2006. "The Stern Review: A Dual Critique." *World Economics* 7, no. 4, 167–98.

DeWitt, C. B. 1994. *Earth-Wise: A Biblical Response to Environmental Issues*. Grand Rapids, MI: CRC Publications.

———. 1997. *Caring for Creation*. Grand Rapids, MI: Baker Books.

Grubb, Michael, and Karsten Neuhoff. 2006. "Allocation and Competitiveness in the EU Emissions Trading Scheme." *Climate Policy* 6, no. 1.

Hay, D. A. 1989. *Economics Today: A Christian Critique*. Leicester, U.K.: Apollos, Inter-Varsity Press. Republished in 2004, Vancouver, B.C.: Regent College Publishing.

Hepburn, C. 2006. "Regulating by Prices, Quantities or Both: An Update and an Overview." *Oxford Review of Economic Policy* 22, no. 2: 226–47.

Houghton, J. T. 2004. *Global Warming: The Complete Briefing*. 3d ed. New York, NY: Cambridge University Press.

IPCC. 2007. Summary for Policymakers. In *Climate Change 2007: The Physical Science Basis. Intergovernmental Panel on Climate Change*. New York, NY: Cambridge University Press. View at www.ipcc.ch.

Lenton, T. M., H. Held, E. Kriegler, J. W. Hall, W. Lucht, S. Rahmstorf, and H. J. Schellnhuber. 2008. "Tipping Elements in the Earth's Climate System." *PNAS* 105, no. 6 (February 12), 1786–93. Proceedings of the National Academy of Sciences.

Nordhaus, W. D. 1994. *Managing the Global Commons: The Economics of Climate Change*. Cambridge, MA and London: MIT Press.

———. 2007. "A Review of the *Stern Review on the Economics of Climate Change*." *Journal of Economic Literature* XLV, no. 3 (September), 686–702.

Sider, R. J. 2000. Biblical Foundations for Creation Care. In Chap. 2 of *The Care of Creation*, edited by R. J. Berry. Leicester, U.K.: Inter-Varsity Press.

Stern, N. 2007. *The Economics of Climate Change: The Stern Review*. New York, NY: Cambridge University Press.

Stott, J. R. W. 1992. *The Contemporary Christian*. Leicester, U.K.: Inter-Varsity Press.

———. 2000. Foreword in *The Care of Creation*, edited by R. J. Berry. Leicester, U.K.: Inter-Varsity Press.

Tol, R. S. J. 2005. "The Marginal Damage Costs of Carbon Dioxide Emissions: An Assessment of the Uncertainties." *Energy Policy* 33: 2064–74.

Weitzman, M. L. 2007. "A Review of the *Stern Review on the Economics of Climate Change*." *Journal of Economic Literature* XLV, no. 3 (September), 703–24.

Van Til, K. A. 2007. *Less Than Two Dollars a Day: A Christian View of World Poverty and the Free Market*. Grand Rapids, MI: Eerdmans.

Wright, C. J. H. 2004. *Old Testament Ethics for the People of God*. Leicester, U.K.: Inter-Varsity Press.

CHAPTER 14

ECONOMIC GROWTH:

IS MORE ALWAYS BETTER?

Bob Goudzwaard

No claims in our modern society are more insistent and compelling than those related to the necessity of continued economic growth. Growth is seen as the basis of almost everything that is good and desirable. It is the basis of more jobs and a reduced public deficit. It is the basis of the maintenance of good health and social security systems. It is the basis of more adequate environmental protection and increased development aid. So it is our culture's common conviction that we have to strive for the highest degree of productivity and competitiveness in our economy—even if this at times requires substantial sacrifices in human relationships and natural resources. This way of thinking, I believe, is one of the roots of the growing dominance of economics in our culture, for in it we allow economic yardsticks to be decisive in most cases. But is this standard way of reasoning correct? Further, is it the only possible way of thinking? Do its underlying theoretical assumptions need critical testing—for instance, from the broader perspective that the Bible provides?

Questions like these have puzzled me for many years. Almost thirty years ago, in my thesis about unpriced scarcity, I began wrestling with these questions academically (Goudzwaard 1970). I have also dealt with them politically as, for example, in 1976 when I wrote the central parts of the program "Not by Bread Alone," the election platform of the Christian political parties in the Netherlands. But these questions have never been as urgent as they are now. We live in a time of intense globalization in which all modern nations feel compelled to maintain and expand their competitive advantage over other nations. Competitiveness and growth have now become the new absolutes for all so-called good government. We have to expand economically simply to exist: "I am growing, therefore I am." And all this is happening at a time when serious warnings can be heard: This competitive struggle between rich countries is diminishing the chances for the poorest countries, and a continuous expansion of production and trade is threatening the diminishing carrying capacity of the earth and destabilizing the world's climates (Witteveen 1998). But, we hear, do we have a choice? Is there any viable alternative at the turn of this millennium? In this spirit, both Shell and the World Trade Organization took over Mrs. Thatcher's well-known TINA slogan: "There Is No Alternative." Their implicit message is that so-called doomsday thinkers should keep their mouths shut.

At this point, the discussion can easily turn grim—as is usually the case when implicit assumptions come to the fore. I am always happy to engage in abstract debate with fellow economists, but in this chapter I propose to widen the discourse by discussing briefly the biblical sources of my own academic inspiration. For it could very well be that exactly those sources are needed to overcome impasses like the ones to which I have been referring and to lead to a fresh reappraisal of some of the most compelling issues of our time.

Let me begin by referring to a spiritual impulse that comes directly from many passages in the New Testament. In his parables, Jesus often spoke about stewards, good stewards and bad stewards (for example, Matthew 20:8; Luke 12:42). And behind his words, you feel a deep respect for the God-given rule of *oikonomia,* the good care that is needed for the *oikos*, the household. For Jesus, the word "economy" (Gk *oikonomia*) was primarily a divine mandate. It included the care of the land and a concern for the well-being of those who live from its fruits. So for Jesus, it was an economic rule, not just an ethical rule, that workers should receive their food on time! Remarkably, in Jesus' words about human economic life there is also an eschatological perspective. The Lord of the land himself will come back to ask all his servants to render account of their style of economic behavior (Luke 16:1ff.). And that accountability is not only required of persons but also of the *ethne*, the peoples or nations of this world (Matthew 25:32). It is not least as the Great Economist that God will judge them all (Meeks 1989).

Now at first glance these references may seem unrelated to the present debate about economic growth. But let us not be too quick to jump to that conclusion. In these New Testament texts, economy, responsibility, and accountability are interrelated; they simply cannot be separated. But, we may ask, how far have we succeeded in separating them, for instance by splitting them into two compartments, physical and metaphysical? This is an intriguing question, for we can ask this equally about scientific economics and about our societies as a whole. On the level of our modern society, the question runs like this: Have we built our society on the silent premise that we can avoid a lot of nasty questions about responsibility and economic accountability— including questions of growth—if we simply turn to the factual world that functions by mechanisms that are in principle infallible? And on the level of economics as a science, the question runs: Have we as economists, precisely because we wanted to be as neutral and as scientifically objective as possible, fallen into a worldview that is too mechanical, that is closed to any kind of value-oriented normativity? One of the main characteristics of our subculture as economists is this: we want above all to be seen and valued as competent scientists. We have wanted this recognition at least since John Stuart Mill, who protested against Auguste Comte's refusal to view economics as a legitimate positive science (Schumpeter 1963, 417).

I believe it is important to ask these critical questions—not least in evaluating economic growth. For if we economists strive for value-freedom at all costs, then, in the first place, we will be unwilling to speak even one critical word about the quantity and quality of what human beings want. We will treat all these desires simply as data, as given factors; so our study of economic growth will concentrate on questions of the use and allocation of means and will avoid the question of the choice of ends. In the second place, because we want to avoid all qualitative and subjective opinions, we, also, will speak only about objectively measurable entities, such as quantities and prices. And thereby our approach as economists to the issue of economic growth becomes shrunken and small. Our main concern is with attaining a maximum expansion of an output that is well allocated; that is, an output in which the allocation of all products is guided by a properly functioning market mechanism.

Do you not agree that in this way a reduction has taken place? This way of thinking regards economic resources like labor and land instrumentally; they become objects of use, not objects of care. This way of thinking, therefore, leads to a lack of an economic critique on the commercially promoted explosion of human needs in our already-rich societies. For needs can be produced just as commodities are produced, notably by the input of the seductive devices offered by mass media. So the result can be that, instead of a decrease of scarcity, an increase of scarcity is taking place. Think here for instance of e-commerce and advertising campaigns that push the level of human needs and desires artificially beyond the level of their possible saturation. And all this is confirmed by what we daily see around us. We live in a post-modern society in which there is both an abundance of information and a growing general sense of scarcity, for which increasingly more growth is needed. Our society is also characterized by a reduced sense of economic accountability and care, for the market mechanism is not the best possible compass to guide us to a good outcome.

However, critique alone does not help. We should therefore not evade the question of alternatives. In a time in which the need for stronger economic growth has become so strongly compelling, is it true that "There Is No Alternative"? Here I draw your attention to a second source of inspiration: the biblical texts relating to the economic life of ancient Israel. I read these texts anew when I, as a young, university lecturer, was asked to teach a course in the theory of economic systems. To my surprise I found that the regulations of the Torah on work and interest, and on land and rest, were the ingredients of a complete and coherent economic system.[1] Then this thought occurred to me: *In this system of Torah economics, is there perhaps a hidden wisdom that might have value for our time?*

Now it may seem absurd even to ask this question. For referring to the Torah means dealing with the rules and institutions of a very different society, which was primarily agricultural. And these rules and institutions are old—four millennia old. But this sense of remoteness may begin to change if we note that every economic system, of whatever historical period, has to find a kind of internal balance between necessary inputs and desirable outputs. In ancient Israel this balance was in some sense unique or, in any case, was remarkably different from all modern market—and planned—economies. Let me try to explain. When we economists refer to the increase of the Gross Domestic Product or the Gross National Product as an index of our economic growth, we know that these indexes represent outputs—the sum of all the values that were added to the economy by the overall expansion of the output-level. But to enable such an increase in *output,* a corresponding rise of *input* is needed in terms of the use of labor, capital, and natural resources. Of course, economic systems can differ markedly in their adherence to either market or planning principles, but they can also differ in their primary orientation to the level of either output or input. In all modern economies, the primary orientation is to the level of output. We want to maximize the growth of our production, and we therefore implement and enforce stringent rules of efficiency and productivity in the area of input. But in ancient Israel, the primary economic orientation was to inputs. Just look what this meant in Israel with regard to the main production factors of labor, nature, and capital. Labor: In Israel it was forbidden to subject any laborer to harsh treatment—a slave was immediately freed if only one tooth was knocked out—and all workers were entitled to enjoy their daily and weekly rest. Further, the land, the vital economic factor in ancient Israel, was protected by numerous legal measures. Every seventh year—the sabbatical year—the land was to be rested from cultivation, while cattle fertilized it, so it would be ready for a new cycle of cultivation. And capital? It was available to all people. This was arranged by an open and public discouragement of any strong accumulation of capital. For example, investing in land was impossible in Israel because the Jubilee laws required land, every forty-nine years, to be returned to its original owner. So the demand for capital and the supply of capital could indeed meet each other around a zero-level of interest. All this made Israel a mainly input-oriented economy: the good and healthy condition of land, labor, capital, and environment was basic to all economic processes and was enabled by an overall preventive care—a care that included even access to land for the poor.

Of course such a radical orientation of an economy toward the preservation and regeneration of inputs has a price: it diminishes the possible final level of output. But in ancient Israel, the height of that level was of secondary importance. For the soil was fertile enough to lead to good harvests, the needs of the people were limited, and extraordinary outputs were seen as surpluses that enabled feasting together, enjoying the abundance of the Lord with all members of the community. For all the Israelites knew, and maybe they knew it better than we do, there can only be a sense of abundance if there is first an awareness of having enough; for, literally, abundance means *overflowing*, having even more than enough.

Let us consider this in light of our contemporary values. At first sight, this looks plain crazy—this attentiveness to the condition of inputs and the apparent recklessness on the output side. But is that true? To put it pointedly: why, when we speak of economic growth, do we talk only about the *volume* of the output side of our economies and never about the *condition of* the input side? Have we, in our Western economies, become so preoccupied with outer growth that we have neglected the possibility of an inner growth of our economies?

I think the answer is an unequivocal "Yes." In our rich societies, we are now even reaching the point—indeed, there are indications that we have already passed it[2]—where the value of further increases of the outer growth is more than offset by reductions in the inner growth of the economy. Just think of the many people in the production process who are working under permanent stress and are facing "burn-out"; in the Netherlands this amounts to one-sixth of the working population. Think also of the millions of people who have become unemployed for similar reasons. And think about the ease with which we accept further burdens on our environment, greater destruction of the fertile topsoil and the build-up of greenhouse gases, merely to reach a somewhat higher level of outer growth. And think, last but not least, about the lack of available and cheap capital, especially for poor people and for the indebted countries, precisely because we, as rich countries, want to give priority to our own consumption and output. In our economies, the balance between inner and outer growth has become distorted; it has shifted far too much to the output side. Somehow, in our modern arrogance, we have missed the wisdom of ancient Israel, whose economy was an economy of abundance (shalom) and inclusion based on limited means. In contrast, ours is an economy of scarcity and exclusion based on an ever-expanding flow of means.

Now this insight could be a key for the liberation of our economies for which so many in our societies are looking. But how can we use that key? We obviously have to redress a balance. But how can we, in our countries and cultures, imagine an alternative? I would like to make two suggestions.

My first suggestion is derived from the wisdom that is evident in every growing tree. The tree grows in height, which relates to outer economic growth; but it also grows inwardly, in the silent process of building its fruit-bearing capacity. This happens by the inclusion of all cells and by an enriching symbiosis with its environment. This combination of inner and outer growth is something we have not been able to realize in our "tunnel economies." For we include some people but exclude others, those who stay unemployed or are living in the poor South; and we increasingly overburden our natural environment and cause stress in a lot of human bodies and souls by the way we are producing things. And so the question occurs: How can a simple tree do what we are unable to do, combining those various goals and keeping the balance? The answer is as simple as it is surprising. The tree is able to do these by using restraint, by refraining from the desire to grow up to the heavens and reach the clouds. At a certain moment, led by what we could call an inbuilt wisdom, the tree reaches maturity; it stops its further vertical growth in order to use its reserves fully to bear fruits and produce seeds.

In my view this analogy contains a valuable lesson for all modern economists and politicians. Only when we exercise restraint, only when we invoke the discipline of withholding, does inner economic growth become a real possibility (Goudzwaard and de Lange 1995, Chap. 8). The wisdom of self-limitation can be partially illustrated by the success of the Dutch *polder* model. This is a model of cooperation, between the organizations of employers and employees, in which they make contracts with each other to create more human-friendly and environmental-friendly workplaces and to uphold essential welfare provisions in the Netherlands, all of this on the basis of openness to restraint in their financial claims. Notably, the labor unions have been willing to support a trade-off between these broader goals and the maximum rise in their own disposable wage-income. Of course, these contracts are sometimes difficult to make; the negotiations can be hard. But experience has shown that it works, even in a highly export-oriented economy like Holland, which will lose out completely if it fails to maintain its high level of competitiveness.

My second suggestion is related to the almost forgotten need for an enlarged, broadened type of economic responsibility. For too long our societies have trusted well-functioning mechanisms, such as the market mechanism, the democratic mechanism, and even the plan mechanism, to produce good outcomes. Mechanisms, however, cannot save us. They can even tempt us to neglect basic responsibilities for our neighbors, for our environment, for the well-being of our children and grandchildren. So while we think that we are wide awake and alert, we can in fact be asleep, hypnotized by the soft, seductive voices that lull us into thinking that we should not fear, because Growth is with us and the staff of the Market will help us and lead us through all valleys of economic death.

But I am convinced that the time has come to wake up. Think of the parable of Jesus (Matthew 25:1ff.) in which those who were fast asleep were awakened with the shout that the Lord was coming. Our situation is analogous. For our environment is in genuine peril, nations in the South are really perishing, and we are overburdening both others and ourselves. So the moment has come for our rich economies to leave childishness behind and to come of age; it is time for us to decide deliberately for enoughness, for contentment, wherever (and whenever) that is needed for the transformation of our economies. For, if such a willingness were to grow in our culture, it could induce at least some, and maybe in the course of time many, producing companies to extend their economic services to the public—producing their goods with better care for the environment, less stressful labor conditions, and a fairer compensation for their trading partners in the South—in exchange for either higher prices or lower wage demands. Labor unions could then consider whether they would be willing to pay for this in terms of a diminution of their wage claims, while consumers would have the choice to opt for a socially and ecologically "better" product in exchange for a somewhat higher price. For "always more" is the silliest formula to live by; and our tasks as Christians are primarily support and restraint.

Likewise, governments, according to a suggestion of George Goyder (1975, 130), could play a part in this. They could designate companies that are pioneers in the field of enlarged and widened forms of social and environmental responsibility with the label "public company," so that these would be clearly recognizable by the public. We should also expect our governments to take action in the international field. Our governments should be willing to cooperate in and conclude global agreements about environmental restraints (Rio, Kyoto), and they should be prepared to meet together for a second Bretton Woods conference on the International Monetary System. In that conference, the turbulent ship of global finance could be re-anchored in solid ground. That ground can be found only if rich countries understand that they have to grow into new patterns of material saturation and serviceable fertility as well as make financial room for the unfulfilled, basic needs of the heavily indebted poorest countries.

Christian students in Surabaya, Indonesia, put it well in their conference about globalization. They declared that TINA, the motto that there is no alternative for our economies, is a lie. In its place they proposed a new slogan: TATA, "There Are Thousands of Alternatives"—especially for those nations and peoples who want to act on the basis of their own true economic responsibility.[3] May their words become our words in this new millennium.

Economic Growth: Is More Always Better?

This chapter originally appeared in Christianity and the Culture of Economics, edited by Donald A. Hay and Alan Kreider (2001). Reprinted with permission from University of Wales Press.

Questions for Review

1. Do you believe economic growth is good? Please explain.

2. Do you believe Christians have been too uncritical about the assumptions underlying economic theory?

3. Regarding the accountability and care for our economic resources, Goudzwaard maintains "the market mechanism is not the best possible compass to guide us to a good outcome." Do you agree? Please explain.

4. What differences would you see in your life, good and bad, if our economy were to change from its current output orientation to an input orientation?

5. Goudzwaard concludes that "always more" is the silliest formula to live by, and that our tasks as Christians are primarily support and restraint. Identify three ways you could specifically promote such a change in perspective.

Notes

[1] See Goudzwaard (1978). There I discuss the hidden economic cohesion between the separate rules of the Torah. Think, for instance, about the strange rule in Deuteronomy 23:20 that says it is generally not permitted to claim interest for loans with the exception of loans to foreigners, whom one may compel to repay: "On loans to a foreigner you may charge interest, but on loans to another Israelite you may not charge interest." That is a text that appears to us to be discriminatory and just plain wrong, until we realize that Israel had to uphold its own distinctive economy in a world in which the payment of high interest was a common practice. If every foreign banker could borrow Israelite money at an interest-level of zero without repayment, just because the law of Israel said so, all Israelite capital would have flowed immediately to the neighboring economies. So we meet here an economic-political provision to keep the necessary capital within the Israelite borders. The system was not meant to remain Utopian; it was obviously designed to work in practice and to lead people to prosperity.

[2] See Daly and Cobb (1989, 453). From 1970 to 1980, there was a very slight decline of the per capita ISEW (index of sustainable economic welfare) by 0.14 percent per year. The decline of the per capita ISEW during the 1980s by the time Daly and Cobb wrote had been 1.26 percent per year.

[3] International Seminar on Alternative Economies in the Global Market System, held in Surabaya, Indonesia, October 1996. Also cited in *Living Together in Plurality and Justice* (SWGF 1999, 30).

References

Daly, Herman E., and John B. Cobb. 1989. *For the Common Good: Redirecting the Economy toward Community, the Environment, and a Sustainable Future.* Boston: Beacon Press.

Goudzwaard, Bob. 1970. Ongeprijsde schaarste, een onderzoek naar de plaats van expretiale of ongecompenseerde effecten in de theoretische economie en de leer der economische politiek. Ph.D. diss., with an English summary. The Hague.

———. 1978. Socioeconomic Life: A Way of Confession. In *Aid for the Overdeveloped West.* Toronto: Wedge Publishing, 22–23.

———, and Harry de Lange. 1995. *Beyond Poverty and Affluence: Toward an Economy of Care.* Grand Rapids, MI: Eerdmans.

Goyder, George. 1975. *The Responsible Worker.* London: Hutchinson. id., 1961. *The Responsible Company.* Oxford: Blackwell.

Meeks, M. Douglas. 1989. *God the Economist: The Doctrine of God and Political Economy.* Minneapolis: Fortress Press.

Schumpeter, Joseph A. 1963. *History of Economic Analysis.* Oxford University Press.

SWGF. 1999. *Living Together in Plurality and Justice*. Solo, Indonesia: Social Welfare Guidance Foundation.

Witteveen, H. Johannes. 1998. Economic Globalization in a Broader, Long-Term Perspective: Some Serious Concerns. In *The Policy Changes of Global Financial Integration*, edited by Jan Joost. The Hague.

LIST OF CONTRIBUTORS

Christopher Barrett is the Stephen B. and Janice G. Ashley Professor of Applied Economics and Management and International Professor of Agriculture at Cornell University where he also serves as the Cornell Center for a Sustainable Future's Associate Director for Economic Development Programs. He teaches and conducts research in the areas of international development, environmental and resource economics, international trade, markets and price analysis, agricultural production and distribution, and applied econometrics. He has published 10 books and more than 170 journal articles and book chapters. He served as editor of the *American Journal of Agricultural Economics* from 2003–2008, is presently an associate editor or editorial board member of the *African Journal of Agricultural and Resource Economics*, *Environment and Development Economics*, the *Journal of African Economies and World Development*, and was previously President of the Association of Christian Economists.

Bradley Christerson is Associate Professor of Sociology at Biola University. He is coauthor of *Against All Odds: The Struggle of Racial Integration in Religious Organizations* (NYU Press, 2005). He has also written numerous journal articles in the areas of ethnicity, globalization, and religious organizations.

Judith M. Dean is currently a Lead International Economist in the Research Division of the Office of Economics, U.S. International Trade Commission. Before joining the ITC, Dr. Dean was an Associate Professor of Economics at SAIS, John Hopkins University, and served as a consultant to the World Bank and the OECD. Dr. Dean received her Ph.D. in economics from Cornell University. She is a former president and active member of the Association of Christian Economists, and serves on the Boards of Gordon College and World Relief. Dr. Dean has an extensive publication record in both the secular and Christian literatures, including the recent book *Attacking Poverty in the Developing World: Christian Practitioners and Academics in Collaboration* (Authentic Media, 2005).

Daniel Finn is both an economist and a theologian. He teaches at St. John's University in Collegeville, Minnesota, where he is Professor of Moral Theology and the William E. and Virginia Clemens Professor of Economics and the Liberal Arts. He is president of the Society of Christian Ethics and a past-president of the Association for Social Economics and the Catholic Theological Society of America. He has published extensively on the relation of ethics and economics, including his latest book entitled *The Moral Ecology of Markets: A Framework for Assessing Justice in Economic Life* (Cambridge, 2006).

Bob Goudzwaard is professor emeritus at the Free University in Amsterdam. He was elected to the Dutch Parliament in the 1970s and served for a time in a Christian policy research institute in The Hague. He is the author of numerous books including *Capitalism and Progress*. His most recent book is *Hope in Troubled Times: A New Vision for Confronting Global Crises* (Baker Academic, 2007).

Donald Hay is now retired. He was head ("Dean") of the Division of Social Sciences at the University of Oxford and a Professorial Fellow of Jesus College, Oxford, from 2000–2005. Previously, he taught and researched in the Department of Economics. His main areas of research and teaching were in industrial organization and economics. He undertook research in Brazil and China, and contributed to academic discussions that led to a major reform of competition policy in the U.K. in 2002. Among his many publications was a major text, co-authored with Derek Morris, *Industrial Economics and Organisation* (2d ed., 1991). He has also written on the interface between Christian theology and economic analysis, with an emphasis on ethical issues, notably *Economics Today: A Christian Critique* (1989) and *Christianity and the Culture of Economics* (2001).

Roland Hoksbergen is Professor of Economics at Calvin College. He earned his Ph.D. in Economics from University of Notre Dame (1986) and his research interests are focused on the areas of Third World development and the role of non-governmental organizations. Before Calvin College, Dr. Hoksbergen worked for the Christian Reformed Church World Relief Committee.

Michael Novak currently holds the George Frederick Jewett Chair in Religion, Philosophy, and Public Policy at the American Enterprise Institute in Washington, D.C. He is the 1994 recipient of the million-dollar Templeton Prize for Progress in Religion. Mr. Novak has written 26 influential books on the philosophy and theology of culture, especially the essential elements of a free society. His writings have appeared in every major Western language and in Bengali, Korean, and Japanese. His masterpiece, *The Spirit of Democratic Capitalism*, was published underground in Poland in 1984, and after 1989, in Czechoslovakia, Germany, China, Hungary, Bangladesh, Korea, and many times in Latin America. His latest book, *No One Sees God: The Dark Night of Atheists and Believers* was published by Doubleday in 2008.

Julius Oladipo is founder and President of Vintage Development Organisation, a Nigeria-based NGO focused on capacity building in Africa. He has a Ph.D. in Statistics (1983) from Bradford University, England. Before founding Vintage Development, he served at Ahmadu

Bello University for 16 years at the Computer Centre, consulting on research projects of professors and graduate students and simultaneous at ABUCONS, the university's consultancy firm. For 5 years afterwards, he was Senior Consultant for BEMS Nigeria, engaged mostly on governmental projects funded by official assistance. He later served for 9 years at CORAT AFRICA, a Pan African training and consultancy organization that serves churches and Christian development organizations. He has vast experience in planning, monitoring, and evaluating development programs; organizational strengthening; leadership development; peace building; and conflict resolution.

J. David Richardson is Senior Fellow Emeritus at the Peterson Institute for International Economics in Washington, D.C., and Professor of Economics and International Relations in the Maxwell School of Citizenship and Public Affairs at Syracuse University. He is a Research Associate of the National Bureau of Economic Research and has written extensively on trade, globalization, and international economic policy issues. He is the author or coauthor of *Why Global Commitment Really Matters!* (2001), *Global Competition Policy* (1997), *Competition Policies for the Global Economy* (1997), *Why Exports Matter: More!* (1996), *Why Exports Really Matter!* (1995), and *Sizing Up U.S. Export Disincentives* (1993).

Steven Rundle is Associate Professor of Economics at Biola University, where he teaches courses in international economics at both the undergraduate and MBA level. He has traveled extensively in the developing world, and most of his publications reflect his interest in the challenges facing those countries. He has published in peer-reviewed journals and books and is lead author of the book *Great Commission Companies: The Emerging Role of Business in Missions* (Intervarsity Press, 2003), which explains how globalization is changing the ministry landscape for Christian businesspeople. He also consults or has cofounded several organizations that aim to see Christian-owned businesses prosper in less-developed countries.

A. Sue Russell is both a theologian and anthropologist. She earned doctorates from La Trobe University and Biola University. She currently has a joint teaching assignment in the Talbot School of Theology and the School of Intercultural Studies at Biola University. Before her graduate studies, Dr. Russell spent seventeen years doing field research with Wycliffe Bible Translators, working with indigenous communities in Southeast Asia. She has published extensively in areas of theology, missiology, and anthropology.

Stephen L. S. Smith is Professor of Economics at Gordon College, where he chairs the Department of Economics and Business. His research in international economics and economic development has been published widely in professional journals. He coedited (with Judith Dean, above, and Julie Schaffner) the book *Attacking Poverty in the Developing World: Christian Practitioners and Academics in Collaboration* (Authentic Media, 2005). From 1987 to 2007, he served as coeditor of *Faith & Economics* and was visiting scholar at the U.S. International Trade Commission in 1990. He earned his Ph.D. in economics at Stanford University.

John P. Tiemstra has taught economics at Calvin College since 1975. He earned his Ph.D. at the Massachusetts Institute of Technology, where his mentor was the late, distinguished economic historian Charles P. Kindleberger. Prof. Tiemstra's research has focused on methodological issues surrounding the integration of Christianity and economics. His institutionalist approach to economics has also informed his research on government regulation of business, globalization, and environmental policy. As a visiting professor, he taught for a semester at Potchefstroom University for Christian Higher Education in South Africa. Major publications include two books: a one-semester textbook, *Economics: A Developmental Approach* (Mohican 1999), and Reforming Economics (Edwin Mellen, 1990), which was a group project of the Calvin Center for Christian Scholarship. His articles have appeared in *International Journal of Social Economics, Cross Currents, Business and*

Society Review, Challenge Magazine, Journal of Income Distribution, and *Christian Scholars' Review,* among others. He served on the Working Group on Ethics and the Earth of the Reformed Church in America. In 2007 he served as President of the Association for Social Economics, an international learned society of economists who are interested in the ethical dimensions of economic theory and policy.